Because of them . . .
"PART OF THE PARADE"
. . . the Parade goes on!

Vince Carocci   **Norm Mawby**

Mawby Project Group

Lenni, Pennsylvania 19052

www.mawbyproject.com

Cover Photo by Dr. William H. Erb

Cover designed by Anita W. Taylor

Table of Contents

Dedication

To the legion of regular folks who...for whatever reason, season after season, game after game...take it upon themselves to make our visits to ballparks, stadiums and arenas across the country such an enjoyable experience. Thank you.

Vince Carocci
July 2009

To my wife, Marietta, who has helped and supported me though this project as well as all else I attempt.

Norm Mawby
July 2009

Acknowledgements

From Norm Mawby: The list of people to thank for their assistance in making this book a reality could be endless. My apologies in advance to anyone I might have missed inadvertently in the process. But specific acknowledgement must go to: The Lamb girls, Emily and Julia, whose "do-everything-and-do-it- with-a-smile" approach to the many and varied tasks asked of them made it a joy just to be in their company; to the Carver boys, Jeremy and Colin, for their computer skills and assistance; to Bruce Mowday for his production and marketing counsel and expertise; and Marilyn Price, my sister, for her encouragement and research.

From the Phillies organization, Leigh and Eric Tobin were always available to answer any and all questions as they arose; to Sal DeAngelis, Mike DiMuzio's valued aide; to Corliss Hobbs, who does everything for everybody who asks at Citizens Bank Park; to Carrie and Jason Adams of the Clearwater, FL, Phillies for their hospitality and their knowledge of baseball; and to Fran Ehly of the ballpark command center who helped in the logistics of getting to the right place at the right time. A special word of appreciation to John Hollinger, my grandson, for his insights and his instincts on the tone and shape this narrative might take. Above all, of course, was the extraordinary cooperation and assistance from Director of Ballpark Operations Mike DiMuzio. They just don't come any better than he in his field.

To Vince Martin and Gopher Young, my thanks for their logistical support and good friendship throughout the years; to transcriptionists Candida Franklin and Jan Kaufman for their skills and their time; to Sean Humsher of Comcast for his research assistance; and to Bill Webster of the Washington Post, whose grandfather, Logan, was an usher at old Forbes Field in Pittsburgh circa the 1920's.

And to Bill Erb, a valued friend and confidant with whom I've shared attendance at countless sporting events over the last 60 years. It's truly been my pleasure.

To one and all, this project could not have been concluded as successfully as it has without the always present support, friendship and the "oh-so-good" advice you rendered throughout. I am in your debt.

—ɯ—

From Vince Carocci: First, thanks must go Philadelphia Phillies management for allowing us unrestricted access to the people and the venues of Citizens Bank Park. While the Phillies may have been subjected to a lot of grandstand analysis from the fans and the media for some of their baseball decisions through the years—it's professional sports, after all—there's one element of their operation which is simply beyond reproach. That is the value they place as an organization on the men and women who lend their time and their labor to make Citizens Bank Park the welcoming environment it is. Special thanks to Mike DiMuzio, the "go-to" guy in our travels around the ballpark. As Norm noted earlier, there's none better at what he does.

To the game day staff who shared their time, their backgrounds and their insights about the Phillies and the ballpark with us. You are the real stars of this story. Without you, there would have been no story line to explore.

A special word of appreciation to Rosie Rahn, a Phillies photographer a number of whose pictures grace these pages. She never saw her first major league baseball game until she interviewed in 1963 at the tender age of 18 with Phillies General Manager John Quinn. One month later she was watching a World Series game in Yankee Stadium with other members of the limited Phillies staff as guests of the ballclub. 46 years later, her affiliation with the organization continues. We thank her for her efforts.

Finally, to my family: To Toni and our four children, Patty, Tom, David and Steve. Your love and steadfast support motivated me to continue, not only with this project but with my previous writing endeavors when the words to tell the stories I wanted to tell just wouldn't come to my satisfaction. I hope I have done them and you justice in the process.

Thank you all.

July 2009

Foreword

You see them the moment you begin to approach the gates to Citizens Bank Park, the South Philadelphia venue the Philadelphia Phillies National League baseball team calls home.

You see them, but their presence doesn't necessarily register immediately with you.

You know what they do...but, more likely than not, you don't know who they are.

You may even know their faces...but unless you're from the neighborhood or have been going to these games for more years than you probably care to admit, you probably don't know their names.

Truth is, you don't have to. After all, you're there for the game and they're not the game.

But without them, the game couldn't go on. Certainly not in the way it does.

Who are they? Well, they're the folks...the nameless, almost faceless folks—teachers, retirees, public servants, businessmen and women, even a school superintendent thrown in for good measure...they're the folks who make certain the wheels at the ballpark turn while you're watching the Phillies do their thing on the field below.

...The ticket sellers and the ticket takers...the ushers and the program vendors...the concessionaires, the groundskeepers. Some are charged with responsibility for security; others walk through the stands hawking their hot dogs, beer, soda, popcorn, pretzels, peanuts, and, of course, crackerjacks. There's even a landscaper or two to beauty up the place and its surroundings.

They're part of the game if not exactly part of the team. They're like stagehands who blend seamlessly into the backdrop while the show goes on. And in the end, if it's a good show and you've enjoyed it...well then, they've done their part.

The late Pat Cassidy, the director of stadium operations in years yore, of whom you will hear much as these pages turn, used to tell his assembled stadium operations staff: "You'll be getting paid $6 a game, and I know that's not much. But you're part of it..."

Mike DiMuzio, a Pat Cassidy protégé and his successor as director of ballpark operations, puts it this way: "We're part of the parade. Nobody needs to know what we do. But as long as it's a great show and people enjoy it, then that's fine with us because we'll know we were part of it."

The 1,200-person ballpark operations staff comes in two distinct assortments. There are, of course, the fulltime Phillies' employees...the "regulars," they're called. And there are the seasonal part timers... in many ways, the heart and soul of ballpark operations. They're called "game-dayers."

By and large, the "game-dayers" have real-life jobs to work day in and day out. Yet 81 times a year, at a minimum, these folks arrange their schedules so that they can fulfill their occupational responsibilities, change clothes, grab something to eat (often on the fly) and get to the ballpark before the fans begin to arrive. And, if it's an extended home stand, they have to do it all over again tomorrow, and the tomorrow after that...for as many tomorrows as the Phillies' home schedule dictates.

A good number of them have been doing this for many, many years.

Why?

Well, you'll hear the answer to that from them, much of it in their own words. But when all's said that needs to be said, it still gets back to what Pat Cassidy told his staff time and time again years ago: They're "part of it"...part of the parade that is Philadelphia Phillies baseball.

This is their story. Enjoy!

Vince Carocci

July 2009

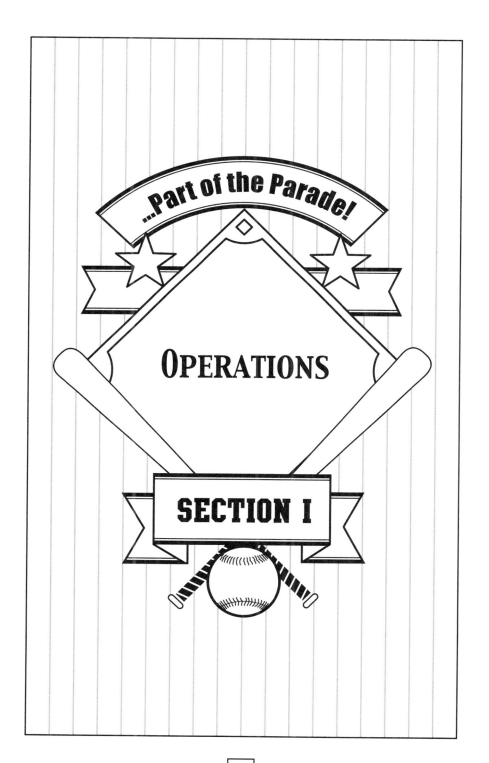

...Part of the Parade!

OPERATIONS

SECTION I

"What's up, Mike?"

April through September…ideally, into October…the bedroom alarm in Mike DiMuzio's Wilmington, Delaware home goes off about 5:45 each morning. For DiMuzio, the Director of Ballpark Operations at Citizens Bank Park, home of the 2008 World Series Champion Philadelphia Phillies, it's time to get up, get showered and get going. Another day at the ball yard awaits.

First, of course, come the morning greetings and conversation with his wife, Debbie, son, Adam, and daughter, Lindsay. (Son Michael, 28, is grown and gone from the household.) Then he's off.

En route, there's the mandatory stop at McDonalds in Chichester for two large coffees…one with cream for his mother, Penny, please; the other with cream and "a lot of sugar" for himself. Penny DiMuzio, approaching her 80th year, has worked in the Phillies Merchandising Department for more than 20 years. She lives about a half-mile from Citizens Bank Park in South Philadelphia where Mike was raised. Daily, they ride to the ballpark together.

It's 8:15 when they pull into the parking lot across the street from the Phillies operations center. DiMuzio knows from his quarter-century-plus on the job that much of what he and his staff encounters that day is what they encounter regularly each day during the season. Some of it, however, will not be. In either case, he's ready to take on the day and what it might bring.

Mike DiMuzio is one of six boys raised by Ted and Penny DiMuzio. He's a graduate of the Bishop John Neumann High School and the University of Delaware. He's been in the employ of the Philadelphia Phillies in one capacity or another for 37 years. He started as a part time groundskeeper while still in high school—"a younger guy running out in the fifth inning sweeping the bases, you know." He then worked his way through the formative years of the merchandising department selling Phillies

Phanatic dolls and also helping out with season-ticket sales in the off-season.

"I went and worked wherever they needed me," he recalls. "So I kind of had my hand in a lot of little things—not that I was good at any one of them. But I guess I was trying to find my niche." Find his niche, he did. In 1982, he was shifted to ballpark operations and he's been there ever since.

It was a hot day in July, 2008, when the Phillies hosted the St. Louis Cardinals in an afternoon finale of a three-game series. After a quick stop in his tight, functional office complex in the Ballpark Operations section of Citizens Bank Park, DiMuzio is ready to begin his rounds to be certain all is in the ready throughout the venue.

This day, however, there's a parental matter which first must be attended to. Daughter Lindsay is an entrant in the Miss Teen Delaware competition. DiMuzio has to put her entry fee in the mail. Father's tend to keep their priorities in order. Once that's done, he's on his way.

Game time is still four hours away. The 43,500-seat stadium is virtually deserted. The quiet of the concourse is interrupted only by the concessionaires gathering their wares for sale, dumping their ice bags into their coolers and preparing their food stands. Soon these same concourses will be bustling shoulder-to-shoulder with a 45,000-sellout crowd. But for the moment, the environment is solitary. Peaceful, actually.

There are the obligatory stops—the command center, for one, where the facility is monitored 365 days a year, 24 hours a day, 7 days a week for any disruptions of service, dislocations or disturbances. It's the command center gate that all employees and the media enter subjecting their bags and their visages to computer and visual ID checks.

As he roams the enterprise, DiMuzio comes on a small leak from an executive suite a level above the main concourse. It's already being addressed. A tiny area is cordoned off from pedestrian traffic. The leak itself, more irritating than debilitating, will be repaired when the Phillies break in three days for the annual Baseball All-Star Game in (the soon-to-be-demolished) Yankee Stadium.

This particular day, television personality Alyssa Milano is at the ballpark to promote a line of baseball women's apparel she designed. DiMuzio stops by the "Star Suite" to be certain all is in order for her and her small entourage. Alyssa Milano being Alyssa Milano, DiMuzio has no shortage of volunteers from the young men on his staff offering to escort her around the premises. "She won't get lost by herself," one prospective escort jokes when the director of ballparks operations asks if everything is going right.

DiMuzio is very much an advocate of "Management by Walking Around" because "walking around" is his best way to assess how ready the park is for the fans. He's dressed in his typical game day garb—slacks, Phillies golf shirt, loafers with no socks. It's functional. It has to be because DiMuzio also is very much a hands-on kind of a guy who'll jump in on any job at any moment if he thinks he can help. "I've ruined a couple of nice pair of dress pants jumping on a forklift," he ruminates to a visitor.

He's also very much a "one of the guys (gals)" kind of manager. He's not much on titles. "Hey, Mike, how's it going?" Or "Hey, Mike, got a minute?" Or just, "What's up Mike?" … that's how he's greeted as he makes his rounds. And he returns the congeniality in kind. He sums up his approach to the job and the employees this way:

"Every job is equally important. If you don't do your job going up the chain, people (meaning, primarily, the most important customers—the fans) will notice. Nobody is lesser than anybody else. Nobody's better than anybody else. We're all stagehands and we help the show go on."

The easy interaction between DiMuzio and the staff is patently transparent. For them, this relationship is more than a mere slogan. It's actually the way they function.

This day, the unexpected arrives early…on very short notice. It usually does. A delegation of 20 or so employees of the Phillies' contract concessionaire gather in the ground floor reception area of the club's administrative offices. They're having problems, at least from their perspective, in their negotiations with their employer and want the Phillies to intervene on their behalf. They inform receptionist Kelly Addario-DiGiacomo they'd like to talk to someone from Phillies management. They also let it be known, politely but firmly, that they don't intend to leave until they do. DiMuzio is requested to handle that assignment.

The meeting is brief and cordial. "Hi, I'm Mike DiMuzio from Ballpark Operations," DiMuzio says in extending his hand to the head of the delegation. "How can I help you?"

A brief conversation ensues. The workers explain that they're dissatisfied with the way their contract negotiations are being conducted. The Phillies are not directly involved. Nonetheless, the union is requesting the organization to intervene by encouraging the concessionaire to engage in—again, from their perspective--more constructive, good faith labor discussions. It's a request they also had made minutes earlier of the Philadelphia Eagles across the street in Lincoln Financial Field. And it is a request they will be making of the Philadelphia 76'ers and Flyers at the nearby Wachovia Center before the morning is out.

They have a letter to that effect and want to be certain it will be delivered to Phillies executives. DiMuzio says he can do that for them. They hand him the letter, thank him for his time and attention and leave the premises quietly. As these things go, it was almost a non-event.

DiMuzio, true to his word, makes his way to the third-floor management suite, hands the letter to a senior vice president and briefs him and Phillies counsel on the gist of the conversation. Obviously, any labor strife for the concessionaire can have ramifications for the club's ballpark operations. The request is certain to be considered in the executive suite. (Editor's note: By December, the concessionaire and the union local had reached a tentative agreement for Citizens Bank Park concession employees. How much the letter contributed definitively, if at all, to the accord could not be determined.)

Next stop, the playing field where the grounds crew under the direction of head groundskeeper Mike Boekholder is at work. Boekholder, five years into his Phillies tenure, is himself handling the hose sprinkling the infield dirt. This being an afternoon game following a night game, there's no batting or infield practice for either the Phillies or the visiting Cardinals. Preparations will conclude just a bit quicker before the 1:05 PM first pitch.

Then it's off to the umpires' dressing room to determine if there are park issues to be addressed. Nothing major, as it turns out. But one ump suggests the ball girls patrolling the foul lines in left and right field be reminded not to reach for a ball before the ball actually has been called foul by the umpiring crew. The evening before a line drive whistled down the right field line; the ball girl instinctively reached for it as it approached. The problem was, the drive was so close it could have hit in fair territory. "Tell 'em to make sure the ball's out of play before they reach for it," DiMuzio is requested. "Will do," he responds. The message will be conveyed before the game starts.

Next it's up to the press box to check on game readiness from the media perch. En route, DiMuzio encounters Harry Kalas, the Phillies Hall of Fame radio and television voice. "Hey, Mike, how's it goin?" Kalas greets as he awaits an elevator to take him to his broadcast booth. "Pretty good, Harry! How 'bout you?" Short but very cordial was this exchange.

Conditions were just fine in the mezzanine level media area overlooking home plate. The reporters were slowly making their way to press row. Some were stopping at the cafeteria area behind the press box to purchase hot or cold food for lunch.

There was still about an hour before game time. DiMuzio makes one last trip to the playing field. There he waits as field preparations are completed and the National Anthem is sung by a visiting Shriners' group. One last meeting with the umpires. It's a warm, sunny afternoon but DiMuzio asks if they wanted the stadium lights rimming the ballpark turned on. "Sometimes they do," he confides to his visitor. Not on this occasion. The crew chief peers over his stylish sunglasses for a moment, surveys the sky and concludes, "No, this is fine."

With that, DiMuzio makes his way back to the press level for a quick lunch as the game gets underway. En route, incidentally, he is reassured the Alyssa Milano contingent is doing just fine, thank you. When he enters the dining area, a number of other Phillies regular employees are eating as well. The ball is in play, the show is on, and their role, if only temporarily, is on idle. Now's their time to grab a bite. Miniature televisions hang from the ceiling for those who care to stay informed about how the game is progressing. Before DiMuzio sits to eat himself, he runs a lunch plate down to his Mother in merchandising, as is his custom.

Once his lunch is over, he's off again on his rounds. First stop is to the reception area where one of his staff is sitting in for the receptionist who had to pick up her young son from baseball camp. "Get something to eat," DiMuzio tells the young man. "Nah, I'm alright and Kelly will be back shortly," the assistant demurs. "Get something to eat," DiMuzio insists. "I'll handle this." And he does with aplomb. "Phillies, how may I help you?" he says in answering one of the several calls which come in during this brief stint at the switchboard. Kelly might do it better, but only slightly.

Next, he's off to visit to the "Eye in the Sky" box located almost adjacent to the giant scoreboard in the left centerfield upper deck. This time, the concourse is jammed shoulder-to-shoulder with this sellout crowd as he makes his way. All is in order in the box, so it's back to the concourse for more patrolling.

That's the way his day plays out during game hours. Once the game is over, it usually takes about an hour to an hour-and-a-half to close the park for the day or the night. This day, however, young kids have been invited to run the bases on the playing field. Last night, there was a fireworks display. In two days, the fireworks event will be repeated. DiMuzio and his staff must work these extracurricular activities, as well. Ballpark Operations stay on the job until the curtain closes for good.

Once that happens, there's usually some time for decompression...maybe a beer with the group...before Ballpark Operations finally calls it a day. After a night game, DiMuzio normally gets back to his Wilmington home between 1 or 2 AM. This day, it probably will be a more reasonable hour of 7 PM.

Tomorrow, when the Arizona Diamondbacks visit, it starts all over. It just as easily could be the Mets or the Braves. The brand of the competition is quite immaterial to Ballpark Operations. Ensuring that the show goes on for the fans without glitches is what commands their focus. "It's marketing's job to get them here," DiMuzio advises. "It's our job to make their visit enjoyable enough that they'll want to come back!" In 2008, the year the Phillies won the National League Pennant and then the World Series (only their second in the last 28 years), the fans certainly did want to come. More than 3 million strong. And Ballpark Operations had the place ready for them each and every time.

For the DiMuzio's of South Philadelphia—St. Edmond's Parish, to be exact, "'cause you always talk parishes in South Philadelphia"--their connection with the Philadelphia Phillies, if not exactly a family affair, certainly has been a long time family proposition.

Mike's been with the Phillies since 1971.

Older brother Tom was there before him—summers while he was a collegian.

Later came brother Ted, now a corporate lawyer, who was a bartender in the super boxes at Veterans Stadium.

Brother Mark sold programs.

Brother Danny is still a game day groundskeeper.

And David, who worked on the Philadelphia Stock Exchange, helped Mike in the 1980s in the merchandising department and is back now with the Phillies assisting in the coordination of program vendor operations.

Even Mike's father, Ted, spent "10-to-12 years" as a night watchman at the Vet after his retirement as a systems analyst with the Signal Corps before deciding he had enough and just wanted to sit home. (Ted passed away in 2007 on son Mike's birthday.)

And there's mother, Penny, a Texan whom Ted met while in the Army, and her two decades of service in the Phillies' merchandising department.

Sport was very much a part of the DiMuzio family culture. Tom was a more than fair-to-middlin' quarterback with the University of Delaware Blue Hens. In his senior year, he finished second team Little All-American behind a fella from Louisiana Tech named Terry Bradshaw. Mike confesses he tried his hand at a variety of sports, but "I wasn't very good at anything. I guess that's why I became a (basketball) referee. Some people say I'm not very good at that either," he jokes in that self-deprecating way of his.

The DiMuzio boys grew in an era when Connie Mack Stadium was for them a two-bus or subway ride up to the North Philly station and then a short walk over Broad and Lehigh to 21st...an era of transistor radios and young boys sneaking a listen in school or under their pillows in bed at night...an era when 9 and 10 year-old boys like Jim and Fred Anton from the Port Richmond section of the city would have their mother pack them a lunch, ride the #60 trolley to 21st street, walk down to Lehigh, pay 50-cents for a bleacher seat and watch Richie Ashburn patrol center field like only he could. It was, they remembered a half-century later, "a blast!"

Mike was just a junior in high school when he applied for a part time grounds crew job with the Phillies. The team was about to move from Connie Mack to Veterans Stadium in their South Philadelphia neighborhood and DiMuzio remembers just how that came about.

"One, I guess the fact that my brother had worked for the Phillies and the Phillies were moving down here (to the city's South Philadelphia sports complex). Two, obviously as parents do, they want to see their kids make out well. So my Mom and Dad had me send in an application to the Phillies when they were about to move… (Work ethic as well as sport also was very much a part of the DiMuzio family culture)."

Mike was one of 15 youngsters the Phillies recruited that year through Bishop Neumann High School to work on the junior ground crew the organization was starting in conjunction with the move to The Vet. The teenagers were to assist the 8 or 9-member regular ground crew who would be relocating with the team from Connie Mack.

"They wanted to kind of complement those gentlemen (I thought of them as older gentlemen at the time and now I'm as old as they were)…They wanted to complement those gentlemen with a new fresher look. They were bringing in the 'hot pants patrol'. They wanted this fresh look of young guys running out in the fifth inning sweeping the field, cleaning the bases, helping the older guys with the tarps, that sort of thing.

"I was fortunate enough to be one of the 15 guys chosen by either the principal or vice principal or whoever they (the Phillies) had gone to at Bishop Neumann. I think two of us lasted the year. And, knock on wood, I'm still here."

Mike established very early on that there wasn't anything he wouldn't do as part of the job. Changing second base in the fifth inning, for one. "Nobody wanted to run out that far 'cause they were too afraid that if they fell, people would make fun of them.

And I guess being the class clown that I was, I said, 'So what, that's a part of life.'"'

DiMuzio remembers his first day with the Phillies as if it were yesterday.

"My first day with the Phillies was April 10, 1971 when we opened the Vet," he recounted. "…The excitement of walking into this new facility…56,000 to 57,000 people…the whole aura of this new happening, particularly in South Philadelphia…really being a part of it. I guess I was sold on that."

His role with the Phillies took its most dramatic turn at the end of the '81 season, in advance of the '82 season, when fate intervened in an unfortunate way. Pat Cassidy, the venerated and to this day revered director of Stadium Operations, had suffered a stroke. DiMuzio was approached by then Executive Vice President David Montgomery, and asked if he would take on some of Cassidy's duties to relieve some of the pressures and stresses on him. He said he would. But before the transition actually could be implemented, Pat Cassidy had a relapse.

So it was that at the tender age of 28, DiMuzio was offered Cassidy's position. "I was nearly floored," he remembered. "I guess it was the fact that I knew a little bit about a lot but didn't know a lot about any one thing. I said, 'I have to talk to my wife.'" Which probably was more a gesture than a fact, because, DiMuzio confesses, 'I think my mind already was made up."

Pat Cassidy remained with the Phillies for another 10-to-12 years in an office services capacity. DiMuzio called him a "huge, huge help to me as I was getting my feet wet." As it turned out, getting his feet "wet" in more ways than one, literally as well as figuratively.

"January 11, 1982," is fixed in DiMuzio's memory bank. "I remember that day specifically—January 11, because we lost every high pressure, high temperature, hot water valve in our office in the building that day. It was about 4-Below and every valve exploded, completely flooding our entire office. Just when all this stuff became my responsibility! I remember saying to my wife, 'If you think I worked long hours as a groundskeeper and merchandising guy…now that a lot of this responsibility is mine, it may be even longer.' And my first day was 30 hours cause I came in at 9 that morning and left about 3 the next afternoon. And

she said, 'You said it would be long but this is a little ridiculous.'"
DiMuzio and his staff spent from January until Opening Day in
April getting their offices in shape. "Opening Day and we're still
laying carpet," he recalled. "And I said to myself, 'it can't get
much worse.'"

The functions which come under the umbrella of Ballpark
Operations are as varied as they are many--ushers and usherettes
(host and hostesses, in modern ballpark terminology); ticket takers
(or greeters as they're now called); security, groundskeepers, guest
services (or fan accommodation personnel). Their responsibilities
can involve everything from leaky toilets to a fan getting hit with
a foul ball. Parking and traffic flow are part of it as well. To
DiMuzio's way of thinking, if it's a concern to a fan, it's a concern
to Ballpark Operations. "Whether we deal with it directly or
indirectly, we have to deal with it because we have to get the
person back here."

This is where the time DiMuzio spent learning from Pat
Cassidy comes into play. He remembers Cassidy's admonition in
his first day as a game-day groundskeeper. Cassidy told his new
crew: "You'll be getting $6 a game and I know it's not much, but
you're a part of it."

DiMuzio enlarged on the theme of his mentor: "That's
what I always remembered. That I was part of it! And that's
the mentality I grew up with first in Stadium Operations (it was
Veterans Stadium, after all) and now Ballpark Operations (because
it's now Citizens Bank Park.) You don't have to be a superstar.
You have to be a stagehand. We're curb sitters. We watch the
parade go by. I'm a curb sitter. I'm part of the parade. Nobody
needs to know what I do.

"When the fans come to the ballpark, it's their nine against the
other nine and whether their nine won or their nine lost. It's not
about the 1,200 people that were here that night putting on that
show. We know what we did, we in the organization. But as long
it's a great show and the people enjoy it, that's what's important.
And that's fine with me."

Veterans Stadium…state of the art when it opened; but to hear its critics, crumbling, antiquated, in a state of serious disrepair when it closed. Don't count Mike DiMuzio among of them.

"You could probably talk to a thousand people about this," he said emphatically, "and there's only going to be one of them who's going to be pro Vet. And that's the guy you're talking to now." Actually, he was off by several in his count. Many of those who spent any time at all at the Vet share his fond memories of the old place. More on that later. For now, DiMuzio has the floor.

"This," he says, gesturing in his surroundings at Citizens Bank Park, "this place is gorgeous, a brand new house; absolutely gorgeous. But to me, it's not home yet. The Vet was home. I grew up at the Vet. I was there for 33 years. I never lived anywhere for 33 years."

As he thought about it, that fact registered even more with him. "You know, I lived with my parents 'til I was 21. I went to college and then got married. And I only lived at another place for about four years before I moved to a house. And I've only lived there for 12. But at the Vet, I was there the entire time—33 years. So I grew to really love the Vet. I knew every nook and cranny at the place."

There's really no way to compare the Vet and Citizens Bank Park. The Vet was round; CBP is more sectioned off. A fan or an employee could start at any point at the Vet, walk around the concourse and get to where he and she were going. Strangers in Citizens Bank Park would do well to have a map or a guide with them. That's not to be critical. Just stating a fact.

The Vet was multi-purpose—one building for two teams and concerts. Citizens Bank was built solely for baseball (although it does host an occasional concert or two when the schedule permits). The Vet was artificial turf. Citzens Bank is retro with its dirt and grass. The Vet was enclosed, CBP more open air with a view of the Philadelphia skyline.

"Could you see the game from the concourse (at the Vet) the way you can here?" DiMuzio mulls aloud. "Obviously not. Were there problems at the Vet? There were. But they weren't as bad as they were reputed to be."

What strikes DiMuzio as curious even to this day was how the perception of the Vet changed dramatically among long time Vet employees as closing day drew closer. "Everybody was saying how bad it was," he recalled, "how bad it was. Yet how the reactions changed in 2003 when we moved out. Now everybody was saying, 'I met my wife there;' or 'I met my husband there;' or, 'I have some great fond memories of this place.' And then that last day, what we did with all the players coming back…then it really hit me, you know…that this place was special."

So special that closing day remains one of DiMuzio's favorite recollections of his experiences with the Phillies. That's because he was chosen to carry the 1971 Phillies' flag during the commemorating ceremonies on that last day. And then, just meeting all of the old players who came back for the occasion, to have them come up and shake his hand, saying, "Thanks for what you did for us," or "the ballpark was really, really special!" Those kind of memories stay with a person and they did with DiMuzio. When it was time for the Vet to be imploded, he went to great lengths to get a bird's eye view of the implosion. "I got to watch it, basically from above. That was pretty special."

He was there the day the Vet opened its gates. He was there when she was blown to the ground. It was a special time…for the city, for the teams it hosted, for the people who worked there, for the fans who watched there. It was really, really special for Mike DiMuzio, who grew up there.

For as much as the ballparks have changed over the last decades, the demographics of Major League Baseball may have changed even more. It's a point not lost on even the most casual of observers. One just has to look over the fans from game to game at CBP to understand what's happening.

"Our crowd has gone from an older crowd to 'This is the happening place to be,'" DiMuzio observes. "It's the younger people who come here. Their ticket is basically their cover charge, as if they're going to a, you know, nightclub or the hotspot that they go to in the summertime. This is the place to meet people. Although they're caught up in the excitement of it, we get a crowd many of whom don't know…some of whom don't really care about what's happening in the game. They're here to be with their friends."

As the demographics of baseball have changed, so, too, have the rules of the business. It's a point DiMuzio and ballpark operations staff must contend with from season to season. Not that it's a problem. Just a reality.

"There's obviously a lot more rules now that Major League Baseball has become involved," he said. "A lot of things are standardized...the pace of the game, time of the game, things to help speed up the game. And a lot of things are run by network TV.

"Before, you were on your own schedule. You televised the game when you felt like televising it; you played the game when you felt like playing it. Now if you wanted to play a day game on this certain day, but a network is doing the game, you know that you wouldn't be able to televise your game. So instead of playing a day game, we'll play a night game. So a lot has changed."

Had the game changed for the better? "In some cases," DiMuzio replied. And then the traditionalist of someone who grew up in the baseball industry surfaces. "I'm still the daytime, you know, particularly from a younger standpoint. It bothers me some when any event, whether its' baseball or basketball, and it's played late at night and the kids that you want to bring to the sport aren't able to watch because it's on the West Coast and it's 9 or 10 o'clock at night and the games are getting over at 12:30 (in the morning)."

Now that he was into it, he warmed a bit more to his subject: "Play the game in the daytime. It's a gorgeous day out today and wouldn't you love to see a double-header? That's another thing that's changed. There are no scheduled double-headers now. I used to love those things at Connie Mack Stadium. And we did it at the Vet for a while. "I understand why (scheduling is as it is). I know that dollars are involved. But ..." There's always a but, isn't there.

DiMuzio's trip down nostalgia lane continued a bit more. "It used to be, you could go to a game, see a game, then go eat (hot dogs at the ballpark) and see another game. That was pretty special. Kids today can't appreciate that because now when there's a double-header, one in the morning or early afternoon, then you clear the ballpark, clean the ballpark and then you've got to come back under another admission."

But it is what it is. And DiMuzio wouldn't change much if at all about how his life in baseball played out.

Particularly the special moments—Opening Day at the Vet; the last day at the Vet; watching the Vet go down. The World Series win in 1980. And, of course, the World Series win in 2008. All that was special.

The 2008 World Series victory may have presented unique problems for Major League Baseball, national television and, most importantly, the fans. But not for DiMuzio and his ballpark operations crew. First, there was the rain delay of Game 3 against the American League Tampa Bay Rays on a Saturday night. To start, the first pitch in World Series games is thrown at 8:35 rather than the usual 7:05 PM to accommodate a prime time national television audience. This night it was raining when the first pitch was to be thrown. The game never started until sometime after 10 PM.

But, to DiMuzio's way of thinking, there was never a doubt the game was going to be played. "We knew when the shower stopped and the front passed, that was going to be it. It was just a question of when it was going to stop." What prolonged the delay was that once the rain ceased, it took 35-to-40 minutes to get the field in playing condition and the players, primarily the starting pitchers, warmed up. But all that would have applied in a regular season rain delay. Inconvenient and discomforting given the time of year for the fans, but not insurmountable for ballpark operations.

The suspension of Game 5 for two nights was another matter. Rain fell so heavily by the 6th inning, the playing field was unplayable. The game had to be stopped. What wasn't generally known was that the Commissioner of baseball had ruled even before the first pitch, when the weather forecast was ominous, that this game would go for nine full innings whether it had to be delayed or suspended. This caused a lot of confusion in a lot of quarters, including the national telecast crew.

Whether the game should have been started at all was at the time, and in some quarters continues to be, a subject of considerable debate within and without baseball circles. If not postponed, another alternative would have been to move the starting time up a couple of hours to beat the storm. But, there again, you have the television factor.

What there was little debate about, given the commissioner's earlier decision to play the game nine full innings, was whether the top of the 6th inning, when Tampa Bay scored a tieing run, should have been started at all. At that point, DiMuzio acknowledges, there was "no way" the field could have been kept in adequate playing condition.

When the game ultimately was called in the middle of the 6th, it never resumed until two nights later. Again, a great inconvenience for the fans. Probably for the Phillies ticket office, as well. But for ballpark operations, it was a challenge they often encountered through the years during the regular season. Getting the stadium ready for the resumption, DiMuzio said, was no different than getting it ready after a regular season rain out.

The game resumed 48 hours later. The Phillies won. All was forgiven. Winning a World Series can do that for you. Particularly when it's been 25 years since Philadelphia and its fans had experienced that championship feeling for any of its professional sports teams.

The World Series win, incidentally, was certainly reason for the city, the fans and the team to celebrate and celebrate they did. But for Ballpark Operations, first there was the job of getting the park set up for the victory ceremony. Once they did, DiMuzio and his staff made their way to the victory procession through the city to Citizens Bank Park. This time they were truly, "part of the parade." And deservedly so.

As special as these events were in DiMuzio's memory collection, so, too, were the players he met and the people he worked with through the years. Richie Allen and Tony Taylor principal among the former; the aforementioned Pat Cassidy and Tom Hudson of the merchandising and advertising department among the latter. And not to forget the ground crew guys he worked with when he was starting out—Wimpy, the guy who worked on the pitchers mound; Joe the guy who worked home plate with Barney; and Charlie, the guy who pulled the hose, and Freddie, the head guy. "I saw them working at Connie Mack and I didn't know who they were. And then I got to meet them and remembered, 'Oh yeah, these are the guys that were there." And the game day employees that he called "near and dear" to him still to this day…the Kenny Bushes and Pete Ceras and Teddy Kesslers, all of the clubhouse guys, Foster at the front desk…all those people who helped me immensely."

But as time passes, so do his associates. "Unfortunately, I've been to five funerals in the last six months, four of which were game day employees. And of those four, three were dressed in their full Phillies employee game day uniforms. The fourth had all his Phillies memorabilia--his hats and pins and stuff. To see that touches me more than anything…that their time with the Phillies meant so much to them. To me, that speaks volumes about the time they spent here."

DiMuzio was asked, "Why, Tony Taylor, why Richie Allen?" He responded: "They're probably the two people who not only you knew as a player and a worker, but as a friend…people who were concerned about your family, always asking, 'How's Mom?" and when my Dad was alive, 'How's Dad?' 'How're the kids?' I developed a pretty close relationship to them. I've done it with a couple of ballplayers, but those two in particular."

To some, the Allen association might seem curious. If his reputation is to be believed, Allen was not the most congenial sort to teammates and fans alike. But he was to DiMuzio. "Dick (notice, Dick not Richie) was what I call a small people, game-day person," DiMuzio explains. "When he came to the ballpark, the first room he stopped in everyday was the ground crew because Dick knew what the ground crew meant to getting the ballgame played. So I got to know him through the older guys on the ground crew. For Dick to take a 17-year old kid like myself and Froggie and some of the other guys as if we had been his long lost buddies was kind of special." (Given that history, then, it should not have been surprising during the Vet's closing day to see Richie—make that, Dick—Allen, accompanied by Jay Johnstone, spontaneously run out with the ground crew to change first base for them during the mid-game infield sweep.)

When Mike's father died, Allen flew in from California for the viewing and the funeral. That's how special their relationship was. Is it any wonder, then, that one of the three signature bats DiMuzio has hanging from his office wall is a Dick Allen Louisville Slugger?

DiMuzio was asked where he saw baseball heading. He paused to reflect, but only for a moment before he responded. "It'll probably go more global. More international stuff. An international team...a road trip to Germany and Spain."

Maybe, maybe not. But the question was posed to him nonetheless:

"Will you still be a part of it?"

His reply: "I'd like to think that I will. Maybe there'll get a point where I'll say, the challenges of my position are such that I can't physically do it anymore. Maybe then I'd look and say, 'Well, I need to do something...selling programs, but something. I'd just want to be a part of it.

"I tell the game day employees, 'When you come to work for the Phillies, as far as I'm concerned you work until you tell us you don't want to, or you give us a (disclipinary) reason not to have you back.'

"As long as the Phillies want me here, I'm going to keep coming to work every day until somebody tells me, 'No!' I've had some offers to go other places. But nothing that wowed me enough to leave...So, if the Phillies want me...well, I've thoroughly enjoyed what I've done from April 10, 1971 until this very moment."

So when the alarm goes off at 5:45 AM at the DiMuzio household in Wilmington, April through September...again, ideally, into October...Mike DiMuzio fully expects to be up for another day at the ballpark. For him though, it's more than just another day at the ballpark. It's a career!

The Grounds Crew

Between them…the four of them…they have 120 years of combined experience with the Philadelphia Phillies grounds crew. They were young men…teenagers, actually…when they started. They're now in their middle-aged years and they're still at it. With, it might be added, no end in sight.

To introduce them, one by one:

First, there's Rob Wright. He was a sophomore in high school when he began working as a part time Phillies grounds keeper. Today, he's a sales representative for a Philadelphia-based food distribution company.

Next, Ed Downs, who as a 15 year-old teenager, was a friend of the son of the director of Stadium Operations at Veterans Stadium. For $15 a game, on "Giveaway Sundays," he would unload the gifts the Phillies were offering to fans and then reload the leftovers once the giveaway was over. Today, he's a heating, ventilating and air conditioning control technician at the University of Pennsylvania.

Steve Mucha was the son of the chief of surgery at the now-gone Philadelphia Naval Hospital across the street from the Vet when he made his connection with the team. Today, he's a Facility and Energy Financial Analyst with a prominent Philadelphia area convenience store chain.

And finally, there's Jeff Wright, Rob's younger brother. He harbored aspirations of becoming a major league baseball player but due to a combination of life circumstances more than lack of skills, necessarily, he ultimately became a full time Phillies grounds keeper.

They've traveled divergent professional paths over the last 30 years. But their mutual attachment to sport in general and Phillies baseball in particular kept their tracks aligned. So there they were again, in the 2008 National League and World Series championship season…getting the Citizens Bank Park playing field ready 81 times a year—more with the play-offs and series factored in--for the Phils and their opposition. Grounds keeping at a major league baseball park, at least for them, remains as contagious today as it was when they started.

Rob Wright, of Wallingford in neighboring Delaware County, was, in a way, a victim of circumstances—but circumstances of his own making. It was 1974. Rob's father—"Chalky," he was called--was the coach of the Nether Providence High School baseball team. Rob, a 10th grader at the time, was an outfielder on the team. But he was caught smoking in one of the high school bathrooms. His father had a number of rules for his players. One of them was, "no smoking!" No smoking, period! Rob was dismissed from the team rather unceremoniously.

"I was home the next day after he threw me off the baseball team," Rob remembers…"ticked off, sitting there watching TV when he (his Dad) walked in the backdoor. I'll never forget this. It's ingrained in my mind. He comes walking in the backdoor, sees me sitting on the couch, looks at me and says: 'If you think for one damned minute you're gonna come home from school every damned day and sit on your can and watch TV, you've got another think coming!!'"

The next day, Rob was out looking for a job.

One of his high school buddies, Joe DiProsperos, was a friend of the family of the aforementioned Pat Cassidy, director of Stadium Operations at the Vet. The friend had a job with the Phillies grounds crew. Rob asked if there were openings. The friend said he would talk to "Mr. Cassidy." It just so happened that one of the grounds crew staff had broken his leg the day before. Cassidy called him in for an interview. The next day, as a 16-year-old kid dressed in his "nice shirt, nice pants," Rob Wright went to meet Pat Cassidy.

Rob recalls: "He said to me, 'So, you want to work on the grounds crew.' And I said, 'I'd really like to do that.' He asked me, why and what happened. And I told him. He said, 'Well, that sounds good enough to me. Take him downstairs, get him a uniform and he'll start working tonight.'" And so it was, two days after his father removed him from the Nether Providence baseball team, Rob Wright started working as a game-day grounds keeper with the Philadelphia Phillies. He subsequently earned a degree in health and physical education in 1980 from West Chester University of Pennsylvania. His offices with C. W. Dunnet, a wholesale food distributor for distributors in the food service industry, are located less than two blocks from Citizens Bank Park.

—m—

Ed Downs had been working full time on the Phillies grounds crew for about a year in 1981 when an opportunity presented itself that he just couldn't resist. Under similar circumstances, who could?

He was 22 at the time. As a high schooler at West Catholic High in Philadelphia and then as a college student at Camden County Junior College in New Jersey, he had played small forward/guard on their respective basketball teams. He was pretty good at it, too.

One day, "out of the blue," Downs remembered, Maje McDonnell of Phillies player lore approached him and asked: 'Would you ever consider traveling with the Glob-ies (the Harlem Globetrotters)? I can get you a tryout.'" McDonald was a Villanova College teammate of Red Klotz. Klotz, of course, was the playing coach of the Washington Generals, the Globetrotters' favorite touring foil. He was always on the lookout for basketball talent and he and McDonald had stayed in touch through the years.

Within 30 days, Downs found himself heading to Margate, N.J., for a tryout under Klotz' supervision. "I'm thinking he's goin' to have me out there with a bunch of guys competing. I was in pretty good shape playing regularly in the summer leagues. So I go to Margate. I show up and it's just me and Red Klotz at a playground. It's like 10 o'clock on a Saturday morning. And he says, 'Let's see what you can do.' So he starts throwing the ball to me and making me run up and down for two hours to see what kind of shape I was in.

"I could run and jump pretty well back then. After about two hours, he said to me, 'Okay, we're goin' to check your records, make sure you're not wanted in any states. We'll be leaving in about a month.'"

So it was that Ed Downs of West Catholic High School found himself in October of 1981 touring the United States for seven months and Europe for two playing against the "Glob-ies" of the Curly Neal and Geese Ausbie era. The dream ended in 1982 when, as Downs succinctly put it, "I got cut." (The Generals would call him back a couple of years later. But by then, he was pursing other full time job avenues. So he declined. It was, for him, a memorable time in his life. But it was over.)

Downs was offered a job with the Phils junior grounds crew at Vet Stadium in 1977. He was in college at the time. He accepted immediately. "I thought it would be a good job," Downs recalls. "I saw it as being around, close to the game…pretty cool for somebody who likes baseball. I played a lot as a kid."

Three years later, he was offered a full time grounds crew position. With the exception of the year off he took (with the Phillies blessing) to tour with the Generals, he remained on the full time crew until 1985. In 1986, he took a two-year leave of absence to pursue a more permanent career path.

He attended Lyons Technical School to learn a trade in heating, ventilating and air conditioning. He found a job as a heating, ventilating and air conditioning controls (HVAC) technician at the Philadelphia International Airport where he worked for 12 years. He later moved to St. Joseph's College (where, incidentally, building on his academics at Camden County, he earned a bachelor's degree in sociology.) In 2007, his career track took him to the University of Pennsylvania.

He returned to the Phillies grounds crew as a game day employee in 1988. "I just bought a house," he explained, "and I could use the extra money, I didn't burn any bridges when I left in '85." 20-some years later, with a wife, Helen, and a three-year old son, Evan, at home, the "extra money" never hurts. But that's not the reason he's stayed with grounds keeping. He just likes it and the people he works with that much. For him, that's reason enough.

Steve Mucha was a college student—a "18 or 19-year-old kid" when in 1978 he had the opportunity to join the Phillies game day ground crew. "We knew one of the equipment people and he mentioned there was an opening," he explained. "I love baseball, I love sports in general. I used to go to a lot of games with my Dad, my brothers. So when I found out there was an opening, I jumped at it."

He spent his youngster years—one of six Mucha children--as a self-acknowledged "Navy brat," traveling with his family to Naval assignments at Camp Lejeune, NC, and Roosevelt Roads Naval Station in Puerto Rico, among other duty stations, before his father was assigned back to Philadelphia in 1967. Puerto Rico, he recalls somewhat wistfully, was a great place for a young boy to be—"a tropical paradise…go to school, come home and go to the beach." His father was promoted to chief of surgery at the Naval Hospital in 1970, a position he held until his retirement in 1978.

Steve was graduated from Gloucester Catholic High School in New Jersey and then enrolled at Rowan University where he earned his degree in Business Administration with a specialization in accounting. (That's the same Rowan which formerly was known as Glassboro State College, when in the mid-'60's it inexplicably was chosen to host an international summit meeting between President Lyndon Johnson and Soviet Premier Alexsei Kosygin. But that was before Mucha's time on the campus.)

Mucha had been working a variety of part time jobs…waiting tables, bartending, etc…at the Naval base officers' club. So, he was asked, why would he opt for the Phillies? He seemed a bit surprised at the question. "Who wouldn't want to jump at something like that if it was presented to them?" he responded. "It didn't take me two seconds to think about it!"

When he started with the Phillies, he was by his own admission, "low man on the totem pole." He'd go out and groom the bases, of course. But he also carried soft drinks and Tastycakes to the left and right field ball girls to take to the umpires as a mid-game refreshment break. Today, his job is a bit more specialized, like laying the foul lines down along first and third base.

Jeff Wright, Rob's brother, is the youngest of the quartet. He's also the only one of the four who made the grounds crew his career. " I liked what I was doing," he recalled some 18 years after his tenure with the Phillies began. "I mean, I'm down on the field, close to the players…I enjoyed what I was doing and just kept doing it. Why not be out there with them instead of inside an office somewhere?"

There was a time when Jeff and his father may have harbored a dream of his becoming a major league player. He played for his Dad at Nether Providence, just like Rob. He was a first baseman. Jeff insists, with Rob sitting at his side, that there never was a chance he'd suffer the same fate as his brother. "My Dad would never throw me off the team," he joked. "I was too good a player!" Of course, if he also smoked in the high school lavatory, he at least never got caught. But this conversation didn't go down that track.

After his graduation from Nether Providence in 1980, he matriculated to the University of Maryland as a soccer recruit in pursuit of a degree in graphic design. Soccer just wasn't for him, however. He wanted to be a baseball player. He tried out for the Maryland team but got cut. "They said they wanted a left-handed first baseman. I was right-handed." Academically, there also was some foul-up with the classes he had been advised to take for a year and one-half—"the classes had nothing to do with my major," he remembers—so he came home to sort things out.

He took a job with the Franklin Mint in nearby Media and was working at that for almost two years when Rob called. "He asked me if I was looking to get a job as a part time, game day grounds keeper," Jeff continued. "I figured why not, I'll make some extra money, get my foot in the door, go back to school, see what happens…"

From 1987-90, he worked as a game day groundskeeper while also re-enrolled as a part time student at Maryland. "I'd come home on weekends when the Phillies were home, I'd work at the Vet and go back down to school"

He finally was graduated with his degree in graphic design in 1989. But his career path took a dramatic change in direction in January of 1990. Mike DiMuzio called, asking if he would be interested in interviewing for a full time position with the grounds crew. Wright told DiMuzio he had his degree in graphic design and also would be interested in doing some "art work for the

Phillies." DiMuzio said, "We'll see what we can do." Meanwhile, Wright intermittently would explore avenues in graphic design, but kept running into stone walls. "You don't have enough experience," was the answer he kept encountering. So it was that Jeff Wright ultimately settled on the Phillies and the ground crew.

The Maryland tryout persuaded him that his aspiration to become a big league baseball player was out of the question. The dream may have died a little harder for his father. But if the subject arises, Jeff reminds his dad: "Look, Dad, I got into the big leagues some how. I don't get paid like some of those guys do. But that's just the way it goes sometime." For Jeff Wright, it seems to have worked out just fine.

It's 9:30 in the morning on a crystal clear, blue-sky day in mid-September in Philadelphia. The Phillies game with the Florida Marlins is still hours away. But the Phillies full time grounds crew already is at work getting the playing field in shape.

Jeff Wright is on his mini-tractor skimming the infield dirt. Head groundskeeper Mike Boekholder is on the big mower cutting the outfield grass, a 1-to1-1/2 hour operation he undertakes every day the Phillies are home—every two or three days when they are away. This day he's cutting in a criss-cross pattern for aesthetic effect.

Citizens Bank Park is virtually deserted at this hour. The only discernible activity in the stands at the moment are the attendants cleaning the windows of the luxury boxes high above field level. Landscaper Pam Hall drives by. She's en route to clipping the plants in the flowerbed above the left field wall, something the umpiring crew requested after the previous day's game.

The permanent grounds crew usually reports to the ballpark between 8 and 9 each morning, earlier if necessary for an afternoon game. Their game-day counterparts will get to the park about 2-to2-1/2 hours before the first pitch fill out the 20-man crew on hand for each game. Regardless of when they arrive, "there's always," in Wright's words, "something to do." And there is.

There are really three components to their job: Pre-game, in-game and post-game. The crew is versatile enough that any one member can do another's job if need be. But each usually finds his niche and stays with it. "You get used to doin' it, and when it's good, then you don't want somebody else doin' it for you," Jeff Wright explains. It seems there's a pride of authorship in more than just literature.

Wright, for example, regularly preps the infield --"skimming the skin," they call it. Boekholder does the outfield mowing. Also hosing the infield dirt—"watering the skin"—before the game. His crew helps him move the heavy hose around. Rob Wright sets up the batter box lines and paints home plate and the pitching rubber. The batting cage and the screens need to be be taken down and stored after BP is completed. Ed Down and Steve Mucha lay the 1st base and right field foul line. There's more than enough to go around.

Pre-game alone there's dragging the infield; cutting the grass (always to a 1-1/18-inch playing height); laying the foul lines; laying the batters box; packing the pitchers mound; getting the bullpens ready; edging the field; cleaning up any loose debris in the warning track and along the foul lines; fluffing the grass where it's been matted to protect against " snakes" when a ball might veer suddenly to the left or right of a charging defender.

The object, always the primary object: To make the playing field a non-factor in the outcome of the contest. "From the minute we get there (to the ballpark), we work to put the field in the best possible playing condition for the players and to make it look like a painted picture for the fans and the television cameras," Jeff Wright explains. If they succeed, as they usually do…well, the grounds crew know they did their job.

The crew has about 30 minutes between the end of batting practice and the first pitch to complete all they have to do. "It's not that hard, physically," Rob Wright acknowledges. "It's very systematic." So systematic it's laid out in the "Game day Grounds Crew Work Assignments," a work sheet posted daily in the grounds crew workroom. It reads like this:

Batting Practice Tear-down--1B Screen; 2B Screen; OF Shag Screen; Foul Territory Mats; Homeplate/Mound; Drag Baselines; Fan Rake; Drag Warning Track; Foul Screens; Cage; Mound/HP (Home Plate) Astroturf; "L" Screen; Pitching Platform; Fungo Mat.

For Pre-game preparation, there's: Drag Infield, Wipe Down Wall Pads, Bases; Hose; Chalk Lines; Broom Edges; Strings and Chalk HP.

Rob Wright, Steve Mucha, Ed Downs, Danny DiMuzio and Andy McMenamin don't have to refer to the assignment sheet very often. They've been at it this grounds keeping thing so long…since their days at the Vet, to be exact…they've come to be called "The Big Five!"—the senior guys on the game-day crew. It's second nature for them to go about what they do game in and game out.

Still, the work sheet has its in-game assignments: Bullpens; Home plate chairs; Clean Room & Shop; 3rd Inning Mat Drag; 6th Inning Mat Drag; Cutouts/Bases; Wash Vehicles. The crew calls it tending to those "little things" which need to be done. And, oh, yes, watch the game a bit if you like.

Jeff Wright makes his way to the bullpen to be available if the mound or the plate need tending; or a door needs opening; or to call into the clubhouse when a player needs something, even something as unusual as sugar for his coffee. Not much heavy lifting, but still…it can have its moments.

Wright remembers to this day the first home stand in 2004 when a brawl between the Marlins and the Phils erupted on the playing field. It started with a "bad brush back" pitch, he recalls. "Next thing you know, I'm standing there with another guy at the door and all of a sudden, you hear these cleats coming down the cement steps. We stepped back, they start pushing the door, the door doesn't go out, you have to open it inward. And they're pushing…

"We hear the crowd going nuts because something's happening on the field. 'Hold it a minute,' I tell them. And I open the door and out they go. 'What'd you do?' the guy I'm with asks me. 'I don't know, I just the opened the door and they go for it.' When their little scruff is over, the players come walking back. It's a long walk to center field. The players, from both teams, are sort of laughing with each other. One of them tells me, "Don't open the door again. It's a long run out there.'" Wright, to the best of his recollection, hasn't had occasion to ever since. Nor does he regret it.

Once the final out is recorded, it's time for the post-game activities to kick in. Again, the assignment sheet spells it out: Back vacuum edges, inside and out; Home plate and mound; Drag skin with Bunker Rake; Mat Drag; Drag Baselines; Moisture Probe; Clumping; Bullpens; Pickup chalk lines; On deck circles/ seeds. The field is covered when necessary because of the threat or forecast of inclement weather.

It's about a ½-to-1-hour proposition to clean the playing field up after a game. Then time, maybe, for a wind down beer with the crew. In their younger days, Steve Mucha acknowledges, the crew could become, if they chose, quite the "connoisseurs" of the various malts. As they've aged, however, he admits there's a lot more "moderation" to that particular activity. One, after all, doesn't bounce back quite as quick as the years pass as one used to. Then it's home, to work the next morning and off to the ballpark again the next evening. Such is the life of a game-day grounds crew member.

When Ed Downs friends asks him how much he gets paid for working on the Phillies grounds crew, he has a stock reply: "I usually say, 'they pay me too much when it doesn't rain and not enough when it does.'"

For a grounds crew, rain is the bane of their profession. Jeff Wright puts it this way: "If it's not going to rain and it's a beautiful day...Hey, you're in a major league ballpark; you're working for a major league team; the smell in the stands of sausages cooking...how can you beat that job? But we love doing this. It's a great thing to do. And everyday without rain is an excellent day here."

Rain, rain delays...even a rain suspension...will linger long in the memories of Phillies fans. How could it not be, what with the rain delay which pushed the scheduled 8:30 start of Game 3 of the 2008 World Series back until 10:30 at night...or the suspension of play for two days after the sixth inning of Game 5?

Yet, this group of grounds crew workers are of the unanimous opinion that neither the Saturday night rain delay, nor the Monday night rain suspension were the two worst inclement weather encounters they had experienced in their long careers. To a man, they agree: The "Joe West Game" of 2007 and a San Diego doubleheader of 1993 were much, much worse to contend with. To recount:

It was September 9, 2007 when the Phillies and the Florida Marlins met. MLB.com baseball writer Ken Mandel described it in his account as "...a steady rain that (had) nearly turned the Citizens Bank Park infield into the Delaware River..." The game played on until a ninth-inning slip by infielder Tadahito Iguchi while trying to cover first base on a sacrifice attempt opened the door to a two-run outburst by the Marlins. Philadelphia lost the game, 4-2.

Jeff Wright remembers that night vividly: "We were out every half-inning for what must have been the entire game. We went through three skids, about 120 bags of calcimined clay ("diamond dry," a drying material, for the uninitiated) that night. It's alright, it's worth it if you win. But if you loose..."

Joe West, the crew chief, was umpiring 2nd base that night and he allowed play to continue. Rob Wright recalled that a day or two later, West "said he made a mistake, he should've called the game." Wright wished West had come to that realization 48 hours earlier. "It was a mess!" he said. "It was a night game. I had to go to work the next day and we didn't get out of here until I can't remember when..."

Their second memorable rain-influenced contest occurred 15 years earlier, in 1993, against the Padres at Veterans Stadium. The first game of the scheduled double-header encountered five rain delays alone. The second game didn't start until 1:15 AM. When the 1:15 starting time was announced over the public address system, many of the diminished fans still in the stands thought that was 1:15 the following afternoon. Wrong. The game finally ended at 4:41 in the morning on a base hit by, of all people, pitcher Mitch Williams—the "Wild Thing" with the bat or the ball. Ed Downs, for one, wished the game might have gone on longer.

"I was hopin' it would go a couple of more innings," he said. "It would've been kinda cool to be there when the sun came up and they're still playing." Not to happen, however.

The World Series, by contrast, posed none of those problems for the caretakers.

The Saturday night rain-delayed game may have caused the fans and the media some grief. Jayson Stark of ESPN.com called it "the madness that unfolded at Citizens Bank Park as a soggy night turned into a madcap Sunday morning." But for the Wrights, Downs, Mucha et al, it was just another rain delay like any regular season rain delay. Business as usual, and it was treated as such in terms of game prep.

In the suspended Monday night game, Jeff Wright maintains that the playing condition on the field looked a lot worse on television than it really was on the ground. "On TV or to the people in the stands, it looked like, man, there's a lot of water out there. But really, there wasn't a lot of water. It was surface water. Underneath, the skin (infield) was pretty dry…well, not dry but stable."

He doesn't dispute the decision to suspend the game, though he and others might have done so a half-inning earlier. Still, he said, the crew could have had the field in playing condition by noon or 1 PM the next day if the weather permitted. But it didn't. The rain continued through Tuesday. The final three innings were resumed two days later, on a Wednesday night. When the Phils won, the suspension became a non-factor. Championships have a way of doing that for players and fans, alike.

Coping with the weather, the crew agrees, is "a lot easier now," thanks to the advanced technology available to them. "There's not much chance we'll be blindsided," Jeff Wright observes. A major league grounds crew must be prepared to play the hand the weather deals them. This crew usually is.

When you've been at it for as long as these four fellas have, it doesn't matter what the venue is. Veterans Stadium or Citizens Bank Park…the job's still the same: Get the playing field in the best condition possible each and every time, each and every game, each and every season.

But there are differences in the different venues, and those differences are not lost on this quartet. Some of the differences are obvious to all. The Vet, for example, was artificial turf; CBP is natural grass. The Vet had cutouts around the bases. CBP is a full infield. You mow the grass at CBP. At the Vet, a motorized brush/sweeper fluffed up the turf.

Other differences are more physical in nature; or more aesthetic; or more atmospheric. Only those working the field might really know.

Jeff Wright had a two-fold observation to offer. "I'll tell you what, since I've been here (at Citizens Bank), I haven't had a bad back because it's softer. I might be in better shape, I don't know. But there I used to get bad backs…" And, the other—the heat on a mid-summer afternoon. "It got a little hot during the day (at the Vet) because you're in a bowl and that black asphalt and all that heat…it seemed like 140 degrees some days, but you just had to deal with it."

For Steve Mucha, it's the atmosphere around the ballyard. "The Vet was so much bigger," he opined. "There's a lot more ballpark atmosphere with Citizens Bank Park. And I think that lends quite a bit to the overall enjoyment of just being there, whether it be from my end or the fans' end. You don't need cowbells to make a lot of noise. And those rally towels are really phenomenal."

Ed Downs remembers the wind and the tarps at Veterans Stadium. "At the Vet, we had two covers. At the new ballpark, we have the one. The two at the Vet were actually heavier. There was a way you had to fold them to keep the infield completely dry. Whereas, the one now is just one bigger one, it's a lighter weight material. Plus, we have more guys, too."

That's true. A typical ground crew at Veterans Stadium was 10-to-12 per game. At Citizens, it's 20-22. That's because, primarily, there's so much more ground to cover…which translates into so much more work to do.

"The Vet was fun in a lot of ways," Rob Wright chimes in. "But there was not a whole lot involved over there. This has turned into a job."

Finally, there's the satisfaction one can take from a job well done.

"We're always getting compliments now about how nice this field (at Citizens Bank) is," Rob Wright explains. "Whether it's from the ballplayers, whether it's from the people in the stands, whether it's friends. We hear, 'How great this field looks' a lot. We never got that at the Vet. I loved the Vet. But talk about going unnoticed."

Their work did not, however, go unnoticed by the people who counted the most…the players, both at Citizens Bank and the Vet. Particularly in 2008 at CBP. "During the Divisional Series and the World Series, just about every player came up to every one of us on the grounds crew and thanked us for the great job we did in getting the field ready," Rob Wright said. "They didn't have to do that. We appreciated it, but they didn't have to do it. It's like Jeff says…it's part of the job. We all have a job to do and we all take pride in what we do. The players have every right to expect the field to be perfect. And that's what we try to do each and every game."

There was a moment, on the last day at the Vet, that will live probably forever in the memory of the grounds crew. The grounds crew was dressed in tuxedos…attire befitting the very special occasion it was. The grounds crew watched from the dugout area as the players, past and present, made their way from the field after the closing ceremonies.

"The players made a turn at the dugout," Jeff Wright recalled. "They all came over and shook our hands and said, 'Great job, great memories, we remember you back in whatever (year it was) when we played here. They remembered us when we had hair, or when we had dark hair.

That was special!"

As notice goes, it doesn't get much better than that.

So, the question arises: After 120 collective years of getting a baseball field, albeit a major league baseball field, into playing condition, how much longer do they intend to stay at it?

For Jeff Wright, the answer is easy. It is, after all, what he does. And what he does is satisfying personally and professionally to him. Grounds keeping got into his blood very early in his career and it's not likely to leave his blood stream any time soon.

He puts it this way: "I'm working in the game. I'm down there by the players doing what I enjoy doing. I enjoy the people I'm working with. We're having fun joking around. Can you beat this job? Well, you can get another job making a lot more money. But we love doing this. It's a great thing to do."

For Rob Wright, Steve Mucha and Ed Downs, it's just not that simple. After all, they have day jobs and family which command their time and attention as much as being at the ballpark 81 times a year.

Afternoon business specials present a particular challenge for them. Rob Wright can count on one hand the number of afternoon games he's been able to make in 34 years as a game-day grounds keeper…"probably less than five in all the years they've had the business person's special. My full time job just has to take precedent."

For Steve Mucha, much depends on the time of the month it is. "Being in accounting, it can be difficult to make a day game in the beginning of the month," he explains. "Other than that, I can use a vacation day. I've got enough of them to use and we're encouraged to use up all our vacation time as possible. So the business man's specials…I probably make about half of them during the season. If there's like eight, I'll probably make four. But if there's a conflict, Wawa always must take precedence."

Ed Down had a unique way to make day games very early in his stint with the ground crew. He called it "blood time" and it worked this way. "When I worked at the airport, they'd bring in the blood mobile and you'd earn four hours vacation when you donated. I would donate three or four times a year easily. Every time there was a business man's special, I'd turn in my four hours blood time." Since his stay at Penn was still in its relative infancy at the time of this conversation, it's not easy for him to make the afternoon games. "I don't have a lot of vacation time (accumulated) so I've missed a lot of them in the last few years," he acknowledges.

But day-game logistics aside, still they persist. The fact that their wives can appreciate what they do and why they do it makes their "fun job" that much easier to do.

"Jeff married Carol, who was an usherette," Steve Mucha explains. "Rob married Diane, who was an usherette; Ed married

Helen, who was an usherette. And I married Donna, who was an usherette. They know we like what we do as much as we do." In terms of domestic tranquility, that is a matter of no small import.

There's also the special satisfaction they can get from the unique role they play with the Phils...satisfaction like inviting youngsters down from the stands to help lay the chalk lines along left and right field; or handing a loose ball to a little boy.

"Since we've been at Citizens Bank Park, we invite a couple of kids on to the field to help us out," Steve Mucha explains. "The kids are like, 'Wow, I'm on the field!' It may be old hat to us, but it's pretty special to them...a Disney World opportunity. And it's special to us to be able to do something like that for them, too."

"Joe McFadden (of the grounds crew) started it," Ed Downs added in a later conversation. "I don't know how he came up with it, but we'll tell the guard, 'Try to pick somebody out, somebody whose parents are there, somebody who has a camera...It's pretty neat. And the parents get as much a kick out of it as the kids."

It's also neat when there's a loose baseball for one of the grounds crew to hand to a youngster as they're clearing the equipment from the field as the game begins. "Did you ever give an 8-year-old a baseball?" Ed Downs asked. "It's a great feeling. There are loose balls that roll around behind our screens or whatever...You see a kid who comes to the ballpark with his dad, and he's got his hat on; he's got his glove. And you just walk up to him, hand him a baseball. You feel like Santa Claus for a few minutes. Steve does it as well as anybody. He'll find the perfect kid. It's a wonderful feeling."

A lot of Rob Wright's pleasures came from watching the Phillies kids grow up. Like batboy Ruben Amaro, the Phils' newly designated general manager going into the 2009 season. Or the Boone brothers, Brett and Aaron, when their father, Bob, was catching for the Phils. And not to forget Gary Mathews Jr., a major leaguer in his own right and the son of Phils' outfielder turned broadcaster Gary Mathews. "We've seen them grow up," Rob says. "That was enjoyable."

So back to the question at hand: How long is each of you going to keep doing this?

Rob Wright answered this way: "In 1980, when I was in college, every year I'd think: 'This is gonna be it for me; this is my last year.' After our first daughter, Chelsey, was born in 1987, I thought that would be it. But here it is. A second daughter (Taylor) and a son (Drew) and I'm still here. I guess I'm just going to keep doing it as long as I can."

Steve Mucha knows that day will come when it's time to put down his chalk. It's just hasn't arrived yet. "As you get older, obviously, it's a lot more difficult to recover," he acknowledges. "But the social aspect, the camaraderie that has developed over the years between the guys. We have a good time down there. I love it, just love it."

Ed Downs comes at it from the same perspective. There will come a time to pass the torch. That registered with him most graphically as the Phils were making their run to the 2008 National League pennant and the World Series championship.

"Seeing the other guys on the crew, Richie Donnelly and Danny Buckley and Scott Anderson…these are kids who are in the mid-twenties who had never seen a championship. Just seeing how they reacted…that was something," he remembers. "Rob and I talked about it. We said, 'You know what, this is their time. We had our time in 1980.' They're in the same position now that we were then. It was really neat to see these young guys enjoy it!"

True enough. But for Downs, Rob Wright and Mucha… well, their time hasn't passed. Not just yet, anyway. As long as their health holds up and they stay in pretty good shape and the demands of job and family permit, they intend to keep doing what they've been doing for so long. For them, for the foreseeable future, a good day at Citizens Bank Park will continue to be a 2-1/2-hour game and a Phillies win. And, oh yes, no rain!!

THE LANDSCAPE MANAGER

The question was pertinent so it was put directly if imprecisely to the woman in question: What's a nice girl like you doing in a place like this?

The lady was Pamela Hall. She's the landscape manager for the Philadelphia Phillies national league baseball team. And the place was Citizens Bank Park, the team's home venue.

So question really was, and it bore repeating: What's a landscape manager doing at a place like a baseball stadium? Pam Hall didn't hesitate in her response.

"I love my job," she replied. And, oh, by the way, she informed, there's a difference…a big difference…between a stadium and a park. And Citizens Bank Park is just that—a ballpark, not a stadium.

Stadiums are coliseum-like in their aesthetics. Big…bold…lots of cement, surrounded by concrete parking lots with a couple of trees thrown in for effect. A place to go (even tailgate if you like), watch a sporting event and leave.

Ballparks, on the other hand, are just that—parks. Parks with trees, flowers, shrubs, ornamental grasses, perennials, ground cover and designed landscaping. Citizens Bank Park qualifies and deliberately so.

"What the Phillies did," Pam Hall explains, "they created a ballpark. It is truly a park; it's 100 acres…just under 2,000 trees here; there's over 5,000 shrubs, different kinds of shrubs. The whole place is landscaped. What the Phillies wanted to do was to create a fun place for people to come. Aesthetically, I think, it (Citizens Bank Park) is a beautiful ballpark inside and out."

To maintain the aesthetic of the place, you require someone who knows what he or she is doing…a landscape manager, a landscape architect. Pam Hall knows what she's doing. So now you know why she's at where's she's at and why she's doing what she's doing.

What you don't know is how she got there. That's part of her story, as well.

—m—

Truth is, Pam Hall took a very circuitous route to Citizens Bank Park.

She was born in New London, Connecticut, and received her undergraduate degree in 1980 from the University of Connecticut—a major in English Literature, a minor in Business Law.

She says she really didn't know what she wanted to do after graduation. Always having been fascinated by "how things work...and putting things together" she took a job as a "ship fitter" with General Dynamics in Groton, Connecticut, the submarine capital of the world. After two years at General Dynamics—"reading plans and implementing those plans for submarines," (including work associated with the Trident nuclear power submarine)—she said to herself: "It's time to go."

Go she did. She arrived in Philadelphia in the early 1980's— "'81, '82, something like that"—and enrolled in the landscape architecture advanced degree program at the University of Pennsylvania. "I was always fascinated with architecture but I knew I didn't want to design buildings," she recalled. "I wanted to something to do outside and I thought about working for the National Park Service. They were looking for a number of landscape architects. I kept bumping into it (landscape architecture)...I thought, 'Okay, this must be a sign.'" So she went to Penn, met the chair of the Landscape Architecture Department, was "taken" by what the program had to offer, applied, was accepted, and earned a Master's Degree in what became her ultimate career track.

Her first stop after graduate school was Cherry Hill, New Jersey, where she served as the township's landscape architect and "learned a lot" about site planning, historic preservation and zoning. Then came a stint with a private sector firm specializing in engineering, planning and landscaping where "I went from site plan review to designing large residential areas, large subdivisions, laying them out." Parks and industrial parks also came under her umbrella.

Back to the public sector she went, doing basically the same thing in Jersey City, New Jersey, when she her career track returned her to Philadelphia. It was while she was doing enterprise zone volunteer work for the West Philadelphia Economic Community that she connected with the Phillies. Indirectly, at first.

Thanks to the network she built while working in the enterprise zone, she was put in touch with John Stranix, the Phillies project manager for the Citizens Bank Park construction. She landed a job with the Philies as Site Work Manager for CBP.

"My job," she explained, "was to act in the Phillies' interest" on a construction contract worth about $100 million. That involved concrete, that involved steel, that involved moving soil down to the Navy Yard temporarily, that involved parking and paving. It also involved having markers set in place in a parking lot across the street from Citizens Bank Park memorializing where home plate and the three bases were situated in what once was Veterans Stadium. Pam Hall wasn't a party to Vet lore. But she understands just how nostalgic the Phils and the fans are about the place. Of the markers, she says: "They're in bronze, bronze markers in the parking lot" for permanent keeping.

When the site work was done, there was the landscaping to be addressed and maintained. Landscape architecture, you see, involves more...much, much more...than just gardens, flora and shrubs. "It starts with soil and geology and hydrology," Hall explains for the uninitiated. "Before you even get to plants, it's what underneath, all of that. Before you get to design, you have to understand your environment."

She recalls how one of her Penn professors..."a British fellow" by the name of Anthony Walmsley...described the profession: "You're like a conductor of an orchestra," he said. "You have to know a number of different things" about the music, the instruments, the sound and how they all resonate together. So it is, Pam Hall continued, with landscape architecture. "You have to know a number of things...like paving, whether it's concrete or pavers, asphalt, granite, brick, what's going to go under, what makes it all stable..."

When CBP opened in April of 2004, there were still some loose ends to be tied. Pam Hall remained as site work manager. "We were still getting our soil back from the Navy Yard, and finishing the parking project. There were a number of contractors still out there, and that meant there was landscaping which still hadn't been completed. We still had curbing to do, we still had concrete work to do." When the touchup was finished, Pam Hall moved from site work to landscape management. Four years later, she still was at it as enthusiastic about what she was doing as ever.

Pam Hall's day during the regular baseball season normally begins about 7 AM and ends about 5 or 6 that evening. There's a lot to do and a game to play. So she and her crew get an early start to address the landscaping issues before the fans start to arrive en masse. For afternoon games, the time to tend to the landscaping is compressed considerably.

It matters little to Hall and her crew, however, whether it's a day game or a night game. What matters more is whether the Phillies are in a home stand or whether they're away on a road trip. Landscaping work during a home stand usually is limited to the basics of having the park ready for that day's crowd. It's on road trips and non-game days when the landscapers can catch up on the things they couldn't get done while the team was at home.

"You're always prepping for the next home stand," she explains one quiet morning in August as the Phils were about to complete a three-game series with the St. Louis Cardinals and head out on the road. "Maybe I've got to replant some of the bullpen. I'm going to do that on non-game days.

"We just bought 20 trees. I'm not going to plant those trees today, but tomorrow. Knowing the team is out of town next week, we'll put all those trees in and get them watered and get them on a watering schedule so we can get them healthy—at least somewhat healthy—before the team's next game and the fans get out in the parking lot."

The plants above the left field wall are the most labor intensive landscaping area in the entire ballpark. "It gets a lot of abuse. Balls drop in there. Batting practice and home runs. Fans reach for them. Plants are pulled up in the process. We have to replace them. The left field wall..we have to rip everything out and replace it a couple of times a year." Also keep it trimmed throughout the season. Pam Hall was spotted clipping the plants in the left field beds before an important series as the season entered the homestretch with the Phils very much in contention for a play-off position. The umpires passed the word, she explained, that some of the plants were growing over the wall—or at least appeared to be from their vantage point--and could come into play. Hence, the clippers at work.

The landscaping budget for the Phillies is no small item...in excess of $1 million each year. Landscaping, to be done the right way, is a big money investment. It also is a high maintenance enterprise.

Hall has a fulltime crew of five at her disposal. Plus 10 high school kids for seven weeks during the summer. Eight of the kids come from Saul Agricultural School in the city. All 10 are youngsters who have demonstrated a serious interest in horticulture, landscape architecture, landscape construction. It's a field they intend to pursue beyond their high school days.

She's also very much a hands-on manager. She's in her mini-Deere motor truck shortly after her arrival making her rounds of the premises. In season, Mondays, Wednesdays and Fridays are watering days. 1,000 gallons of water dispensed by three trucks—a 500-gallon truck, a 300-gallon truck and a 200-gallon truck.

The first location to be tended is the bullpen area where there are plants and hanging baskets to be watered. The 40 large containers in the front of Citizens Bank Park also all need watered. The largest truck, as might be expected, is assigned to the places where there are biggest beds; the smaller trucks are used for the "smaller places" around the ballpark.

Her clippers and her shears are very much at hand as Pam Hall circles the exterior and interior of the park. She's not beyond taking a clipper from one of her high school students and snip a shrub or two to demonstrate how the bushes should be clipped. Later, she'll be on the concourse or in the mezzanine supervising the replacement of plants which are delivered to the location on a truck cart.

She's also very much a teacher for her high school staff. "The students usually are interested in design, or at least think they are," she explains. "I say to them, 'This is your palette. This is what's in our nursery. What are you going to do? What do you want to do here? It's fun because a lot of time, most kids will say, 'Well, I would put three over here and three over there.

"And that's fine. Except that's residential. I used to do residential and this is not residential here. In this space alone you need a couple of hundred…not three. So it's helping them with scale. This is a huge place. It sucks up a lot of plants. So we're designing something all the time."

Hall constantly is on the alert in her daily travels about the premises for plants which need replacing. She's also very conscious of the color scheme visible from different locations throughout the ballpark. The colors, she says, help to "soften the atmosphere" of the place, an objective she takes most seriously.

She wants the ballpark to be soft…"a nice entrance for people…pleasant for people to come into. You feel like you can have a picnic here." Well, not quite, but close enough. Similarly, Hall is very conscious of the people who work in the ballpark. She wants their surroundings to be as pleasant as possible, as well. "People who work here spend a great deal of time here, a lot of hours, 10 to 12 hours a day," she explains. I feel a responsibility to make it pleasant for them. I want it to be pleasant for them to come into and for them to leave. We want them all (fans and employees alike) to enjoy the park while they're here."

Some things are beyond Hall and her crew's control. Early on in the life of Citizens Bank Park, for example, 45 oak trees had to be replaced. "They weren't going to make it," she remembers. "There are some things that look great on paper, on the design. But when you put them out on the field, some things just may not work." So it was that 45 of the original oak trees were out.

More recently, the summer of 2008, to be exact, the city of Philadelphia undertook a paving project on Pattison Avenue adjoining the ballpark. The heat of the paving machines singed "a lot" of the trees. "Half our trees had turned brown from the heat that came up from these machines.   It takes a lot of time to get these trees to 3-years-old and in a healthy condition. Within a half-hour, they were singed. So what we had to do was trim them, keep them watered and keep them coming back. Aesthetically, it didn't look so great. But there are some things (man made or from

Mother Nature) you can't control. I've learned on this job that if I can't do anything about it I just have to let it go, replace it the best I can. But you have to move on."

And there's the weeding...there's always weeding to be done. While some of the crew is watering, others will be weeding. Hall will do some of it herself as she moves about the exterior of the park. "There are a lot of weeds," she says. "It's a constant for us. Weeding and taking out the plants, the shrubs that have died."

In the summer, it's also making certain the mulch is kept damp. "As the summer gets hotter and hotter, the mulch gets dryer and dryer. A lot of times we'll have trucks on the mulch. Or someone will discard a cigarette. So you have to keep things a little bit damp in some areas around the border of the park."

Hall understands that dealing with 3 million people who pass through the Citizens Bank Park turnstiles each year, there are landscaping issues she and her crew will have to deal with several times each season. "Fan traffic can be a little destructive. There're going to be things that just have to be taken care of, things that are going to have to be replanted. I tell my crew, don't get upset if things get torn out or whatever. We just replace it. People are here to watch a ballgame. This isn't Longwood Gardens. It's a ballpark."

Summer may be for watering and weeding. Winter is for ordering. Spring and Fall are for planting. "In the Spring, we are planting biannuals. And when we plant them, we're also planting about 6,000 pansies. In the Fall, we're planting bulbs, hundreds of bulbs that will go in front of our building. We're also planting pansies. You get a lot of bang for your buck with pansies. They bloom a long time. You can plant them in the Fall. They'll also bloom again in the Spring."

In the Fall of the regular season, like the World Series year of 2008, Hall and her crew are particularly attentive to the Phillies play-off position in the standings. "We have to pay attention to whether or not the Phillies make the play-offs. If it looks like we're about to make the play-offs, we're going to change things up. Like the left field wall, the bullpen. We're showing color all the time, trying to show the ballpark at its best."

Truth is, when the home team wins the World Series as the Phils did in 2008, the ballpark always looks good. But rest assured, Pam Hall and her crew did more than their part to keep it that way.

—m—

One might think when the season is over and Winter sets in, the landscaping staff might enjoy some down time. Wrong. Between November and February, Hall says, "we're extremely busy. As soon as we finish our Fall planting, which is, again, bulbs and annuals, we're going into the holiday season. Holiday season means that we decorate inside and outside. This ballpark is never closed. There are parties, bar mitzvahs, weddings, holiday parties. We are decorating. And we recognize all holidays… Christmas, Hanukkah, Kwanza, Three Kings Day…."

So it was that one week after the 2008 World Series had concluded so gloriously on the playing field at Citizens Bank Park, Pam Hall was busy working with the city and the carpenters and the electricians getting ready for the holidays. "And," she reminded herself, "everything has to come down in January."

Except for a three-week stretch heading into February, there's not much slack in the schedule. Come February, and it's getting ready for the Spring all over again.

Pam Hall knows the role landscaping plays in the environment in and around Citizens Bank Park. She isn't presumptuous enough to suggest it's started a trend in baseball construction around the country, although she remembers the Washington Nationals had a delegation check the park out in the design stage for its new stadium. "I met with them about what we had done here," she says, but hasn't been to Washington to see for herself what the Nationals did in this regard.

But trend or not, it doesn't matter to her. It's her job to keep Citizens Bank Park in Philadelphia exactly what it was intended to be--a park, not a stadium. And, to coin an old baseball expression, she won't take her eye off the ball.

"The Eye in the Sky"

The gates to Citizens Bank Park do not open until Wes Whittington gets the okay.

In most cases, it's a rather routine process. On the very rarest of occasions, it is not. But in either case, until Whittington gets an all-clear, the gates won't open.

Whittington has been director of Communications for the Philadelphia Phillies since 1971. "Communications" is the official title. But not in the traditional definition of the word. In Whittington's case, and in layman's terminology, he's more of a trouble-shooter, a problem solver…and a coordinator.

Whittington is seated in his glass-paneled booth high above Citizens Bank Park adjacent to the giant Phanavision scoreboard in left field. It's called the "Eye in the Sky" box among the Phillies family of game day employees. And rightfully so. It gives him a wonderful panorama of the ballpark.

Whittington assumes his post each home game about ½ hour before the scheduled gate openings. For Ashburn Alley--the park's signature general admission attraction along the main concourse overlooking the home and visitors' bullpens--that's normally 4:30 for a 7:05 regular season night game. For all other gates, it's a 5:30 opening.

The first thing Whittington needs to hear is an "All Clear!" from the 20-to-25 supervisors stationed strategically throughout the park. "What that's saying to me," he explains "is that 'I have checked my area; there's no packages; there's no boxes, no hoses, nothing that anybody could trip over…but most of all there's no boxes, no backpacks, okay. Once they check for that, they'll call me. I'll check them off. When we hear from all of them, we know it's okay to open the gates. If we don't hear from one supervisor, the gates will not open until we do."

More than 90 per cent of the time, the process works flawlessly. Oh, sometimes a forecast of serious rain will cause a delay in the gate opening. Or a report of a section of the ballpark that is just not ready yet for fan traffic. And sometime—not often, but sometime—something more serious occurs. When it does, all precautions, extraordinary and otherwise, are taken. If, for security reasons, the police are summoned, all decisions are deferred to them.

(One such occasion occurred during the final days of the 2008 regular season. Ashburn Alley already had already been opened and the teams were taking batting practice when three suspicious packages—about 8-to-10 inches long, 5-to-6 inches wide, each wrapped in duct tape—were found in the vicinity of the first base gate. The area was cordoned off, all other gates were ordered to remain closed, police were called and ultimately, the bomb squad was summoned. A wider area along the first base line was cleared, half of the building evacuated and the packages were detonated on site without harm to property and person. It ultimately was determined the packages were hot dogs used in an advertising shoot for television and left by mistake where they were discovered.)

Wes Whittington was a North Carolinian before he was a Philadelphian. He was just a young boy when his parents migrated to the city from Ashville, North Carolina—"too young," he remembers "to say where I wanted to go." Still, he settled in. Became a product of the West Philadelphia public school system, began a career in auto body repair, married and, ultimately, in 1973, moved to Buena, New Jersey with his bride, there to remain to this day. For he and his family, the move to Pennsylvania worked better than even he might have anticipated.

He was just a growing boy when he became attracted to the auto body repair business. He remembers precisely how it happened. "My father had an accident and we used to go to check on the car. And I'd say, 'Woo, how'd they do that?' And, 'Wow, how'd they do that?' I was just amazed. Drawing blueprints and stuff like that (in high school)...that was boring compared to what I saw in that auto body repair shop. So, I said to myself, 'I want to learn how to do auto body.'"' And he did. At a General Motors training school. A career was born.

Whittington found a job with a well-established family auto body shop in the city. He was an employee "for 12, 13 years," if memory serves him right, before buying into the business as a partner in 1978. Twelve years later, 1990, he bought the business outright and ran it as the sole proprietor until he sold it in 2003.

Whittington was deep into auto repair when his love of baseball took him down a second career track…this time with the Phillies.

"I was coming out to the games (at Connie Mack Stadium) two or three times a week…a paying customer," he recalls, when his brother-in-law first raised the notion of working for the team with him. The brother-in-law was a Phillies usher. "He says, 'Hey, look, you want to get a job?' I say, Wait a minute. You mean getting paid to watch the Phillies? He says, 'Yes.' I say, Yes, I'll take a job. I mean, they're going to pay me to watch the ballgame. I'll take it!"

Whittington started with the Phillies in 1964 as an usher in the seats along the third base line at Connie Mack. He truly enjoyed it, he says. "I was in a permanent section and all my fans, every year they'd come back. 'Hey Wes, how you doin? How was your winter?' And we'd just carry on. Every day, they would come in and we would have good baseball conversations."

Shortly before the Phillies moved to Veterans Stadium in 1971, Whittington was asked to move from his usher's position into security. He initially was reluctant to do so.

"They (the Phillies, Pat Cassidy in particular) called me in the winter and said, 'Wes, we're starting something new. We're starting our own security and Joe Yang was going to be heading the unit. Joe wants you to become a security guard. We're only picking a select group and he wants you to be a part of that group.'

"I said, Well, I've been an usher all my life. I don't know anything about being a security guard. Let me sleep on it and I'll call you back in the morning."

Sleep on it, he did. The next morning he calls Pat Cassidy back and responds: "Look, if Joe Yang and you want me to become a security guard, I'll do it." But, he had a caveat. "If I don't like it, I want to go back to being an usher because I had a section I liked. I knew everyone, all my season ticket holders and it was a lot of fun."

It was an option neither Whittington nor the Phillies had to explore. Whittington joined the security staff on opening day in 1971. A mere 14 days later, he was switched to still another function—trouble-shooting, problem solving, coordinating. He's been at it ever since.

From his perch in his narrow booth—25 feet long, 10 feet wide—high above the main concourse, Wes Whittington has an unobstructed view of the playing field below him and the grandstands in front of him.

His communications links are in easy reach beside him—the two-way radio, the phones, the beepers and the binoculars. To his left, Frank Diskerman is manning his portable laptop to flash the advertising displays on the electronic field level panels in the left and right field corners. To his right, Scott Finzen or Bill Graves (or someone else from the 24/7 command center staff) is working the six cameras which constantly scan the ballpark and the crowd for signs of problems or trouble.

If not for the fact there was a job to do, it would be an absolutely ideal spot from which to watch a ballgame. But Whittington and his associates know why they're located where they are with such a premier view of all that transpires before them. They're very vigilant about what they do. So much so, in fact, it's not unusual for one to ask another: "Hey, how'd the Marlins get 2 runs?"

When Whittington started on the job, he didn't have the view, the electronic access or the communication tools he has today. When he first accepted Pat Cassidy's offer to leave his gate security position to become a response coordinator, his first station was in the 200 level of Veterans Stadium in the vicinity of the centerfield scoreboard.

He had a desk, two phones, and walkie talkies. What he didn't have was a clear view of the field. When problems arose, he often was flying in the blind to start. "Actually," he remembered, "I often had to leave my desk and run through the opening which we called the bombatory to look out. When he looked out, he remembered, he was in "dead centerfield." On those occasions when he could or would remain at his desk: "I used to have to call to the scoreboard and say, 'Do me a favor. Take a look at Section 541 and tell me what's going on…whether I need to send some security over there, or whatever. And they would look for me and they would say, 'Yeah, Wes, you do have a problem.' Or, 'No, you do not have a problem.' They were my 'eye-in-the-sky,' so to speak. That's where the designation came from."

At times, Whittington took it upon himself to walk around Veterans Stadium, his two-way radio holstered conveniently in his belt. "What I would do is sit at my desk for an hour, an hour-and-one half, then I would leave.

"I would actually start all the way up on the 700 level and walk all the way around the 600 level, the 500 level. Unless there was a problem, I'd stop for something to eat on 400. If there was a problem, I'd go directly to the problem."

When he came upon a problem like an altercation or such, he had a standard line to talk the issue down. "I'd say to the troublemakers: Look,. If I can't resolve this, I'll get security. If that doesn't work, I'll get the police. If that doesn't work, I'll get the National Guard. And if that doesn't work, I'll get the Marine Corps. So there's no way you can win this. So you might as well sit down and enjoy the game and relax because it's going to happen that I have to get this resolved."

Most problems, he found, were resolvable. But not all. The security staff was well aware: "If Wes calls security, he's in trouble!" And reinforcements would know to head to the trouble spot on the double. It didn't happened all that often. But when it did, security at the Vet knew not to take the call casually. It wasn't.

It's not necessary anymore for Wes Whittington to leave his post. With his "eye in the sky" view, the cameras at his command, his binoculars, and his radio and cell communications with the hosts, supervisors and security located throughout the ball park, problems can be addressed almost instantly.

The security cameras are surveying the stands when the radio to Whittington's right crackles. It's a host reporting a spill of French Fries on the concourse. Whittington immediately contacts the facilities department to dispatch a cleanup crew. One problem addressed.

There will be others before the game is over. There always are. Medical problems are of constant concern. With 45,000 or more people in the stands each night or afternoon, they're impossible to avoid.

Each host and hostesses is equipped with a pager that instantly alerts Whittington and the medical unit simultaneously of any ailments a fan in the stands may be experiencing. The pager will flash "Medical." A response is set in motion immediately. Whittington has the cameras focus instantly on the area. The hosts or hostesses have a yellow card to hold up for easy detection. Whittington will tell them to move the card around so they can more easily be spotted by the binoculars or the cameras. Medical support is on its way.

Fights…now that's another matter. Altercations, in fact, are a little easier for Whittington to detect. When a scrap breaks out, people are usually standing up. There's a lot of pushing and shoving in the area. It's not very hard from Whittington's perch to locate the trouble spot. Security is dispatched immediately to restore order. Reinforcements will be called in, if necessary. The magic of electronic advancements makes it possible to respond so much faster than it used to be.

Signs, as mundane as they might seem, also command the attention of the "Eye in the Sky" booth. Graves' cameras spot a sign in the upper deck, Section 309. The cameras can't capture the wording precisely. Whittington asks a host to check it out. Signs obstructing another fan's line of sight, or signs with offensive language, will be addressed. This one proves harmless. "Circle me!" it reads, with a circle around the appeal. "Somebody wants to get on television," Whittington and the section staff concludes. It's not bothering anyone. So it was left unattended.

Whittington also knows from years of experience when certain events are likely to be problematic and when they are not.

Afternoon business specials usually are very routine and trouble free.

College nights are not. Not when the beer in the parking lots adjacent and across the street from the ballpark flow much freer than usual. Coupled that with the natural exuberance of youth... well, college nights always seem to be more active than one might hope.

And then, there are the Met games. Always the Met games.

Philadelphia fans are renowned nationwide for their passion for their sports teams. Visiting teams know full well to bring their thick skins if not their earplugs when they come to town. Met fans are no less passionate and competitively driven. When the Mets and Phillies faithful mix, whether in Philadelphia or New York, the electricity in the air is transparent.

Whittington knows it's going to be a busy afternoon or night when the Mets are the opposition. . The last time the Mets were in Philly, his incident report covered three pages, including 10 altercations. This particular afternoon, a business person's special against the St. Louis Cardinals, there were only four incidents on his report midway through the game. And two of them were minor medical matters. Such is the nature of the competition.

Make no mistake, Wes Whittington certainly enjoys his new surroundings at Citizens Bank Park. But like so many others with his many years of service with the Phillies, he misses Veterans Stadium in so many ways.

What he misses most is the daily contact he would have with his game-day counterparts. Now, despite all its modern amenities, his "Eye in the Sky" box is just not on folks' normal traffic patterns.

He welcomed those occasions at the Vet where he could sit one-on-one with a host or hostess and just talk...or be a father-confessor of sorts, when need be. "Many times I was like a priest," he says. "People used to come in and tell me their problems because they knew it would stay with me at my desk. If you wanted to air it out about something, I had a chair there and you could come there and I'd let you blast me with their problem." He helped them simply by being a good listener. "I miss that!" he observes.

"The Vet" also had "so many memories," for him. One he would have preferred not to experience.

"A guy fell down into a pit near where our scoreboards where," he remembers. "It had to be 80-90 feet. He was intoxicated. He fell into this pit. They call me. I had to call a helicopter (for medical assistance). It was at the end of the game. I went over and I looked at the guy down on that concrete. I didn't sleep that night. I was very sorry I looked at that guy down on that concrete. But, it was part of my job."

Whittington's other memories have a distinctly more pleasant theme to them. One special one stands out. It was the Phillies World Series win in 1980. Whittington's job, he remembers, "was to go out onto the field and stand behind the pitcher's mound. I ran out onto the field after we won the World Series and I'm standing there. They're (the players) are jumping on top of each other 5, 10 feet from me."

Why were you out on the field, he was asked? He replied: "I guess just to make sure there were no fans running out there to interrupt the celebration. We had police of there, certainly. But that was my job. And I'm standing out there and I can see the reaction from the crowd. There was no one who had the view I had…the entire stadium, the ballplayers, the fans reaction…it was unbelievable!"

Whittington's picture even made Time Magazine's coverage of the World Series clinching game. And people would say to him, "How come you wouldn't smile?" And he'd tell them: "Because I could not believe the site I was at and what I was seeing. I could not believe the sight I was seeing." It was a scene the Phillies wouldn't relive for 28 years. No wonder it's so indelibly imprinted in Whittington's memory file.

Like so many of his game-day counterparts, Wes Whittington puts in long days with the Phillies. It starts with his hour-to-hour-and-one half drive from his New Jersey home to Citizens

Bank Park. He's at his sky-box desk by 4 PM for a 7:05 PM start. Then there's the game. Then there's a sweep of the ballpark to be certain no one's in the rest room or any of the shopping venues before the ballpark is put to bed for the night. Then the incident reports to complete. Usually, it's an hour or so after the last out before Whittington can head home, only to start in an extended home stand all over again the next day.

It's certainly been easier for him since he sold his business. But even with the auto repair shop to run, Whittington's been very diligent about his responsibilities with the Phillies. He could afford to be because the good reputation of his business preceded him.

"We had three generations (of customers) coming into my business," he recalls. "People who would say to their sons and daughters, 'Look take it over there, see Wes. I don't have to go.' You know how most fathers have to go with their sons. No, it wasn't like that with us. 'Just go over there and see Wes. I know it's going to be done right and the price is going to be right.'" So he seldom encountered a potential conflict on where he needed to be on a given day. His shop was in good hands while he was at the ballpark.

And how much longer will he be at it?

Whittington doesn't know.

"There comes a point every year when you say, 'This is my last year,'" he admits. "But then Spring rolls around and you're right back in the groove. People ask, 'Are they going to win? Are you ready?' And my first instinct is to say, 'No, I'm not ready.' But once I get in, the first call I get on the walkie-talkie, the first call I get on the phone...By the end of the day, it's like I never left. I'm right back in it."

Will he know when it's time to stop?

"I would like to think so. Right now, I feel like I can go on forever. I'm 67 years old. I'm in good health. But how long can I go? Honestly, I don't know."

The steps might tell him.

Whittington has an aversion to elevators. So every day or night, he climbs three flights up 75 steps or so to arrive at his perch high above Citizens Bank Park. The last 25 steps are the most difficult to maneuver. They're in enclosed area. They're steel and they're narrow. Wide enough for only one shoe at the time. It's no walk in the park to climb them at any time. 81 or more times a year certainly can take their toll. "If anything," he confides to a visitor, "those steps...the steps you came up...those steps might wear me out. Those steps could take away a lot of years."

But until they do...until he concludes he just can't climb them any more...rest assured: When you're seated in Citizens Bank Park...anywhere is Citizens Bank Park...Wes Whittington has you covered from his "Eye in the Sky!"

Security

Joe DeJulius worked on the construction crew that laid the brick as Veterans Stadium was going up. (Actually, he stipulates in the interest of accuracy, it wasn't brick so much as it was cinder block "They didn't have too much brick, but they had block... most everything was block over there," he says.) Brick or block, he helped build the stadium. So it only stood to reason that he would be there 35 years later to see the place come tumbling down. Little did he realize that in the interim it would become almost like a second home to him.

Sam Kline, a life-long Phillies fan and a game-day security supervisor at Citizens Bank Park, remembers the night he had to eject an unruly patron from the premises. Little did he know that the man in question would almost immediately become a passing friend of his.

Nick Schmanek, another security supervisor, still recalls those rare occasions in his early days with the Phillies when, among other assignments, he had to chase disruptive fans who made their way for whatever silly reason on to the Vet playing field. "I took that personal," he says. "I'm not a muscle guy but I could always run." Today, removed from field level to the Citizens Bank Park main concourse, he considers it a good day if all he has to talk to the fans about is the game.

And DeWitt Hobbs, from the isolated bowels of CBP at the entry to the visiting club house, still likes to reminisce about watching Pete Rose Jr. walk the halls of the Vet...or Bob Boone's boys—Aaron and Brett—bouncing a rubber ball against the wall outside the Phillies locker room in the early 1970's.

Joe DiJulius; Sam Kline; Nick Schmanek; DeWitt Hobbs... four different men, with four different backgrounds, from four different locales in and around Philadelphia. But four men who come together at Citizens Bank Park at least 81 times a year as members of the Philadelphia Phillies ballpark security staff with one common purpose: To keep things orderly throughout the park so the fans can enjoy the contest in front of them without disruption or distraction.

Joe DiJulius was 4 years old when, in 1936, his family migrated to Philadelphia from Tamaqua in the heart of the Northeast Pennsylvania coal region. His father had to be hospitalized for a variety of ailments he suffered after his long years in the coal mines. Tamaqua had no facility that was up to the task at the time. So Mr. DiJulius was transferred to Philly to be admitted to the hospital at the Philadelphia Naval Shipyard. "It was too much going back and forth to Tamaqua," he remembers in explaining the relocation. Regrettably, his father passed away when DiJulius was 6. His family never returned to his roots. Today, as a security host, he's stationed down in the field level seats in Section 132A along the 3rd base line, just left of the visiting team dugout, tending particularly to the needs of physically disabled fans who are seated in the section.

Sam Kline is a Philadelphian through and through. Philadelphia born, Philadelphia bred, married a local girl and raised with her a daughter and two sons—the youngest of whom in 2008 was serving his second combat tour with U.S. Special Forces in the cauldron that is the Middle East—first in Afghanistan and then Iraq. "You think of them every day, but you have to put 'em in God's hands," he murmured reflectively. Sam Kline and his security associates work the pavilion level of Citizens Bank Park, Sections 201 and 301 to Sections 210 and 310 during Phillies home stands.

Nick Schmanek, another security supervisor, patrols the concourse with his staff in the area which is probably the "hottest spot" in the ballpark…the bullpen area off Ashburn Alley. It's in easy view and shouting distance for the throngs of those vocal Phillies fans who constantly pass through for most if not all a nine-inning game. It is, in short, a place ripe for potential verbal turmoil by the very fact of its proximity. "We get a lot of people in a very small area," Schmanek explains. Most games, he thinks it's going to be a good night if he makes it through the 5th inning without a verbal incident. When the Mets are in town, make that the 1st inning.

DeWitt Hobbs, meanwhile, is stationed in the relative calm outside the visiting team locker room beneath the stands, far removed from the daily fan traffic. Technically, he's more of an attendant than a security guard. But it's his function to make certain no unauthorized person invades the privacy of the visiting clubhouse. He's been doing that for the Phils since the club moved from Connie Mack to the Vet in 1971. And quiet and unassuming though he is, he's good at what he does.

Three of the four…DiJulius, Schmanek and Hobbs, readily admit they had economics in mind when they went to work for the Phillies (DiJulius in 1989, Schmanek in 1994 and Hobbs in '57): Earning extra money to supplement their family income. Kline says he applied as "sort of a lark."

As they tell it, It happened this way.

"We were a little slow in brickwork," DiJulius recalls. "A neighbor of mine (who was a Phillies game day employee) asked if I wanted to go to work for them, too. I said, 'Okay.' Came down and was hired on the spot. Been here ever since." It wasn't too long after he was hired that he got himself a nickname. "Coal miner," they called him. It was an obvious reference to his Tamaqua roots. But there also was another reason, he explained. "We had too many, Joe's." DiJulius retired as bricklayer in 1996— "I got my 50-year pin this year (2008)," he is proud to inform—but he was concerned from day one about the consequences of inactivity in retirement. "I've seen too many people fade away when they retired," he declares. "Fading away" was not for him. It still isn't.

Nick Schmanek wasn't contemplating retirement when he applied with the Phillies. Not with "three young kids and a fourth on the way." For him, it was more a matter of "necessity." Having cut his teeth in the boiler room of what is Philadelphia city politics—he's director of constituent services for Philadelphia City Councilman Frank DiCicco when he spoke--the Phillies offered not only an income supplement; but also, a diversion. "I'm a people kind of a guy," he acknowledges. "I enjoy the give and take with the fans, so long as it doesn't get out of hand. This job's not complicated…just keep it orderly." And most of the time he does.

DeWitt Hobbs was a welder and shop planner at the Philadelphia Naval Shipyard before retiring after 38-1/2 years in the Navy's employ. His family lived three blocks from Connie Mack Stadium. His brother worked for the Phils for a year before he, with his brother's help, became a Phillies game-dayer, too. He's still at it because, like DiJulius, he simply likes what he does. "It keeps my mind goin'" he declares. Besides, there's "no stress" involved. A pretty good combination at this stage in his life, he believes.

Sam Kline…now that's a different story. It was 1997 and a co-worker of his at Philadelphia Traffic Court where he has been employed for 17 years mentioned that he had a friend who worked with the Phillies. So just sort of kidding around, Kline said: 'Well, listen. Next time you talk to him, if they need an extra set of hands down there, have 'em give me a call.' The next thing I know, I got an application to fill out. Three weeks later, I got a call. I came down for an interview and here I am." And, as a life-long Phillies fan, here he intends to stay.

Kline and Schmanek might conventionally be described as two of the "law and order" guys stationed strategically around Citizens Bank Park. They and their security staff patrol their areas with a detail of Philadelphia police in position to assist if necessary. "We wear quite a few hats," they explained. "We're there to watch out…to make sure the policies and the procedures of the ballclub are followed for the comfort and security of the fans. We're up there to answer questions, to locate lost children, to deal with medical emergencies, crowd control…basically, just making sure everything's secure for the fans."

Every so often, not regularly (maybe three or four times a season by Kline's count)…but every so often, they have to physically confront fans who believe the rules and regulations of the ballpark don't apply to them. "We always try to talk the situation down first," Kline said. "But some people don't want to cooperate. They feel as though they're being picked on. Before we eject anybody, they've been given two or three warnings about their behavior, their language, whatever. If it comes to an ejection, basically, the fan made the decision to push it that far."

One ejection will remain with Sam Kline forever. "It was back at the Vet," he remembers. "One night I got a complaint from a couple of fans and one of the hosts that a fellow in Section 527 was being disorderly. He had been warned about his mouth and his actions and whatnot. But he had a few too many drinks. So finally, enough was enough. The hosts came and got me. I got a couple of other security people and we went down and got him out of his seat. He was being belligerent…beer muscles and bottle courage, you know. We told him he had been warned, and that he had to be ejected. He really got nasty about it, but we did manage to get him out of the ballpark.

The story continues. "Two nights later, I'm standing at my post and this fellow walks up to me. He said: 'Remember me?' I said, 'Yes, I did.' And he said: 'I just felt as though I needed to come back to you and apologize for my behavior. Regardless of whether or not I was drinking, I had no right to talk to you the way I did.' And I said, 'No problem. Don't worry about it. Just sit, enjoy the game, just remember you have other people sitting around you.'

"It came to the point that every time that fellow came to the ballgame, he would come over and say, 'Hi' and we'd talk a bit. When we got to the new ballpark, he came up to me one night all panicked. 'Sam,' he said, 'you gotta help me.' What's the problem I asked? He said, 'I've got an engagement package here tonight and I don't know where I'm supposed to be. I said, 'You have what?' He was going to get engaged down here at the ballpark. I said, 'Okay,' let me take you to the people who're going to take care of this for you. They'll tell us what to do.'

"So I took him to guest services. They explained what he had to do and where he had to be. Basically, they told him just to go back to his seats and everything will be taken care of from that point. They told him, the only thing that he would have to do is just show her the ring and ask her to marry him.

"I took him back to his seat, back to his section. I told him to sit down and just watch. Our people would take care of everything. I said, 'Take it easy. I'll be watching you on Phanavision.' He said, 'Please, please, stay with me.' So I stood at the top of the steps of his section while all this was going on. The staff came down, he proposed to her on camera and she said, 'Yes!' She accepted the ring. Then he brought his whole family up from the seats and introduced me to them. They greeted me like I was part of the family.

"Then he introduced me to his fiancée. And she said, 'You're Sam?' I said, 'Yes, I am.' And she said, 'You're the one who threw him out of the ballpark that night, aren't you?' And I said, 'Yep, I'm the guy.' She said, 'Every time we come to the ballgame he talks about you.' You just never know. Something that started out on a really bad, sour note, turned into something sort of like a friendship. I still see him. Once or twice a season, he'll come in. And we'll talk a bit."

—m—

DiJulius doesn't have any confrontations he particularly cares to talk about. But he does remember the scalpers outside Vet Stadium and how he dealt with them early on in his Philly employ. "We had these ramps that people would go up on their way into the stadium," he explains. "I'd be at the top of a ramp. And I used to tell the scalpers…'From here to here (the top of the ramp to the bottom), this is my house. I don't want you in my house. And we'd chase 'em down the ramp if we had to." It must have worked. "As long as they listened, I got along with the scalpers. We got along very, very good, in fact."

DiJulius doesn't come in contact with scalpers in any more. Not in Section 132 A. But he does have to be on the alert. Mostly for line drives. Sometimes, even a broken bat. Of that, he knows (and painfully so) first hand.

The exact date escapes him, but the details don't. It was a night that Aaron Rowland's bat splintered and flew toward DiJuluis' section. "I was watching this disabled fan and I thought the bat was gonna hit her," he recalled. In trying to protect her, he took the hit on his left knee.

He was taken by ambulance to nearby Methodist Hospital. (The Phils are pretty quick to get medical assistance to a person in distress, he noted). He was accompanied by his son, Joe, who works the upper level club suites for the Phils. He required six stitches before he was released. "No fracture, just stitches," he recalls. "I missed a couple of games…just a couple of games."

Was he nervous when he returned to his station? "Mmmm, nah," he responded. "Broken bats are rarely a problem. It's those line drives that come at you pretty fast. You have to stay alert!" Especially when (the now departed) Pat Burrell was at bat. "Phew, he had some line drives in there," DiJulius exclaims. The rare broken bat or the blazing line drive not withstanding, DiJulius never asked the Phillies to move him. And he doesn't intend to.

It's impossible to do what these four have done for so many years with out some favorite recollections or reminiscences. Here are just some of them.

DeWitt Hobbs is pretty much alone outside the visitor's locker. He has a small television to watch the game and keep him some company. One thing he misses from Veterans Stadium was seeing players from both squads pass by. "At the Vet, all the players from both teams had to walk by to go to the batting cage," he explained. "That's how I got to know some of them." But only in a passing way. "I'd say hello, they'd say, 'hello.' That was about it." Still it was something. So was the time Hobbs and his wife of 60 years, Geraldine, went at Phillies expense to watch the team at its spring training camp in Clearwater. Now that was a time to remember for both of them.

Joe DiJulius experienced a moment worth remembering during 2008 World Series, Phils vs. Tampa Bay. That's when one "coal miner" Joe got to greet another "coal miner" Joe. That would be Rays Manager Joe Madden, a native of Hazleton. DiJulius is close to the visiting players by virtue of his station near third base and the visitor's dugout. But he doesn't often exchange pleasantries—no fraternizing, after all. Sometimes, he'd offer to hold a visitor's glove while the player signed autographs for the fans. But not that often.

Still when the Rays visited, he couldn't resist saying something to Madden. As he remembered it a month or so after the series, that exchange went something like this: "I said, 'What are you doing you coal collector, you?'"

Madden looked surprised. "How do you know?" he asked DiJulius.

"Well, I'm below you, from Tamaqua," DiJulius responded.

"Get out of here," Madden said. "'Yeah,' I said. And we started talking. 'Hazleton's nice, Tamaqua's nice,'" he said. "Yeah," DiJulius replied, "but it's changed a little bit, you know."

Joe Madden, in Joe DiJulius' book, is "very nice, a very nice fellow." If anybody should say anything different with earshot of DiJulius, DiJulius will be very quick to disabuse him of the notion.

Ask Nick Schmanek what events or incidents have stayed with him over his 14-year association with the Phillies, and three come to mind.

There was the time he served as a security custodian for the reputedly ill-tempered Barry Bonds during the All-Star game Philadelphia hosted. Bonds, contrary to his popular reputation, Schmanek recalled, was very pleasant with the fans and a willing autograph signer.

Then there was the time he was working the field and got hit in the shin by a batting practice ball off the bat of Houston's Craig Biggio. His shin had the welt to prove it, in case his City Hall co-workers had reason to doubt it.

And there was the night in the mid-90's in a deserted Veterans Stadium when the Phils were playing out the string on their season before a meager turnout of 12,000 people. An amorous couple was caught on Phanavision under a blanket in the deserted upper deck. It would have been hard for the cameras to miss. "We had to get up there and break it up," Schmanek reported. "When we asked why, the guy said he always had this fantasy of making love down at the Vet." The moment remains a legend in Philly fan lore.

DiJulius and Hobbs were rather explicit about their intentions to continue in their retirement years as Phillies game-dayers. They were there for as long as they're health permitted and the Phillies would have them.

But what about Schmanek and Kline, who, after all, still had day jobs to tend to?

"I'm going to play it by ear," Schmanek replied. "I have a lot of friends here. It's like a neighborhood…like a family. I'll stop when it's not fun anymore. But I'll tell you this. I'm comin' back next year!"

Mark Sam Kline down the same way. He's so into the Phillies he has to be careful sometimes to remember he's an employee and not a fan when he's at the ballpark. "I gotta watch my mouth…gotta watch my mouth…" he confesses. And he usually does, though he admits the World Series win was particularly challenging in that regard. He sums up his Philly experience this way:

"I've had a lot of exciting and happy moments in my life… getting married, the birth of my children, watching our children married and our grandchildren come along. This (working for the Phils) is another rung, another facet of excitement."

So much so that he advised he had just turned in his uniform the evening before and already he was anticipating the new season ahead. "I was talking to one of the directors upstairs and I told him, 'Now listen, when orientation comes around in March for the new people, keep me on the list and I'll come down and help with orientation. Here it is, the season has just ended and I'm already psychologically setting myself up to return in the season ahead."

"As long as they keep asking me to come back, I'll keep coming back."

By all accounts, plenty of his game-day associates are of like mind.

"The Phillies.
How May I Help You?"

Kelly Addario DiGiacomo was just a young girl…18, maybe 19, as she recollects…when she took the call from the White House. It was President Reagan calling to congratulate Pete Rose for breaking Stan Musial's Major league record for career base hits at 3,631.

Actually, she probably shouldn't have been in that position in the first place. She was, after all, only a parttime Phillies employee at the time. She was sitting in for the regular switchboard operator who was on a break. And what's more, she had no forewarning about what was to transpire.

It was unnerving to say the least. "I was so nervous," she confesses. "I couldn't believe it was really the White House calling."

But that was then. This is now. Kelly Addario DiGiacomo doesn't get unnerved anymore in dealing with the people… celebrities or non-celebrities, alike…who have business…official or otherwise…with the world champion Philadelphia Phillies.

She is, you see, the Phillies fulltime receptionist/switchboard operator. Walk into the lobby of Citizens Bank Park…or call the Phillies central switchboard, and the first person you see…or the first voice you hear, likely is that of Kelly Addario DiGiacomo.

For many fans or patrons, the first impression they form of the Phillies may well depend on how she greets them. She is particularly sensitive to that reality. Hence, she is unfailingly professional, unfailingly polite and unfailingly pleasant to visitors and callers regardless of their stations in life.

"You're the first person that anybody sees when they come into the building," she says. "You have to be totally aware of who you're dealing with and who you are. If not, you won't handle yourself properly."

Kelly Addario DiGiacomo must have been very good at handling herself. February 15, 2009, she celebrated her 25th anniversary as a salaried employee of the Philadelphia Phillies. It was a prospect she hardly could have envisioned 28 years ago when she took that call from the White House.

The date was August 10, 1981. The Phillies had prearranged for the President to place a congratulatory call to Rose when Musial's record was broken. Getting the call through, even for the President of the United States, was more than routine as it turned out. It was rather comic as a matter of fact.

"I couldn't transfer," Addario DiGiacomo reflected. "I didn't know how to do it. I was trying to get someone down stairs to pick up the phone and they weren't picking it up." For its part, the White House wasn't having any more success of its own in placing the call. "The operators must be on strike," Rose quipped, Musial and Baseball Commissioner Bowie Kuhn at his side laughing.

As the misconnect persisted, Rose, ever aware of the national spotlight that was on him, joked to the assembled media: "Good thing there's not a missile on the way." At another point: "I think I got a recording here." And still after yet another failed try, "I'll give him my home number if he wants."

When the President finally came on the line, he told Rose: "It took me almost as long to make this connection as it did for you to break the record."

Rose responded: "We were goin' give 5 more minutes and that was it!" The media ate the moment up.

While the principals may have had a good laugh about the comedy of events that night at veterans stadium, It was anything but a laughing matter for Addario DiGiacomo. In many ways, it still isn't. She smiles in reliving the moment. But she doesn't laugh.

The DiGiacomo family...Kelly, her husband, Michael, their 11-year-old son, Brady, and their eight-year-old daughter, Brogan...live in suburban Delaware County--Norwood, to be exact, about a 25-minute car ride (on a good day) down I-95 to Citizens Bank Park. But Kelly was, is and always will be a Philadelphian--more specifically, a South Philadelphian-- in heart and soul.

She was born in South Philly, moved to Southwest Philadelphia when she was three.

When a visitor to the city asked her what the difference between South Philadelphia and Southwest Philadelphia was, she replied: "Just a bridge, the Passyunk Bridge." Visitors learn very quickly that being from South Philadelphia is more of a mindset than a location.

"My parents are South Philadelphia people," she says. "We lived in South Philadelphia. As a young girl, I'd ride my bike 15 minutes over the Bridge to play in South Philadelphia." She met Michael—"He's awesome!" she declares—in South Philadelphia. Brady plays teener baseball for the Philadelphia Stars in South Philadelphia. Brogan goes to ballet school at the Pennsport School of Dance in South Philadelphia. And, of course, Kelly's worked the last 28 years in South Philadelphia.

(Curiously, Michael and she were married in St. Michaels, Maryland, a year to the day after their first lunch date. Why St. Michaels and not Philly? Well, she concedes, she's always had a bit of the "Rebel" in her. But, she's quick to add, they had their marriage blessed in Philadelphia to acknowledge their city roots and, it might be added, to keep the peace in the family.)

The idea that it might be nice to work for the Phils first registered with teenaged Kelly Addario during the team's 1980 World Series Parade.

"A bunch of us ditched school for the day to go to the parade," she relates. "I saw a girl from my neighborhood who was wearing a Phillies jacket. I asked her if she worked for the Phillies. She said she was an usherette…the hot pants patrol. I said, 'How do you get a job like that?'"

It wasn't long thereafter that she was filling out an application. She had a two-part interview. The first with Tom Hudson of the

Phillies facility staff; the second with Phillies then President Bill Giles ("I had no idea who he was," she confesses.) Both went well. She was offered the job a few days later.

Actually, as she thought about it, she may have had a notion she wanted to work for the Phillies long before that World Series parade but not have realized it. As a youngster she used to dress up as a 'hot pants girl" for Halloween. One of the homes in the neighborhood she would visit to trick or treat belonged to none other than Pat Cassidy ("Mr. Cassidy" to her). "He used to tell me, 'Come back when you 18.' When I did, I saw him and said, 'I'm back!' and he said, 'Wow, that was pretty literal.'"

Kelly started with the Phils in 1981 as a game-day usherette at Veterans Stadium. It wasn't exactly an auspicious debut. The first two home games with the Montreal Expos were snowed out. She was on the "Hot Pants Patrol" for only two or three years. But that was time enough for her to have been asked occasionally to substitute for the fulltime receptionist when the receptionist was off the job or away from her desk. When the receptionist moved to another position with the Phillies in 1984, Kelly was offered the job as her replacement. (She suspects her neighbor, "Mr. Cassidy", may have had something to do with that). Regardless, when the offer was extended, she accepted immediately.

The decision didn't sit well with her parents, initially. They had hoped she had other plans for her life. Actually, as she tells it, she did. She enrolled in the Philadelphia College of Art after her graduation from West Catholic High School. But it wasn't for her. Asked what she did at Philadelphia College of Art, the cynic in her replied tersely: "Took up a lot of space. I hated it." When the offer to work for the Phillies fulltime came down, Her parents "were furious" she didn't go back to school. To calm her parents, she promised she would continue her education in some way, even while working fulltime for the Phils. So she enrolled in cosmetology school.

She, in fact, became a trained hair dresser. But there's little reason, not to mention opportunity, for a fulltime receptionist with the Philadelphia Phillies to cut hair. For Kelly Addario DiGiacomo, cosmetology over time became an avocation. The Phillies were her true vocation.

Ask Kelly Addario DiGiacomo her name, and the response you get is, "Kelly Addario DiGiacomo." Always, "Kelly Addario DiGiacomo." For good reason. Names have special meaning for her and her family.

"Kelly" is her Irish mother's family surname. "Addario" is her father's surname. And "DiGiacomo" is, of course, her husband's surname. She explains it this way:

"I am the first grandchild. My first name is Kelly because my grandmother told my mother all the time that whoever has the first child has to carry the name on. I couldn't take Addario out in honor of my father. And so, I use my mother's maiden name, my dad's name and my husband's name. My three favorite people."

The legacy of what's in a name was passed on to her children, as well. Though she jokes initially that Brady was named after a Baltimore Orioles outfielder, Brady Anderson, she quickly corrects the record. Brady is her mother's Godfather's name.

And Brogan? Brogan, Kelly explains," was named after a nun in my mother's family."

Speaking of names, Kelly Addario DiGiacomo can name more than a few prominent personalities who have passed her desk or called her switchboard during her long tenure as a receptionist/ operator with the Phillies.

There was, of course, the aforementioned call from the White House. It wouldn't be the last celebrity she would encounter through the years.

Celebrities like…oh, Michael Jordan, calling to talk to his friend, former Phillies Manager Terry Francona. "He was very nice to talk to," she says of Jordan.

And others, of course…Roman Gabriel and Donovan McNabb of the Philadelphia Eagles…

Ron Howard and Bill Cosby of the entertainment world. Even the guy from the old Budweiser beer commercial…you remember, the "I love you man!" guy. Sure enough, when he walked by Kelly's reception desk one game day, he blurted out: "I love you man!" That's one she won't forget anytime soon.

Her favorite, however, was the call she took from Philadelphia Flyers goalie, Bernie Parent. "I was the biggest Bernie Parent fan growing up." she explained. "When he called and said, 'This is Bernie Parent,' I couldn't believe it. That was the best. It still is the best for me."

Kelly Addario DiGiacomo knows full well that because of her position with the Phillies, she's had opportunity to greet personalities most of us commoners can only imagine meeting. "Sometimes I wonder what it might have been like if I had gotten another position," she reflects. "But when I look back, I think I am a very lucky person. I see all the action. I've met people other people can only dream to meet. I see things other people will never see…"

Some things she's seen from her receptionist's desk perhaps are better left unspoken.

Like the time Kelsey Grammar…oh well, that's one thing better left unsaid.

Or the look on all-star pitcher-turned-broadcaster Jim Palmer's face when he had to stand in the rain in a taxi line with the rest of the folks to hail a cab as he was leaving after a Vet Stadium telecast. "Furious" might be one way to describe it.

Just the day before this conversation, Kelly had fielded a call from Phils free agent acquisition, Raul Ibanez—penciled in the 2009 spring chatter to be the departed Pat Burrell's replacement in left field. He wanted to talk to his new team trainer. Kelly, of course, put him right through.

It is, as she said, being aware at the reception desk or on the switchboard…being aware of who you're dealing with and why… whether it's a celebrity, or just a fan calling in to inquire or, very often, to vent.

The protocols for the celebs are pretty standard. It's the fans who require special care. They are, after all, the ones who pay the bills. And sometimes they can be the most challenging.

How, for example, do you tell a fan (politely, of course) team president Dave Montgomery…or team chairman Bill Giles or

Manager Charlie Manuel…just aren't available at the moment to take the call about…

…Why some of the players seemed to be drinking on the flatbeds carrying them through the city during on the 2008 World Series victory parade?

…Or Chase Utley's ill-timed, ill-advised expletive caught in full volume in the emotion of the moment during the victory ceremonies at Citizens Bank Park…

…Or why the players weren't dressed in their uniforms instead of their jeans and sweat shirts for the parade?

Philadelphia fans have earned a justifiable collective reputation as being high among the most passionate in the nation about their sports teams. They also are among the most critical, the most demanding in the nation…World Series Champions, or not.

And it falls to employes like Kelly Addario DiGiacomo and her colleagues to remember, always and always, the fans are, after all, the base. You treat the base politely, pleasantly and professionally.

Fortunately Addario DiGiacomo is well suited by temprament and personality to do just that with her customary aplomb.

Her voice has a musical lilt to it when she greets a visitor or answers the phone.

"Good morning, the Phillies," she asks a caller. "How may I help you?"

The greeting changed as the 2008 season wound down to its triumphal conclusion.

First, it was, "National League Champion Phillies, How may I help you."

When Chase Utley heard that when he called in the morning of the day the Phils were about to win their first world Series in 28 years, he told Kelly: "I like that!"

"Well, call me tomorrow," she told Utley confidently.

The very next morning, after the clinching victory in the rain-suspended fifth game, she answered the phone:

"The World Champion Phillies!"

Now that had a nice ring to it! A very nice ring, indeed! But it was to be enjoyed only for a moment.

Once the calendar turned from 2008 to 2009, Manager Charlie Manuel let his team know it was "time to turn the page." No resting on any laurels. The word filtered through the Phillies administrative offices. And Kelly Addario DiGiacomo was back in the Spring of 2009, in that pleasant voice of hers, answering the phone:

"The Phillies. How may I help you?"

CHAPTER
7

Bernie

Bernadette "Bernie" Mansi may be one of those fortunate few…the fortunate few for whom a job lay-off worked to her ultimate advantage. It happened 33 years ago and it happened this way.

Bernie Mansi had lost her position as a drafting technician in a small firm run by a family friend right down the street from her Delaware County home. Her unemployment compensation was running out.

As fate at the time would have it, her oldest son, Ben, was working night home games on the Philies junior grounds crew. He'd been hired (no surprise here) by stadium operations director Pat Cassidy, a passing friend of the Mansi family. Cassidy was telling Ben that he had just lost his secretary. Ben told Cassidy… well, his mother was on the job market.

One thing led to another. Bernie Mansi eventually was invited in for an interview with Phillies chief executive, Bill Giles. She was hired. She started as Cassidy's secretary in the operations department in January of 1976.

Technically, she was hired as a secretary. But almost immediately, her duties deviated from strictly secretarial tasks. Like helping with the payroll. "When I started in payroll, it was all manual," she recalled. "The adding machine--me and the adding machine. Fun time when you couldn't balance. But I loved it. I loved doing payroll. It's a lot more complicated now." Indeed it is.

She also handled, in those early years, assignment of handicapped parking spaces. "All the disabled people who needed to park close to the stadium, I would get the call," she recounted. "They would give me the date. I had certain spots right outside. And if not there, we would work them in other spots that were not taken that particular night. It's very different today. But it was a job that I totally enjoyed and made a lot of friends. I met a lot of nice people, really, really nice people."

And then there was uniform distribution…uniform distribution for the game day employees (300 in all at the moment). Khaki pants for the hosts, hostesses and security personnel; light blue oxford shirts with the Phillies logo for the hosts and hostesses; dark blue shirts for security; white for the supervisors; dark blue sweater vests for premium seating attendants. And jackets/windbreakers for the cooler weather.

Uniform distribution and collection, in fact, has become a principal responsibility for Bernie Mansi and her good friend and associate, Corliss Hobbs. Might seem rather routine on the surface, but it is logistically cumbersome in practice. It also could have its moments.

Like the rain-suspended Game 5 in the 2008 World Series. "I can't tell you how many of our security personnel came in dripping," she related. "I mean they were dripping wet. They had to change their entire uniforms. Even if the pants weren't hemmed. They had to have something." The wet clothes? Well, they were thrown in a big dryer to be recycled in the event further replacements were needed. They weren't, thankfully…not after play was halted in the 6h inning.

When Pat Cassidy assigned Mansi to uniform distribution very early in her Phillies employ, she was a self-described novice in the assignment. Neither could she have known what she was to confront when the Phillies switched to their "Hot Pants Patrol" uniforms for the women usherettes. "They had measured all the girls (approximately 150 in all) for these uniforms," she recalls. "They brought all these uniforms in and I said to Pat, 'Why are there so many big uniforms? Why do we have so many big sizes?' I knew most of the girls by then and it turned out not one uniform fit one girl."

Even Bill Giles had to see what the problem was for himself. "He came down from his office and he was, like, speechless," Bernie Mansi remembers. "We had this sweet woman who was a seamstress. A lot of the girls had to go to her to be measured again. Meanwhile, they had to go back to the original uniform to open the season until the new uniforms arrived." The dilemma eventually resolved itself over time. But there for a moment, it was, in Mansi's words, "a nightmare."

By coincidence, Mansi and Hobbs, had just collected the uniforms from the 2008 game day employees the night before she sat down for this November discussion. Now they were in the process of inventorying the supply, evaluating what was in good shape, what needed to be replaced and what new orders had to be placed. It's not their ultimate decision. But the process starts with them. And every March, during the orientation sessions for the new season, it starts all over again.

Ask Bernie Mansi what she does with the Phillies and she tells you she's a secretary in the ballpark operations department. ("It's part of me," she says). But there's another term that more precisely describes what she does. That term is, "den mother"... den mother to 100 or so game day hostesses 81 home games or, in a good season, more a year. What's involved? A little bit of everything. From sign-in to scheduling; from payroll to union dues and seniority lists. Even a little bit of social director thrown in for good measure.

Bernie and Corliss can be found on home game dates at the table in the front of the "briefing room" where the game-dayers report to receive their assignment for the night. Joe McDermott (the "den father?") is there for the men.

The procedure's a lot different at Citizens Bank Park than it was at Veterans Stadium. At the Vet, the men and women reported to separate locations. "We had our room by the super box area," Mansi explains. "We loved it. It was fun. It was great. We had nice couches and a big coffee table. It was very homey. When the ladies would come in for their breaks, it was very comfortable."

It took some doing, Mansi admits, for every one to adjust to the coed reporting room at Citizens Bank Park. "It was hard at first," she remembers, "because we were such a close group. I think the men felt the same way because they had their own groups and they enjoyed their privacy, too. It took, maybe, two years to get used to. But now we get to know each other a lot better as employees. And I think that's a very good thing."

Some things never change, however, co-mingled or not. Like where the employees sit. Mostly, the men still sit together—hosts here, security there, supervisors over there. The ladies, too. "It's like going to church," Mansi observes. "Everybody has their place where they sit in church. And they just enjoy that. Sometimes, some of the men will come over and sit with the ladies. But they usually sit where they're most comfortable."

There's another staple to the season. It's the party the hostesses have at the end of each year. "It's a tradition that started at Connie Mack Stadium," Mansi explains. "It's a girl's party and it's really fun. Everybody signs up to bring food, a special dish, whatever. Everybody contributes. It's kind of our goodbye for the year to each other." The party carried over from Connie Mack to the Vet to Citizens Bank Park. "When we came over here (to CBP), I will tell you," Bernie says, "I would still hear: 'Are we still having our party? Can we have our party?' And I said, 'We are definitely having our party.'"

The men, incidentally, haven't picked up on the season-end party concept. Perhaps they're not as socially bent as the ladies. Perhaps they have other interests or occupations that consume their time. Who knows? Whatever the reason, this function remains a women-only event. Nobody seems the worse for it.

Bernie Mansi wasn't, by her own admission, active in sports as a young girl advancing academically through St. Charles Elementary School and Notre Dame High School in suburban Philadelphia. But she was aware. She had to be. Her father was a rabid Phillies fan.

"He always, always had the games on," she said, reflecting on her youthful years in the family's Clifton Heights row home. "That's how I came to love the game...through my Dad."

Her Dad, "Rookie" Berry, by name, wasn't the easiest person to live with when the Phillies weren't going good. But, his daughter remembered, "when I got this job, my father and mother were both thrilled, just thrilled." So much so that her father regularly used to visit with Pat Cassidy before heading home after a game. She suspects they may have had a snort or two of liquid refreshment before he began to trek back to Delaware County.

Mansi married her husband, Benjamin, an assistant chemist with DuPont at Grey's Ferry Avenue in the city, in 1957. (They celebrated their 50th wedding anniversary the year before this discussion.) Together, they parented two sons, Ben and James, and a daughter, Lisa; and became the proud grandparents of 9 grandchildren.

Professionally, she worked for General Electric in Philadelphia for five years before her wedding and then held several different jobs (including one at the Philadelphia airport) before that fateful lay-off from the neighbor's small drafting firm. Once she was hired by the Phillies, she found her niche. Never once in the intervening years did she ever want to leave. So she hasn't.

It's inevitable, when one spends 30 years and more with a single organization…it's inevitable that the memory bank gets filled with memorable moments. Bernie Mansi has her share, of course. Interestingly, none of her favorites has anything to do with the game of baseball.

Among them: A family friend, Myrtle Merkins, by name, was riding on an elevator with Bernie. Phillies pitcher Tug McGraw happened to be a third passenger in the car. "She was so excited, so excited!" Bernie recalled. "I thought she was going to faint. A drink couldn't have made her fly as high as she was flying. Even Tug was laughing about that."

Then there was the time she brought her two-year-old granddaughter, Christy, to the stadium. "We were in the hostess room and she was playing there," Mansi recalls. "All of a sudden, we hear, 'Mum, Mum.' "We're all looking at each other, going: 'My God! Where's Christy, where's Christy?' We found her in a locker. She got in a locker and pulled it shut. Later on, when she became a hostess, I have a picture of her in that locker… sitting there with her one leg down and her other leg in the air. It's the greatest." (Christy, was a nurse at Children's Hospital in 2008, preparing for her wedding in August of 2009. Clearly, she suffered no lingering after-effects from her locker shut-in as a young child.)

There was a day, however, Mansi would just as soon forget. It was the day in the early 1980's when Pat Cassidy suffered his first stroke. Bernie had ridden to the ballpark with Cassidy that morning because she was without her car. She thought he wasn't driving all that well. And when they arrived, she noticed, he was having difficulty walking. "I finally said, 'Pat, are you having a problem?' And he started telling me that some days, in the morning, he had a hard time getting dressed…couldn't button his buttons. I said, 'Let me take you to the doctor.' And he said, 'No, it's going to pass.'"

It, unfortunately, didn't pass. Bernie brought him a coffee. He had problems handling it. So she took matters into her own hands. She called his doctor and told him of the symptoms Cassidy was experiencing. The doctor ordered him to the hospital immediately. It was the beginning of the end of the Cassidy era with the Phillies. But what an era it was in the minds of so many who worked for and with him daily at the ballpark.

"He was remarkable," Mansi opines. "He had a wonderful way with people. He would call all the game employees, 'My People.' And everybody loved him in return. He would have to be tough with them, and he was when need be. But he always stood by them. Back then, if a fight would break out among the fans in the stands, he'd get right in there. I'd tell him, 'Pat, you can't be doing that.' And he'd say, 'Yes, I can. I have to be with my guys. I have a great bunch of guys!'"

Bernie Mansi, at age 73, knows the time might be approaching when she has to call it a game with the Phillies. She'd like to finish another season or two at the very least. But when and if it should come to that…for her to leave…she knows just how difficult it will be for her. "When you're involved with so many people, the thought all of a sudden of not being involved any more is hard to contemplate."

As she looks back on her 32 years with the Phillies, she realizes even more how fortunate she was to have landed where she did when she did from the ranks of the unemployed. Not just to have found a job. But to have found a job with the Phillies. "I worked in different jobs," she says, "and there is nothing to compare with working for the Phillies.

"They really care about you. That's impressed me more than anything. You have your job to do and you don't have anybody over your shoulder constantly looking to see if that job is getting done. It's up to you to get that job done. And that's the way it's been for all the years that I've been here.

"The other places that I've worked, they were always coming over to look and see if you were getting it done. Of course, it was different kind of work. But it's hard to explain. It's just that everybody seems to enjoy each other."

It was hard for Mansi in the early years, when the Phillies were down, to hear or read the critics among the fan base and the media. "That was tough," she remembers. "When we were losing, you kept to yourself. You'd read something in the papers and it would set you off."

But now that the Phillies were winning?

"Everybody's in a good frame of mind." Even more so as the Phils moved to the 2008 World Series championship. "You could actually feel the electricity. Everybody was so up. It was almost as though you just knew it had to happen this year."

Mansi's family was in the stands for the World Series clincher. She stayed up in the briefing room, however, with Corliss and others in the Phillies operation staff. "I'm with these people 81 games a year and I wanted to be here with them when this happened. When it happened, Corliss and I were sitting down and we looked at each other. It was like, 'We won! We won! It really happened!' It was a great, great feeling!"

Now that's a memorable moment!

...Part of the Parade!

FAN
ACCOMMODATIONS

SECTION II

"Courtesy Tom"

"Courtesy Tom" Reiter is, by his own admission, a collector at heart. And he has any number of collectibles to prove it. Not the least of which are the autographs of not one, but two Mrs. Pete Rose. Now, that's a collectible or two for you.

Of course, Tom Reiter's in a unique position to gather all of this memorabilia. That's because he is the courtesy ticket dispenser for the Philadelphia Phillies. Has been since 1971. Which not only put him in contact with any number of celebrities through the years; it also explains how he came by the moniker that identifies him in his Phillies gig.

You can find "Courtesy Tom" at Citizens Bank Park, Window 29, 81 home games a year. It's the last of nine ticket windows outside the first base gates. But you can't buy a ticket at Window 29. It's only for those who have been "comped" by the players, management or designated staff, the visiting team…even the umpires.

His digs at Citizens Bank Park are very different from his digs at Veterans Stadium. At the Vet, Tom operated from a small room and solitary window at Gate A across the street from the Spectrum on Pattison Avenue. You identified it by the red canopy and the shingle which marked its location. (The shingle and his ticket rack, are, not so incidentally, among the collectibles which Tom keeps in his South Jersey home.)

In those days, just about anybody who had courtesy access to the game…players wives, guests, family, personalities, politicians, scouts, whomever…they came by Tom's booth to pick up his or her tickets. For the longest while, it had no air conditioning or TV. But, in Tom's words, "I was in heaven!" For a life-long Phillies fan, who wouldn't be. "Every complimentary ticket any one picked up at the Vet, they picked up from me," he remembers. "The scouts would pick up their tickets and come in to chat baseball. The players' wives would come by with their kids. I always had candy ready for the little ones."

Much of that has changed since the move to CBP in 2004. Now, for example, the wives tickets are delivered to the wives' lounge. The scouts pick up their ticket at the press gate, where they enter to receive their credentials. Tom may miss the contact. But he understands it is not his to reason why. Nor does he.

Still, like so many of his game-day associates, he revels a bit in his memories of the Vet. "The only problems I had at the Vet were the scammers who tried to con me for comps," he declares. "Guys would drop names...especially when the Dodgers were in town. The LaSorda brothers owned a restaurant in Blue Bell, and I swear they invited half the county to Dodgers games. 'Smokey' sent me,' they'd say. 'Or, Harry told me I had tickets.'" More often than not, if Smokey or Harry weren't in the neighborhood to vouch for their "guests" when they appeared at Tom Reiter's window...well, it was usually possible for them to purchase a ticket for the night.

Tom Reiter was 73 at the time of this conversation, silver-haired but still teenaged-thin. He and Winnie, his wife of 53 years, moved to Washington Township in Jersey in 2001, about a 20-minute drive from the South Philadelphia sports complex. Tom describes his relocated neighborhood as an "active 55-and-over adult community." And he certainly fits right in. He's a regular player in the community's bocce league and he bowls twice a week. He bowled a 299 game in 2007—missed "the dreaded 10 pin," he smiles—and he proudly wears a "299" ring commemorating the occasion.

But for the first 67 years of his life, he was Philadelphia born and Philadelphia bred—a Philadelphian through and through. And, in the 1940's and '50's, in his neighborhood, as you grew up, you were either a Phillies fan or an A's fan. "I was a Phillies fan," he proclaims. "It was a family thing, you know. Just like Republicans or Democrats."

Tom was graduated from Roman Catholic High School in 1952, took up a trade as a Machinist Apprentice at the Defense

Department's old Frankford Arsenal where he worked for 20 years; advanced to toolmaker and ultimately into procurement before he retired after another 22 years at the Naval Air Development Center at Warminster in neighboring Bucks County. Through the years, Winnie and he became the parents of five children (four girls and a boy) and the grandparents of 11 (seven boys and four girls).

He started his game-day job with the Phillies in 1962 at Connie Mack Stadium. When he was asked, "What prompted you to go to work with the Phillies?" his response should have come as no great surprise. "Pat Cassidy" was his succinct answer. He explained:

"I worked with Pat Cassidy at the Arsenal before he went to work for the Phillies. We were very good friends there, very good friends. Pat was supervisor of ushers back in those days. And he used to get me comps for me and my family. And, just as a natural progression, I suppose, one day, he says to me: 'Why don't you get a part time job as an usher?'

"So, in '62, I started as a temporary usher. I got $6 a game. You would go to the ballpark as an extra usher, sign in and wait with maybe 30 other guys. Mel Moore (of the Phils staff) would look at all his temps…he looked at his list…and according to how big he expected the crowd to be, he'd say: 'You, you, you, you, you can stay.' Just like the union at the docks. 'And the rest of you, go home!'

"And then he would assign you to a section. Well, that went on for, maybe a year. Then, I guess with Pat's help, he gave me a regular usher job and a section of my own. You'd wipe the seats for the big shots that had the deluxe boxes. You would do six chairs and one of them would flip you a quarter. That was fun."

When the Phillies moved to Veterans Stadium, Tom Reiter moved from ushering to ticket distribution. He was assigned to help Chuck Avery, a retired school principal, dispense courtesy tickets in the Pattison Avenue booth. At Connie Mack, Avery had the job of changing the centerfield scoreboard numbers. When the club moved to the Vet, the Phillies organization gave him an easier job, "just handing out the comp tickets," Reiter recalls. When Avery retired a couple of years later, Reiter became, by his own description, "Courtesy Tom without a helper."

Tom Reiter opens Window 29 for business 90 minutes before game time. It's a sunny August afternoon, Phils vs. the Marlins. Phils are 2-1/2 games up on the Marlins; 3 on the Mets. 45,521 fans will show up for this game, the third-largest crowd in CBP's four-year existence. Tom Reiter knows it's going to be a busy afternoon at the ticket window. But he puts on his pleasant face, nonetheless, as he goes about his business.

Some of his customers he knows by name, and addresses them that way: "OK, Darlene; good to see you, dear. Stay cool." Those he doesn't he congenially asks for ID and the name of his or her host. "OK, you're good to go. Have fun, enjoy the game," he says as he hands the tickets through the window. If a child accompanies the guest, he hands the youngster a couple of Phillies schedules with the player of the month on the cover. Chase Utley and Pat Burrell had adorned previous schedules. The flavor this month is Brad Lidge, just after he agreed to a $13 million contract extension (a fortuitous pact for both the player and the club as events played out in the 2008 championship season).

Reiter works from four basic guest lists…the club and its staff; the Phillies' players; the visiting team; and the umpires. Bill Beck, the Marlins' traveling secretary, drops his list off. Tom and he exchange pleasantries.

"How's your daughter?" Reiter asks. "Fine," Beck replies. "She's recovering from a broken ankle."

Reiter: "Sorry to hear that. Tell her to get well quick."

Beck" "Thanks, I will. See you next trip."

Just that short, but a very genuine exchange on both parts.

Reiter works with a slot box hanging above his chair to his right. The tickets are paired in envelopes identifying the guest and the sponsor. If the fan doesn't offer who left the tickets, Reiter will ask. Most of the distribution goes smoothly. He gets their name, hands them their envelope and sends them on their way.

Some hitches inevitably occur, however. A young man in his early 30's wearing an Ohio State T-shirt appears at Tom's window. He asks for his tickets and has an e-mail confirming the order. But

Tom doesn't have them. Nor are they are on his list. He suggests the fan call his contact for more specific information. Ohio State reaches for his cell phone as he steps away from the window. Minutes later, he reappears. "It's from Pepsi Cola," he informs Tom. Pepsi, a major league baseball corporate sponsor, reserved the tickets through MLB. Pepsi "comped" the guy, but paid for the tickets. Reiter understands what's happened immediately. He directs him one window down where pre-paid tickets—there's a difference between pre-paid tickets and complimentary tickets—are dispensed. The man's name is run through the computer and his tickets are handed him. Problem solved.

Most of them are. This day, the Phillies guest tickets were late arriving. One guest shows up before all the tickets are in Reiter's possession. A call is made to the sponsoring employee. The tickets were still on her desk. Minutes later, she appears. The guest is happily sent on his way.

Were it that all such issues are settled so readily. To their credit, the Phillies ticket sellers go to great lengths to satisfy their customers. No fans are dismissed or brushed off...never told, in effect...sorry, no tickets here, now beat it. If the problem is solvable, the ticket windows will work to solve it for them.

One such case: A guest arrived at Tom's window. Problem was his comps were for the game two days earlier. Reiter asks him to hold on for a moment. He takes the matter to a ticket manager in the office behind the booth. The manager has a small reserve set aside for contingencies such as this. Reiter reappears with two tickets. Fan walks into the ballgame, a satisfied customer.

Others, however, simply are not resolvable. Most frequently, these instances involve on-line, private-party sales where the seller either scams the purchaser or fails to forward the tickets to the pick-up windows at CBP. In those instances, the buyer has no recourse but to communicate with the seller. Or buy a ticket to the game. That situation is simply out of the Phillies hands.

By the end of the 4th inning, the guest tickets usually are dispensed and Tom Reiter closes the courtesy window and leaves for his South Jersey home. The next game, the next day, "Courtesy Tom" will be back at his stand doing his thing. And doing it with a smile and a welcome.

But back to the collectibles.

Baseballs, envelopes, autographs, baseball cards...they're all part of the memorabilia Tom Reiter has accumulated in his lifetime with the Phillies. One of his first souvenirs was a baseball he received from one of the Phillies grounds crew—"Reds" by name.

"Reds took a liking to me," Reiter recalls. "He gave me my first autographed baseball. It had Stan Musial on the sweet spot." "Reds" and Tom kept getting the ball signed, but only by the "stars." Tom calls it his "Hall of Fame ball." "We only got the big names...Musial, Warren Spahn, Hank Aaron, Willie Mays, Roger Maris, Nolan Ryan, Johnny Bench, Tom Seaver, Eddie Matthews, Steve Carlton, Mike Schmidt...

"I still have that ball. It will go to my son."

Then, through the years, single ball autographs...Joe DiMaggio, Ted Williams, Robin Roberts, Richie Ashburn, Johnny Podres, Pete Rose. Soon, Reiter started collecting autographs from the celebrities who paused to sign their envelopes as they picked up their tickets: Mike Douglas, and the guests he would bring from his local TV show; Carly Simon, Donald Sutherland, Jerry Vale; James Darren; George Wendt, Don Knotts, Buddy Hackett, Danny DeVito, Danny Glover...

Or athletic personalities like Charles Barkley, Mo Cheeks... Bobby Clarke, Bill Bergey, Billy Cunningham...Joe Frazier, Wayne Gretzky, Maury Wills...Bobby Thompson...or golfers like Nancy Lopez; and, of course, politicians like then Mayor Ed Rendell...

Not to forget the scouts, most of them former players turned talent evaluators, some of Reiter's favorite baseball people...like Charlie Wagner of Reading, a Boston Red Sox roommate of Ted Williams; Ed Liberatore, "a very close friend of Joe Dimaggio;" Dick Gernert; Lou Boudreau; Tom Ferrick; Ken Griffey Sr.; Art Howe; Whitey Lockman; Frank Malzone; Danny Murtaugh; Bill Rigney...Reiter has 'em all on paper somewhere.

In the process, he also had to learn how to deal with players and the sense of humor they exhibited when it came to comps. Sparky Lyle in particular. He'd regularly made up names and

Published 8/12/08

▶ SPEAK OUT

Great Jobs

We know you're way too young to work, but what job do you think would be most fun? Go to *www.kidspost.com* and vote:

■ **A fun job for me would be working:**
A. At a baseball stadium
B. At a candy store
C. At an amusement park
D. At a swimming pool
E. Some other job

At a baseball stadium	44.5%
At a candy store	8.1%
At an amusement park	13.3%
At a swimming pool	9.0%
At some other job	25.1%

SURVEY SAYS

The Washington Post - Bill Webster

N. Mawby

*Mike DiMuzio
Director, Ballpark Operations*

R. Rahn

The Wright Brothers
Jeff & Rob - Grounds Crew

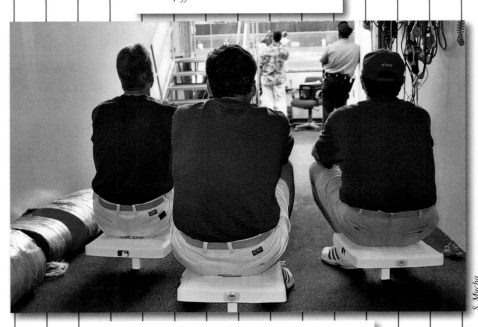

S. Mucha

"Men on Base"
Ed Downs, Rob Wright, and Andy McMeniman

S. Mucha

Ed and Evan Downs
Grounds Crew

S. Mucha

Steve Mucha, Grounds Crew
Dallas Green, A Visitor

N. Mawby

CBP Tarp-Center Field Garden

N. Mawby

Pam Hall - Manager, Landscaping

N. Mawby

Kelly Addario-DiGiacomo - "Kelly" - Receptionist Ballpark Operations

N. Mawby

*Harry Kalas Signature Memorial Tribute from the Phillies organization;
painted by Jeremy Wilt; 1st & 3rd base lines*

R. Rahn

Wes Whittington
"The eye in the sky"

N. Mawby

"The View"

N. Mawby

Sam Kline
Security Supervisor
Right Field, Foul Pole
Sections 201-205

Nick Schmanek
Security Supervisor
Ashburn Alley, Bullpen Area

N. Mawby

R. Rahn

Joe DeJulius - "Coalman Joe"
Security T.V. Camera Dugout, Handicap Seating

R. Rahn

DeWitt Hobbs
Visitor Clubhouse Security - 52 years with the Phillies

N. Mawby

Bernie Mansi - Secretary Ballpark Operations

N. Mawby

Tom Reiter - "Courtesy Tom"
Courtesy Ticket Window

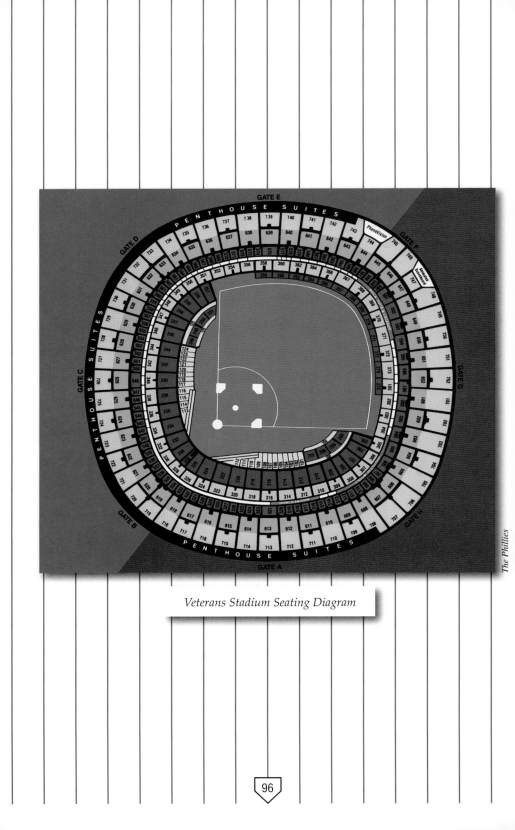

Veterans Stadium Seating Diagram

N. Mawby

Larry McNamee - Greeter, First Base

The Phillies

Shibe Park, Connie Mack Stadium
21st & Lehigh, Philadelphia

N. Mawby

Eric Hartmann - Greeter, Third Base

N. Mawby

Ed Smith - Director of Gates

N. Mawby

John Franzini
Gate Supervisor Third Base, McFaddens

R. Rahn

Rose Ferraro
Assistant Director of Gates

Ellison "Rick" Richardson - Gate Supervisor, Left Field

Lisa Wilson - "Lisa in Right Field" - Gate Supervisor, Right Field

N. Mawby

Tom Payne - "Tommy Programs"
Ashburn Alley-Stands

N. Mawby

Dave DiMuzio, Carman Maniaci - Programs

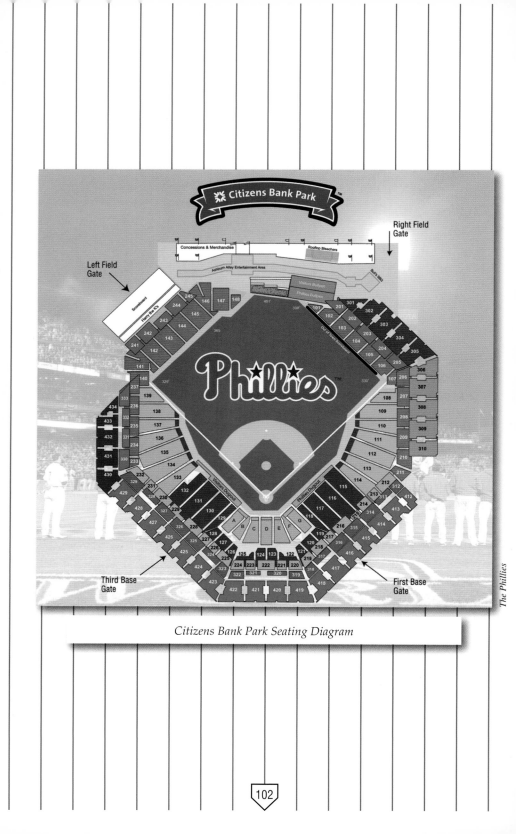

Citizens Bank Park Seating Diagram

put them on his comp list…names like Rocky Balboa; or "Kinky" Denise. Once he even had a Carmen Miranda. Bet on it. If Carmen showed up at his window, Tom Reiter would have found her tickets.

For Curt Schilling, however, leaving a "comp" has a special significance. "Every day Curt was slated to start," Reiter reveals, "he'd leave a comp ticket for his Dad. Curt's Dad is no longer with us. But there was always a seat waiting for him at every park on the day that his son pitched."

Finally, the two Mrs. Rose…wife one, Karolyn ("a great lady"); and wife two, Carol ("a Playboy bunny, a beautiful girl"), both of whom, Reiter says, always were more than cordial with him. Reiter never met Rose, himself—"I have his autograph somewhere,"—but he was the one player Reiter would stay to watch play after he closed his booth.

Why Rose, he was asked. "Just the way he played the game," he replied. "He played any position, he ran everything out, he even ran out walks…His personal life was crap. I think what really jammed him up is that he was obstinate and so full of himself that I'm sure he got in debt so deep that somebody 'dimed' him out…he just messed himself up."

Well, considering the gambling and all, should Rose be admitted to the Hall of Fame?

Absolutely!" was Reiter unequivocal response. "On the field he was a great player." That was enough in Tom Reiter's view to qualify Pete Rose for the Hall.

Understandably, Tom Reiter has had more than his share of lingering memories…fond memories…to reflect on over his 46 years as a game day employee of the Philadelphia Phillies. Memories like…

…Sitting on a wooden bench with the grounds crew at Connie Mack Stadium and helping them put on the tarp—"the damn thing was very heavy"—when it rained and taking it off when it stopped, earning an extra $1 a game for the effort.

...The intimacy of Connie Mack Stadium where his section was next to the Phillies dugout and he could hear the players and coaches screaming at the opposition...

...Getting an "up-close-and-personal" view of the 1964 Phillies pennant collapse, suffering a personal painful affliction in the process...("One morning I woke up with hundreds of itching pimples around my stomach. I went to work, then the dispensary. The nurse told me I had shingles. I'll never forget her words to me: 'Are you having any high stress in your life right now?' I told her I worked for the Phillies. She was a fan and said, 'That's it!' She laughed. The '64 Phillies gave me shingles.")

...The last season at the Vet in 2003...

...The 2005 employee profile in the "Phillies" magazine in which he observed that "New Yorkers are the worst for name-dropping, but it's all about knowing how to handle things and always treating people with respect..."

None of this, "Courtesy Tom" takes pains to emphasize for his visitor...none of this could have happened if Winnie weren't okay with it. "I love this job and I love the people I work with," he acknowledges. "It's a brotherhood of people...a family of employees. And the Phillies organization, they've been good with the people who work here. But I couldn't have done any of this for all these years without Winnie and her consent and cooperation."

So it was fitting that his most indelible memory would come on April 16, 2003, the year the Vet closed. April 16 also just happened to be their 48th wedding anniversary. Tom had planned to take the day off so that Winnie and he could "do something special." But two days earlier, a call came from the Phillies front office. He had been selected, as one of the Phillies longest serving employees, to remove the vinyl shingle on the outfield wall listing how many games remained to be played in the stadium.

"I could invite Winnie and all the children to witness this event. That became our special night. I worked the booth for three innings and then went to our seats in right field. After the 6th inning I went down to the right field tunnel. The Phanatic was waiting in his Phanatic-mobile with the sidecar. I got in and we went flying out between innings to right field when I got out and nervously removed the number 73 and replaced it with number 72.

"The family's flash bulbs were flashing while we took a drive around the Vet with me smiling and waving like some kind of celebrity. What a night and I have a pictures to prove it."

Now there's memorabilia that, for the Reiter family, at least will last more than a lifetime.

Reiter completed his 46th season with the Phillies in 2008, 37 of them in the courtesy ticket window. In all that time, there was only one occasion where he seriously had to consider whether he had to give up his game job with the organization. That was in 1974 when he left Frankford Arsenal, a half-hour drive to the Vet, to go to work for the Naval development center in Bucks County, a good hour away in brutal traffic, especially on a Friday.

"The first day I took that drive from my house to Warminster, I'm saying to myself: 'How the hell am I gonna get to the ballpark? Am I going to take a job all the way up in Warminster that will give me a long drive to the ballpark?' But I really had to take that job. I was too young to retire and we had a family to raise…"

Which brought the conversation back to Winnie. Tom closed it this way: "She's scheduled every summer around the Phillies for the last 47 years. She's listened to many stories of some of the 'unhappy customers' that weren't satisfied with the location or number of the comp seats they received…or the waiting time for the tickets to arrive. She reared five great children."

Winnie, Reiter noted, "is herself a huge Phillies fan. Thank the Lord for that!"

Larry and Eric

Larry McNamee was a young intern with the old Philadelphia Athletics when he met the iconic Connie Mack. Eric Hartmann was in the Philadelphia Phillies business office when he met a young intern assigned to the Phillies mailroom who would, years later, become general manager of the ball club. His name was Ed Wade.

Those encounters occurred years and years ago. But if you're around professional baseball long enough, these are the kind of memories that are possible to collect and store. Larry McNamee and Eric Hartman were. They still are, for that matter. You can find them before every Phillies home game pacing the pavement at the first and third base ticket windows, meeting and greeting fans as they enter the ballpark. More on that later. First, their reminiscences.

Larry McNamee was a teenaged, non-paid volunteer with the A's in the late 40's, early 50's when he first came in the company of the legendary Mack. His high school baseball coach was a friend of the Mack family, and Mack—the A's do-it-all owner/manager--always was on the lookout for volunteer assistants. When the coach asked McNamee if he might be interested in interning with the team, McNamee immediately said yes.

So it came to pass that he found himself mailing player pictures to youngsters who wrote in requesting them. "They were free," he recalls. "I believe the children were allowed to write in for three to five, something like that, and we would send them out. By the volume I handled, I would get complimentary tickets for the ballgames."

Once McNamee started down memory lane, the stories kept coming.

"Connie Mack was such a gentleman," he recalled. "He was involved in all of the day-to-day operations of his ball club. I think he was quite able to raise his voice if he had to. But I never got in trouble so he had no reason to, at least with me. He wasn't stand-offish at all. Any time he would pass, he would tap you on the shoulder and say, 'Things going well?' He never made anyone feel that they were less important than he was."

60 years after the fact, McNamee still remembers the best piece of advice Mack gave him as that teenaged intern. Simply put, it was this: "You never bring an umbrella to the ballpark." And this is the way McNamee tells it:

"I had worked maybe two, three days and it was a rainy day. I ride the bus to the ballpark and had an umbrella with me when I went into work. Connie Mack puts his arms around me. He called me, 'Kid' and he says to me…'Kid, we never bring an umbrella to the ballpark because it never rains on our ballpark. If you need an umbrella, stay home!'

"To this day, I do not carry an umbrella to the ballpark. At the (Shibe Park) gate, the fans were told if they came with an umbrella, they had to leave it outside. We had a barrel we put it in. In those days, when you left the umbrella it was still there when you came out. You could reclaim it."

McNamee interned with the A's in 1949, '50 and'51. But even someone as novice as he could see the team's inevitable end coming. "They weren't playing good ball. I remember in the last year watching a night game and I think he announced the attendance at being something like 223. I don't know where they got that. They were counting arms and legs because it sure didn't look like that many people." In November, 1954 the A's were sold and moved to Kansas City.

McNamee's one lingering regret through the years was that he never thought to get Connie Mack's autograph. "But it's a thing that at the time, you don't realize in whose presence you are," he admits. He doesn't have that autograph, but he still has those memories. And they've lasted him a lifetime.

Eric Hartmann's encounters with Ed Wade were neither so prolonged nor so extensive. They were, however, still worth recalling.

Hartmann was an accountant in the Phillies front office. It was the late 1960's, early 1970's. Wade was a college student--Temple, Hartmann believes. "A very personable young man," he said. "He worked out of the mailroom delivering mail at the time, then he moved on to public relations. Occasionally, I would take him home to Cherry Hill (New Jersey) if he needed a ride."

On that ride, Hartmann said, they didn't "do much talking about baseball." So it came as somewhat of a surprise that Wade later moved to the player/personnel side of the game. "He was a very popular person," Hartmann observes. "I would have thought he would have stayed in the public relations department. I know Larry (Shenk) liked him very much. But, yes, I would never have known at the time that he would get into the baseball end because it was so early in his career."

Wade's tenure as the Phillies GM ended on a somewhat down note. By the time the Phillies won the 2008 National League Pennant and World Series, he was gone (later to resurrect his career as GM of the Houston Astros). But Pat Gillick, who succeeded him in Philadelphia, was quick to credit Wade for much of the team's success by setting in place the pieces that made the 2008 run possible. In the Phillies baseball suite, it seems, Ed Wade was still very much a "popular person."

Larry McNamee and Eric Hartmann casually patrol their respective walkways outside the first and third base ticket windows in their distinctive blue shirts, kakhi pants, sneakers and Phillies cap. They're there, primarily, to be of assistance to the paying customers if need be.

Looking for a will call window, they can direct you. Want to pick up a pre-purchased ticket through one of the kiosks located conveniently outside the gates, they can help you. Need a wheelchair to assist an elderly or injured fan, they can get one for you. Which gate are you looking for? Right this way, sir (or madam).

They've been doing this since the Phillies second year at Citizens Bank Park. Management decided it would be good for customer relations to, in Hartmann's words, "to have someone out there, greet the people, kind of schmooze them in a nice way...

let 'em know the Phillies appreciated there being there." How McNamee and Hartman got to this place at this time is a story in itself for each of them.

Larry McNamee has spent most of his adult life around ticket sales in professional sport. Fifty years ago, he thought he wanted to be a health and physical education teacher and enrolled at the former West Chester State Teachers College to do just that. But two years into it, he became convinced that was not the course for him. So he joined the Marines to sort his prospective career track out. West Chester was not a wasted experience for him, however. He met his wife, Blanche, at the college. They were married in 1955 while he was in the Marines.

When his three-year enlistment was over, McNamee says he wasn't any more certain about the career track he wanted to pursue, "but I knew it was not teaching." So he took a job as a teller trainee with a regional bank. 12 years and two banks later (both of which are now extinct, though he says he hopes he "had nothing to do with that") he became the executive director of the Grocers Association in New Jersey. Like West Chester, that, too, was short-lived. "I soon learned there was a lot of politics" to the trade association industry, he laments.

Fortunately, he had begun picking up part time jobs in the ticket field. He was, in fact, the first ticket manager of the old New Jersey Devils of the Eastern Hockey League. They played in the "Ice House" before it became the Cherry Hill Arena.

It was while he was at Cherry Hill that McNamee secured a part time position with the National Skating Derby—"Roller Derby" to you and me. The Derby was expanding to the East Coast from Hollywood, California and settled on Philadelphia as its eastern home base. "After about a year," he related, "the Derby decided they were going to stay in the area and they were looking for full time people. So they asked if I was interested in the positions of Box Office Manager and Business Manager, and I said, 'Sure.'" He stayed with the skating derby until 1973.

McNamee is a native of Delaware County. Blanche and he moved with their two boys to New Jersey in 1960, across the Walt

Whitman Bridge mere minutes away from the South Philadelphia Sports Complex. They're also about 50 miles from the Jersey Shore, which explains their affinity for Jersey. ("Once you get the sand between your toes, you don't go back," McNamee offers.)

Since the Derby was "more or less a night job," McNamee also started a small ticket brokerage in Jersey. About the same time, in the early '70's, he also took a volunteer job with the Phillies selling advertising.

"When I started the ticket brokerage in New Jersey, I came to the Phillies to see if I could sell tickets for them," McNamee explains. "That's the way I started in the ticket business as such. I sold tickets out of a store front over in Woodbury for the Phillies and worked on the advertising on a complimentary ticket basis."

Each season, he would buy small blocks of tickets for the 300, 500, 600 and 700 levels at Veterans Stadium. He sold them to his customers on a game-to-game basis, at face value. No surcharges here, he emphasized. "There had been no (Phillies) ticket office or resell office in New Jersey at the time," he remembers. "I was the pioneer, I guess you would say. And it built up over the years." Blanche and he would run the ticket office by day. By night, he would head over to the Cherry Hill Arena or where ever the Roller Derby was performing, to handle ticket sales there.

Truth is, ticket sales became Larry McNamee's way of life. He's sold tickets on a part time basis for the Eagles and the Flyers and 76'ers. Also for Temple University at the Liacouris Center and Penn football in the Fall. Even Blanche got involved. She started selling tickets at the Spectrum in 1971. 37 years later she was still working 40 hours a week at Wachovia Center ticket office. And, energetic lady that she is, she fills in at a Phillies ticket window when needed. "It keeps her young," Larry McNamee smiles. In 1988, after he closed his ticket brokerage, he started selling Phillies tickets at the Vet. He stayed at the ticket window until the Phils move him outside to "meet and greet" the fans. Good thing, too, he says. Those computer screens were starting to get to his eyes.

Eric Hartman took a different path from Larry McNamee to the pavement outside the third base ticket windows at CBP.

Hartmann, born in Camden, New Jersey, received an associate degree in business administration from Temple in 1958. His first job was as an accountant with a New Jersey oil company, then with Insurance Company of North America.

In March, 1969, he went to work as an accountant in the Phillies business office. He was hired by George Harrison, the Phillies vice president for Finance. He worked directly under the supervision of Harrison's son, Ted, the Phillies controller, doing financial statements and the books. On the side, as a favor, and if requested, he also would help Phillies players manage their money.

Baseball was a lean business 40 years ago, he remembers. "I don't think we had 26 people. We had calculators, that's all. We didn't have computers. The payroll guy would do the payroll manually. I did the financial statements."

For the 11 years he was doing the financial statement, Hartmann said, he never saw a player's contract. "All I got from Ted Harrison was a number to put in for players' salaries. I never had a hand in developing the number myself. It could be $2 million, but I never knew what Mike Schmidt might have made. Or Steve Carlton or any of those guys. Confidentiality was very, very important."

In 1980, Eric Hartmann did something he wishes to this day he had not. "I just got up and walked out," he mused in a conversation almost 30 years later. "I had trouble, I guess, with the work load. You talk about an unusual situation, an unusual day. It was no reflection on the Phillies. It was just my own problem. I left on my own volition, and I've regretted it ever since."

It was during this episode in his life that Eric Hartmann experienced a Connie Mack moment of his own. Only this time, Connie Mack came in the person of Phillies principal owner, Bill Giles. Giles called him after his walkout, Hartmann revealed, and asked: "Eric, can I help you? Can I do anything for you?" It was a gesture of concern that registered beyond words with Hartmann. "He didn't have to do that," he says. "He's a marvelous man. I can't say enough about him. He's done a great job for this organization. I'm just sorry he didn't get more credit than he did for what he's done."

The Giles intervention aside, Eric Hartmann moved on with his professional life. He ran a frozen donut franchise for five years with a company called Donuts Galore. It didn't work out, he admits. "It was the wrong time. Everybody's trying to lose weight, and all. I just couldn't keep it going anymore."

So Eric Hartmann went back to tax accounting. With a company called Automatic Data Processing, ADP, an organization he describes as now one of the largest payroll companies in the world. It was started by an entrepreneur named Frank Laudenberg. His name might be familiar. He's served two separate tenures representing the state of New Jersey in the United State Senate. Eric Hartman, meanwhile, in 1996, at the age of 62, retired.

It was while Hartmann was with the Phillies business office that he also would volunteer at the "will-call" ticket window. He liked it. So, 1970, at the suggestion of Ted Harrison to "see what was going on," not to mention getting paid in the process, he joined the ticket sellers' union. "At 5 o'clock, I would jump down to the box office. I made a few extra dollars. It worked out very nicely."

Hartmann doesn't know exactly why, but in 2001, a lady ticket seller called him asking whether he might be interested in selling Phillies tickets again. "Nobody particularly associated with the organization," he says, "just another ticket seller. 'How'd you like to come back to the Phillies?' she said to me. And I said, 'Yeah!' 20 years later, I still felt I did the wrong thing by leaving the way I did. So I said, 'Yeah, I gotta go back.' So I showed up and they put me on and I started back at the Vet."

Thus it was that Eric Hartmann was back in the place where years later he still believes he should never have left. "You hear how Tom LaSorda bleeds Dodger blue," he asks. "Well, I bleed Phillies red. I really mean that, too. I love this game and I love this team. It's worked out very well."

So the question was put directly to both men: "What's the most pronounced change that's registered with you about baseball and/or professional sport as an entertainment medium?"

Not suprisingly, for Larry McNamee, it had to do with tickets. "Well," he replied, "first of all, the cost to the fan to have a night's entertainment. Baseball is probably the least expensive from a point of ticket prices rising compared to most other sports. But prices are really up.

"When we (Blanche and he) moved five years ago…I was cleaning out a lot of things you wonder why you ever kept. I found a (Philadelphia) Flyers (hockey) ticket from the early years. The ticket price was $7.50. Today, I believe that seat goes for $125."

Eric Hartmann, again perhaps predictably, was taken by how the nature and the magnitude of the business had changed and multiplied so dramatically. "When I was part of the front office, as I said, there was only 26 people. Today, I couldn't even guess how many there are because of the way the sport has grown. I think Mr. Harrison would turn over in his grave if he saw how this industry has grown today. He really would."

Both Hartmann and McNamee, self-described "people" persons, also are very aware of just how the fan base has changed through the years—in attitude, in approach…even in attire.

"Very few people are not nice to you," Eric Hartmann stipulates. "Most people who come here come here to have a good time. The exception is if we have a window that doesn't open on time. Some people get upset if something's not open on time. But most people are very good. If somebody comes up to you with an attitude and you don't give them an attitude back… well, the situation usually resolves itself."

Except, perhaps, when the New York Mets are in town.

"Historically, they've always been our toughest fans to deal with, the Mets fans" Larry McNamee relates. In the four years he's been pacing the entranceway to the first base gates, he said, he's only experienced one altercation. It happened as the crowd was entering the ballpark for a Mets game.

"I had a young…I want to say, 'punk,' but let's say a young gentleman from New York, probably in his early 20's…may have bent his elbow once too many…who picked on an older gentleman. They had been bantering back and forth---'Go, Mets, go; We're goin' to beat the Phillies; We gonna beat their asses, blah, blah, blah'…that sort of thing.

"And the old man said, 'Ah, just go away. Get away from me. You're drunk' or something like that. And he (the 20-year-old) took offense. I did have to get involved that time. But that's the only altercation that I've encountered. For every schmuck you meet, you meet a thousand nice people."

Since Larry McNamee came from the stiff high collar era of Connie Mack, he also can't help but notice how fan dress and demographics has changed through the years. "Back then, when I was working for Connie, it seems like that was older crowd and they were dressed to the hilt...shirts, ties, suits, hats," McNamee reminisced. "Not the casual attire you've come to expect at the ballpark today...T-shirts, shorts, cut-offs, flip flops. Not that there's anything wrong with it, but it certainly has changed."

And what do they like most in what they're doing?

Kibitzing with the people, primarily.

"I love it," Eric Hartmann says emphatically. "I just love it!" What he particularly loves is seeing parents and their children coming to the ballpark together. "To see a mother and a father out there...little children and the babies in Phillies uniforms. I don't know that there's another sport where you see families like that. Baseball's just so good with that. It's heartwarming."

McNamee would agree. But there's one additional component he would factor in his enjoyment equation. It's the Connie Mack statute. "I'm just so glad they kept Connie Mack when they moved here. I thought maybe when they came to the new ball park, maybe it would just be stored somewhere. It would have been easy to do because he was so long ago and he was from the other league. But they didn't forget him."

No, they didn't. The likeness of Connie Mack, an imposing figure from the past, stands across from the third base ticket windows at Citizens Bank Park taking it all in...the panorama of the ballpark, the vendors, the fans, the traffic. And there's not an umbrella in sight.

Tickets, Please

In another age, another era of professional sports, they used to be called "ticket takers." That's really what they did: Take your ticket and pass you through the turnstiles. But no more.

Electronic scanners and computerized turnstiles have rendered the term if not the people all but obsolete. Now they're called "greeters." Because, among other things, that's what they do at 21st century ballparks, stadiums and arenas across the country. They greet you...welcoming you as you enter the venue, thanking you as you depart and wishing you a safe trip to your destination.

There are approximately 40 "greeters" working the turnstiles at Citizens Bank Park for the Philadelphia Phillies. They're game day employees. If this were a military unit, their field captains would be Ed Smith and Rose Ferraro, the director and assistant director of gates, respectively. And gate supervisors John Franzini, Lisa Mary Wilson and Ellison "Rick" Richardson would be three lieutenants monitoring access and egress and assisting as need be the men and women who work the turnstiles. There are others in the unit, of course. But for purposes of this narrative, these five collectively are representative of their class and what they do.

And what exactly is that? It's simple: To get the fans in and out of the ballpark as expeditiously, as easily and as orderly as possible. Most of the time it's a relatively routine procedure. The fan approaches the gate and inserts his or her ticket into the scanner slot; the scanner reads the bar code; the turnstile clicks; the fan enters. No fuss, no muss. That's the idea.

But when you draw 40,000 or so people to the ballpark each night, as the Phillies have done of late, it's inevitable that some issues arise. Like what can or cannot come into the park. (Cans, bottles, even a broom or two cannot. Homemade signs, tastefully done and shaped so as not to interfere with another fan's view, can.) Alcohol is a definite no-no!

When there are issues, it falls first to the likes of a Franzini, Richardson or Wilson to resolve. If a problem can't be handled at that level, Smith and/or Ferraro are called in. If it's still unresolvable, security might be called. Or upper management. Fortunately, few rise to that level of concern.

The greeters are in place when the gates to Citizens Bank Park open. They're on the job until they close. It makes for a long day. But this quintet has been at it for several years now. So the hours clearly are not a problem.

—∿—

Ed Smith spent most of his professional life as a printer. Most of that with the old Philadelphia Bulletin before the paper went out of business in 1982. It was, in fact, the demise of the Bulletin which led Smith to the Phillies. He was 43 at the time.

"I was sitting at home," he recollects. "I was the youngest of eight kids. My older brother would say, 'let's go play golf in Florida.' He lived down there, but it wasn't for me. I just couldn't go to Florida to have fun. I needed to do something. I just can't sit around. I did it for the month of February. In March, I said I'd like to get a job with the Phillies."

As fate would have it, Smith had some homegrown advice on how to go about it. Three of his sons--Eddie Junior, Fran and Steve--already were Phillies game day employees. They worked security at the gates. With them for counsel, Smith applied and was hired, also in security. He had to break up a minor scuffle his first night on the job. Nothing major, he stipulates. But still, an interesting introduction to what life at the ballpark could be like.

Meanwhile, Smith also found employment in the printing operations of two Philadelphia insurance companies. But having landed a spot with the Phillies, he wasn't about to let that go, either. "I said to my wife, 'You know, I love this job. I am not going to give it up. If I get another night job (offer), I'm not going to take it.' She looked at me like I was nuts. But I said, 'Something will work out.'" It did.

Smith retired from the printing business in April of 2007. His tenure with the Phillies went uninterrupted for 27 years. Now, beyond his family, it's the sole consumer of his time.

In retrospect, John Franzini took a very similar path to Phillies employ. He, too, was out of a job when he decided to apply.

Franzini was a machinist with a Westinghouse plant in the city until it closed in 1986. He immediately applied to the U.S. Postal Service for a position as a mail carrier. He was put on a waiting list. Meanwhile, a friend told him about part time employment opportunities with the Phillies. He pursued the option and was hired in the Spring of 1987 as a gate security agent. The very next year, his appointment with the Post Office came though.

Franzini worked as a mail carrier for 18 years before he retired in 2006. Like Smith, he did double duty with the Phillies throughout. "I liked being around the ballpark so much, when I got my fulltime job at the post office, I kept working with the Phillies," he said. "I like baseball and I like the guests who come to the ballpark. You see a lot of the same faces and we just talk baseball. I just like being around the game."

Rick Richardson grew up at 19th and Lehigh, two blocks from the old Connie Mack Stadium. He remembers he could see the right field foul line and the batter's box from his third floor bedroom window. As an eight-year old, he would help a vendor sell pretzels and peanuts for a nickel or a dime near the gates leading into the old ballyard. "That's how I got the love for working at the ballpark," he reveals. When the Phillies abandoned Connie Mack for Veterans Stadium, he admits, he cried.

He said he wanted to work for the Phillies since the time he was old enough to go to the stadium by himself. He started with the club in 1988 as an usher. He moved to a ticket-taker—make that, a "greeter"-- and then a gate supervisor through the ensuing years.

Rick Richardson, in his other life's work, is a full time driver for Federal Express. When the Phillies are at home, he heads straight for Citizens Bank Park once his Fed Ex shift is over. On a good day, he usually arrives about 3:30 PM. And there he stays until the park is closed for the night—11-to-11:30 on the average. The next morning, on a Phillies home stand, he's up and at 'em again for another long day.

Rose Ferraro started as a hostess with the Phillies in 1988. Actually, she originally planned on applying for a position on the "Hot Pants Patrol" in the 1970s. But a job opportunity took her to New York, instead. The Phillies weren't in her cards for a time.

When she returned to Philadelphia, she pursued her Phillies ambition. Why? "I knew people who worked here and they kept asking me to come and work with them," she explained. "Every year I'd say, maybe next year, maybe next year. So one year I just did!"

She moved to the gates as a supervisor and then, in 2001, was named assistant gate supervisor. That's her side job.

Her real job is an office manager for a New Jersey construction company. On game days, she has an agreement with her employer that she leaves at 3:30 so she can make the 20-minute drive from Jersey to the ballpark in plenty of time to take on her Phillies duties. If it's a day game, she will use her vacation time. The Phillies are that important in her life.

"When I first took this job (with the Phillies), I thought I'd be here 2 or 3 years. 20 years later, I'm still here. I love it. I love the people. I love the atmosphere. I love the Phillies. As far as I'm concerned, I'm never leaving."

Ferraro acknowledges that doing the double duty can wear on a body during an extended home stand. "You do get tired," she says. "It can wear you down, but you keep pushing." At season's end, one would think she'd be ready for a break. No so, she says. "Most people, myself included, actually will start feeling a little bit bad that it is coming to an end. I've tried to explain that to people who aren't here. But it's hard to explain. You just have to experience it to appreciate it."

Lisa Mary Wilson took it as a personal challenge when, at the encouragement of a friend, she applied for her job with the Phillies.

"I was pretty shy," she admits. "So I thought this may be a good arena to help me get out of my shell, to help me interact with people on a one-on-one basis…different types of people, from different cultural backgrounds on a regular basis. I thought it would be beneficial and it was. It really helped."

Interacting with people…young people, at that…is a very important aspect of Lisa Mary Wilson's professional career.

She is, you see, a teacher by day…the Upper Darby School District in suburban Philadelphia. She was graduated cum laude with a B.A. in Education from Temple University. While pursuing her master's degree (again at Temple) in Vocational, Technical Training, she never earned a grade less than an A. .

She was hired by the Phillies as an usher at Veterans Stadium in1991, a job she says had her working on every level of the complex. She remembers cleaning seats in the 500 and 600 levels of the Vet upper tiers in advance of the fans arrival even when attendance might not have warranted such attention. But she thought otherwise. "The fans pay a price to get into the stadium," she explains. "I felt they were entitled to the full baseball experience no matter where they sat."

Lisa Mary Wilson has been teaching business courses at Upper Darby since 1998. She's at her school desk at 7 o'clock each morning and leaves about 3:05 in the afternoon. When the Phils are home, she stops at a South Philadelphia residence for a change of clothes and some dinner before making her 10-minute way to Citizens Bank Park.

Attendance, preparation and effective utilization of her down time are very important to her ability to work two jobs with demanding hours.

"I have perfect attendance at work," she proclaims. "I just never call out. I love my jobs. I prepare ahead of time. My students come first, of course. I am always telling them, 'Proper preparation prevents poor performance.' On evenings when I know the next day I have to do the Phillies as well as teach, I will prepare my uniform ahead of time. I will make lunch ahead of time. I try to get those little things in order so that I can give 110 percent to my teaching and 110 to the Phillies. I have never failed to give my students back their papers the next day. It doesn't matter if the game ends at 2 AM. I tell my students, I will be here and your papers will be graded."

Lisa Wilson has earned 18 credits toward her doctorate degree. But that was on hold as she planned for her wedding in 2009. How much will her schedule change after she's married? Not too much, she thinks.

"My fiancée knows how important this job (with the Phillies) is to me," she said. "I said to him, 'Give me your honest opinion. Do you want me to quit?' And he said, 'No, you love it. It's part of you.'"

So at least as the 2009 baseball season approached, soon-to-be married Lisa Wilson planned again to teach by day and greet Phillies fans at night.

Ed Smith is what is called in the trade a "walk-around" manager. Because once the gate assignments are shared with his staff, that's what he does a lot…a lot of walking around.

At least once a every night—sometimes twice, but certainly at least once-- about 6:10 PM for a 7 o'clock game, Smith makes it a point to walk to each of the turnstile gates just to see for himself how smoothly the fans entry is going.

"I walk around…walk around the outside of the building," he explains, "checking, but not really checking…I just want to see how our people are doin'. I walk by and I talk to them. I ask, 'How's it goin' tonight? Any problems? You don't feel good? Why don't you go to first aid?

"I like to catch a problem or a situation if it is building before it gets too far. So I go by and I talk to them…the greeters. You want them to get to know you. You want them to know you want to know them. If I don't know someone, I'll ask. What's his name? What's her name? And I'll talk to them by their name."

It's important that Smith knows his people because for them to work well, they need to get along with each other. "We need them to work as a group," he says. "If two people can't get along, then I'll move them. You're always trying to get a group that can work together."

Making his rounds one summer night in 2008, Smith encounters 87-year-old George Lawler. Lawler is working the turnstiles at the premium seating entry section. It's covered and it's air-conditioned. There's also a portable television within easy view, something the outside gate greeters don't enjoy.

Lawler's been working for the Phillies for 37 years. "I started out trying to make ends meet," he tells a visitor. "I'm still doing it 'cause I like it." Smith inquires: "Everything okay, George?" Lawler assures him it. Smith smiles, "Atta boy," and moves on. Lawler is stationed where he is in deference to his age and his years of service with the Phillies. He is one of five seniors (affectionately labeled, "the grandfathers,") who work the turnstiles on home stands. He and the other four have one additional privilege. Where the other greeters stay until game's end to greet the fans as they leave—"Thanks, for coming; Have a good night; Drive carefully"--the "grandfathers" are allowed to go home after the fourth inning.

Rose Ferraro sees her role much like Smith does. "My job is to go out to make sure the greeters and the supervisors are not having any problems or issues," she says. "If they are, my job is to help them solve it if we can. But they're pretty good at it. I can't say enough about just how good they are. They do a good job."

There are occasions, however, where a problem has to be kicked upstairs...what can or cannot get into the ballpark; ticket issues. "Sometimes we have counterfeit tickets; sometimes we have problems with scalpers. Sometimes a customer will have a complaint about something. Usually, the supervisors can solve it. If they can't, I will try to help out." If that doesn't work, then the issue has to be kicked upstairs to someone with a higher pay grade than either Ferraro or Smith.

Alcohol when it rears its head is a constant source of concern because the Phillies organization is very protective of securing a fan friendly environment. "Occasionally, we may have someone who has had a little too much to drink trying to get into the ballpark," Ferraro concedes. "We try not to permit those people into the ballpark. We strive to make this family friendly. If we feel that the person is intoxicated...that they're staggering...that you can smell the alcohol on them...

"Well, we would check to make sure they're not driving...ask a friend to take them back to their car to sober up or whatever; or have someone pick them up. If it comes to the worse case, we'll actually put them in a taxi and the Phillies will pay for that and send them home."

The staff is very serious about their security responsibilities, particularly in the aftermath of September 11, 2001. There are training films to view; there are regular meetings to discuss current issues or potential problems. Alerts to be shared and watched for. When a fan is stopped to have a bag or purse checked, it's not to be simply bothersome or harassing. "We are looking in there for everyone's safety," Ferraro stipulates. "There's a very serious side to what we do, and our people take it very seriously as they should. We have very thorough training on those things. We're being very careful to make sure that our fans are being taken care of and protected to the best of our ability."

John Franzini, Rick Richardson and Lisa Mary Wilson know exactly of where Rose Ferraro speaks. As gate supervisors, they are positioned with the greeters game in and game out.

"The gate supervisor's responsible for everything that's at the gate," Franzini says. "If anybody has like a problem or something, they send them to you and you try to take care of the problem."

Like what?

Franzini explains: "Like somebody might have a ticket and it's what they call a reprint ticket...a ticket that was sold as original but it might have gotten lost in the mail. Or it could have been stolen and (in this technological age) they reprint the ticket. Reprint tickets aren't going to work here."

So what happens? "The greeter sends them to us and then we would try to help them get it straightened out. Most likely we would send them to the sales office or ticket window. We try to expedite or facilitate the resolution to the problem."

Other examples: "Well, one of the guests might try to sneak in some alcohol or stuff like that. And we would stop them. Or they might want to bring a cooler in. We don't allow the hard coolers. But where a person could be a diabetic or something, we might allow them for problems like that."

And what if the problem can't be easily fixed? Encounter many of those?

"Not really," Franzini responds. "If we have a problem with a certain guest who starts carrying on and we can't handle it, and it looks like some kind of disturbance might result, we can call for security. And security usually brings a police officer along and they would take care of that type of problem."

Franzini probably knows better than most where that kind of situation might occur. That's because he works the sections where a privately owned bar/restaurant adjoins the ballpark with three direct entry ways into the stands.

He has 5 greeters—all of them men (I'm always concerned some drunk might take a swing at a greeters, so it's all men, no women," explains Ed Smith) … two on the patio area outside the restaurant; 2 in the hallways; and 1 at the backdoor which exits the restaurant into the concourse.

Each of the greeters has hand-held scanners which function exactly as the turnstiles. Read the bar code, confirm the validity of the ticket, gain entry. They also have exit scanners at their disposal so a fan can migrate from the park to the restaurant and back without leaving the premises.

If anyone is going to try to beat the system (and with 40,000 people a night, "there's always somebody trying to beat the system," Franzini concedes) it's most likely to occur in this area. As Franzini puts it: "We do from time to time deal with somebody trying to sneak into the ballpark. If you have four guys come to the ballpark and only three have tickets. They'll tell the fourth to go into the restaurant from the street entry. The three will come into the ballpark. Then one will go to the restaurant with one of the three tickets in his pocket to pick up his buddy. The only problem is that the ticket he scanned when he left the park to go to the restaurant will read 'good' when he reenters. His buddy's, however, won't. It'll read, 'already in.'

"So we have problems in that respect. Sometimes, I have to make a judgment call. It's possible that we missed a scan or something. And if we did, the scan would read 'already in.' So I have to make the judgment call. I can almost always tell who's being honest and who's not. People who try to beat the system that way don't have much luck. Not much luck at all!"

Oh, yes… Those fans who might stay in the bar too long before coming back into the park won't make it if they show any signs in inebriation. "Some times a fan will have been at the bar too long, it's the 6th or 7th inning and they look kind or drunk…or we've been waiting through a long rain delay…Well, the potential for problems are too obvious. We won't let them back in and if we have to get security or the police to deal with it, we will."

For Franzini, in particular…but Wilson and Richardson as well…they usually can anticipate when it's not going to be "just another night" at the ballpark. "Hot Dog Night" and the attendant exuberance of the college crowd it always seems to attract is one. And, need it be said? When the Mets are in town… well, that's likely to be another.

"It's not that the New York fans are bad people," Franzini demurs. "It's just when Philly fans get together with New York fans, they can sort of bother each other. They like to get on each other." Add alcohol to the mix and an already competitive situation can get even potentially more combustible and easily out of hand.

Lisa Mary Wilson has a much more sedate environment at the Right Field gate that she supervises. But she still brings the same enthusiasm and commitment with her that she displays every day in her classroom and that she displayed when she still dusted those empty seats in the 500 and 600 levels of the Vet.

"It's all about providing customer service," she proclaimed as she warmed to her description of what she does. "You are trying to help everyone have an enjoyable experience."

Then the schoolmarm in her takes over: "In the classroom, I like to touch (figuratively rather than literally) people. I want each student to walk away with…'Wow, she really responded to me.' That is the same thing I bring to the ballpark. I don't drink. I don't even drink coffee. I go from one job to the other, and my adrenalin is high. I love what I do. I absolutely love what I do without hesitation." Since she's been doing it for quite a long time and enjoying it, as well, it's obviously a formula and a lifestyle that clearly works for her.

So, once again, as it so often does with their game day associates, the question arises for these five: How much longer are the Phillies in their future?

For Ed Smith, the question need not be asked. He is, by his own admission, an active person. Idleness doesn't sit well with him (he also works in the baseball off-season for the Philadelphia Flyers and 76ers). He has an affinity for sport. As a teenager he was a pretty good shooter in basketball. But he wasn't very good defensively. He actively sought out some coaching on his defensive techniques…"grabbing the pants, stepping on shoes, that sort of thing." His playing days ended when he went into the printing profession but his love for sports didn't. Besides, he's also a self-described people person. "I've always loved people, being around people…I never had a problem walking into a room without knowing people. I could walk into a room and 10 minutes later, I know everybody."

So Ed Smith intends to be around for a while. It will be difficult, he admits, to exceed the excitement of a World Series season. But he was late in 2008 already looking forward to 2009 and what it might bring.

Rose Ferraro, meanwhile, already was contemplating the 2009 trip she and a group of 30 co-workers take annually to Clearwater, Florida for Phillies Spring Training. "Some nights I'm at home 1, 1:30 in the morning. You can't go right to bed. You aren't tired and you have to unwind for an hour or two. There are many nights when I'm operating on two hours of sleep…gone to my other job and then come here. You're very tired, but you do it because you love it. I really love it. We have a great family connection here that you don't find in many places." The Spring training trip serves as her warm up for the season ahead.

Nor is John Franzini planning to leave anytime soon. "I like Citizens Bank Park a lot," he says. "I like the people. It seems like almost every night we're sold out. The park is a beautiful park. And this park keeps me busier than when I was over at the Vet." Strange as it may seem, Franzini gets to see none of the game, except when he passes a television monitor as he makes his way around his station. But he adds: "I look forward to coming in. When they're on the road, I'm looking forward to them coming back so I can come into the ballpark." When he worked at the Post Office and started at 6:15 each morning, he'd get home at 3:30 in the afternoon. His wife would have dinner on the table for him, he'd take a shower and head into the park. "It used to bother her when I was working both the post office and the Phillies and was away from home so much," he concedes. "But now that I'm home a lot, I think she wants to see me go."

Between Fed Ex and the Phillies, Rick Richardson knows what to expect when the team is at home. He's at his day job at 6 each morning. He's at the ballpark by 3:30 each home afternoon to prepare for the gates opening to Ashburn Alley. And he doesn't leave until the ballpark has been checked for any delinquent fans exiting the park. "We check the bathrooms and the gift shops, Harry the K's," he explains. "Last week there was a rainout and there were still a bunch of people in there eating at Harry the K's. So I had to wait until everybody finished their dinner to lock the gates up."

For an average 3-hour nine-inning game, Richardson doesn't get home until 11:15 or so each night. And, like Rose Ferraro, he needs time to unwind. But he's up at 5 AM and back at it again. Fortunately for him, his body chemistry seems to handle the time demands just fine. "I don't get tired unless there's a 14-game home stand," he says. "I'll start getting tired about game 10. But that's rare." So he does it season after season. "I like what I do. I like being part of the sports scene."

There was a time in Lisa Wilson's life when her Phillies co-workers were very much her personal support group. She lost her father, Robert, in 1992, her brother, Robert Jr., to a fishing accident in 1998, and her mother, Frances, in January of 2007. "Losing my mother is one of the hardest things I've ever had to go through in my life. And my family here at this place helped me through in every possible way. And when my father passed away in '92, it was amazing because when I took time off, when I came back their support helped me get through it. I just couldn't believe it."

Working at Citizens Bank Park is also good for the genes, she believes. "This place is almost like a fountain of youth. Think about it. I work along side people who are in their 70's, 80's…I had one worker in his 90's. The enthusiasm, the adrenalin. The excitement they bring to the game…You can't help but catch it. It is wonderful. It's not like coming to work. It's like coming to be with your family."

That, for Lisa Mary Wilson and so many of her game day associates, is what makes it all worthwhile.

11

"May I Help You to Your Seats?"

They're on the "front lines" of the customer service brigade at Citizens Bank Park…the ground troops in the trenches, so to speak.

They welcome you to the boxes, the grandstand and the bleachers; they show you to your seats; they wipe them for you if they haven't been wiped already; they invite you to enjoy yourself and the ballgame; and they're ready to answer your questions or give you directions if you're in need of either or both.

Like their ticket taker counterparts, they've had a change in their terminology. They used to be called ushers (or, in the case of the ladies, usherettes). Today, however, in the lexicon of modern professional sports, they're called host or hostesses, respectively. The Philadelphia Phillies employ some 250 of them for at least the 81 home games the team plays each year…more when the club makes the play-offs.

Pat McCoy of Drexel Hill is one of their representative number.

Ask her what it is the host and hostesses do, and she has this very precise reply.

"We're out there with the people. Basically, we try to make the fans feel welcome. And they depend on us for things like how to get around the ballpark; to tell them where things are; to seat them; to tell them what's going on throughout the ballpark.

"We're the first people they come to for, you know, this question or that: What happens if it gets rained out? What do we do with our tickets? Where can I go for this? What time is the game goin' to start? What are they doing now? Where's the restroom? What section has the food they want? How to get there? Where can I get souvenirs?

"We only work six months a year. But for those six months, we're out there with the fans. In the cold and the rain; and the

128

heat and the humidity. Once the season starts, we are the front line for the fans. We try to be as helpful as we can. We want to treat them like we'd wanted to be treated ourselves if we came to the ballpark."

Helpful, polite, pleasant and professional...that about sums up what the hosts and hostesses do. And, in the main, they're very good at it.

—◊◊◊—

Pat McCoy wanted to work for the Philadelphia Phillies so bad she interrupted a Florida vacation in 1996 to fly back and interview for the job.

It may have been the last night of the scheduled interviews. In any event, she remembered: "I called up here and they said, 'No, we're sorry. If you can't come this night, that's it.' So I flew up and interviewed." As she recalled, it wasn't so much of an interview as it was a conversation. "We talked for close to an hour about the Phillies. We started with the '50 team and worked our way up from '80 to the present (at that time). This was a Tuesday night. They said I'd hear by Friday. I actually heard by Thursday."

There was, of course, a bit more to the interview process than just talk. The Phillies asked why she wanted the job. "I told them I loved baseball." What was she doing professionally at the time? "I dealt with the public...a service representative with the Philadelphia office of the U.S. Social Security Administration." (To this day, incidentally, McCoy believes her experience "dealing with the public all those years at Social Security" prepared her better than she could have anticipated to deal with the fans at Citizens Bank Park.)

There was, Pat McCoy acknowledges 12 years after the fact, an ulterior motive for interviewing with the Phillies. "It was the All-Star year (in Philadelphia)," she admits. "I thought I really wanted to come to the All-Star game. But it's always so hard to get tickets. So, I thought: 'Let's find a job with the Phillies. That way, I guarantee I get in.' Which is exactly what I did. Here it is 13 years later, and I'm still here."

Those who know Pat McCoy aren't surprised at all. She's been a devoted Phillies fan for most of her life.

"I literally value this team," she proclaims. "I've been a big fan since I was 9. Don't know exactly why. Guess it was because I was a tomboy. I just played baseball all day during the summer. I used to come down here in South Philadelphia. This was when kids could travel by themselves when they were younger. My cousins lived down here. And we used to play half-ball; pimple ball, they called it.

"And the boys would want me on their team because I was so good! I could really hit that half ball with a broomstick handle."

Pat McCoy saw her first major league baseball game (the Phillies, of course) as a young girl of 10. A neighborhood swim club was sponsoring a trip to the ballpark. McCoy wasn't a swim club member, but a ticket became available. She was asked her to go along. She accepted.

So it was that on September 15, 1955—she remembers the date precisely because she "was so excited I thought I died and went to heaven"—Pat McCoy found herself seated in the centerfield bleachers of Connie Mack Stadium, "dead centerfield," to be exact. It was the Phillies of the Stan Lopata—"I just loved Stan Lopata"--Willie 'Puddinhead' Jones, Del Ennis era. Robin Roberts, also. although her recollection was that he was nearing the end of his career and "might have" been traded shortly thereafter. "

For as excited as she was that day, Pat McCoy didn't make it back to another Phillies game until after her graduation from high school. Her dedication to the Phillies, however, never faltered. "I always followed them, whether it was on radio or TV," she says. "My parents weren't sports fans. All I remember is that I used to monopolize the TV. So much so that my parents bought another one so they could see their programs and I could have my own TV to watch baseball."

If you haven't encountered Pat McCoy personally at Citizens Bank Park, by now you at least might have an idea of her personality. She's a Type A, for sure.

"I'm a very intense and emotional person," she acknowledges in a moment of introspection. "As I got older, I thought my enthusiasm for baseball would dwindle over the years. But it never did. I like being at the games with everybody. I like left field because that's where everybody gathers for batting practice and I like chit-chatting with them. I like talking to the fans. I like talking baseball. I love atmosphere."

On occasion, she's also an ambassador for her city and her team at one and the same time.

The night of the rain-delayed World Series game, for example. Five Philly fans from Texas showed up in her section. "It was the night we didn't get out until 2:30 in the morning. I'm walking across Broad and Pattison and there's the five of them, looking for a cab. 'You're not going to get a cab over here,' I tell them. 'Where you going?' They said the Sheraton. I said, 'Come on, get in my van, I'll take you.' So they walk with me to the parking lot and Mary, my friend from England, and I took them to the Sheraton on my way home. They wanted to pay me. I said, no. I know I would have loved for somebody to offer to help me at quarter to three in the morning."

There also was the time in 2001 when she befriended a family from Endicott, N.Y. whose young son was being treated at DuPont Children's Hospital in Wilmington, DE. "When they had to stay overnight (in the Ronald McDonald House in Delaware), they would bring him up to the baseball game because he liked baseball. He became an avid Phillies fan."

The first time they met, the family was attempting to get their wheelchair bound youngster to the 700 level of Veterans Stadium. They asked Pat McCoy how to go about it. She told them it was next to impossible to get a wheelchair to the 700 level. She invited them, instead, to stay in her section to watch the game.

That encounter blossomed into a friendship. When Pat McCoy visits with the family, she always has Phillies memorabilia for the young boy. She also met the family's parish priest, an avid Met fan.

That's where her impish side frequently manifests itself.

"He loves to rub it in when the Mets beat the Phillies," she says. "When we finished ahead of the Mets two years in a row, I told Markie (the boy), 'Make sure you wear your Phillies shirt to church and show Father.' I also sent Father a sympathy card. Last year I sent him a 2007 National League East Division Champion bumper sticker. This year I'm going to send him one that reads, 'World Champion.'"

There are two no-no's if you happen to be seated in the section of Citizens Bank Park that Pat McCoy is working…make that, hosting. Booing and swearing.

"I don't like booing," she proclaims. "I don't like it when the fans come down on the team. I don't like losing. But I can't stand booing. The fans aren't really that bad, they're not that bad at all. And all I do is go down to them and say, you know, 'Come on guys. Keep it down. Watch you're language!' And most often, they'll say, 'Okay, I'm sorry. Sorry.'"

What Pat McCoy does like is the relationship that develops over the course of the season between the Phillies game day employees. "I like the family we become for six months of the year. I like seeing everybody. I look forward to that. I've gotten a lot of good friendships out of it. Good, close friendships, so close that we see each other outside the season."

She's also been known to share a hug or two with the fans and her Phillies contemporaries celebrating Phillies success. "The night we won (the World Series), I walked around the 100 level and hugged everybody. I just wanted to share it with everybody." There was plenty for her to celebrate in 2008.

For as outgoing as Pat McCoy is, Stephen Apfum is quiet and unassuming. He's also a prince of a fella. Literally as well as figuratively. He was, you see, born into it.

His father, Moses Komble Apfum, was the king of a small village—4,000 or 5,000 people—in the Volte region of Gana in West Africa. Stephen is its prince and he and his family visit their homeland for a month or so at least once a year to see how the village is doing, and if there's anything he can do to assist.

Stephen Prince Apfum migrated with his wife, Theresa, and daughters Victoria and Jeurnte, to Philadelphia in 1971 in search of an education for himself and economic opportunity for his family. Why Philadelphia? Because his brother, Fred Eidoo, already lived there.

His original goal was to train in computer science and find a job in the profession. After two years at the Institute of Computer Science and another two years at Temple University, it didn't quite work out the way he had planned.

He found a position, instead, at the University of Pennsylvania Hospital as a medical aide transporting patients to and from the operating room. He also doubled as a film file clerk in the X-ray department until the economic downturn of 1991 forced a 200-person lay-off at the hospital.

Apfum accepted an early retirement at age 52. But he knew he couldn't to retire in the purest definition of the word. "I was a family man," he recalled. "I had a wife and two children. My income was not very good. I started looking for a job. I remember very well."

He found part time work at Melrose Country Club in Cheltenham "setting up tables for functions, for weddings." It was while he was at Melrose in 2005 that he came upon his opportunity to work for the Phillies.

"I had a friend I was working with at Melrose," Apfum recalled. "Joseph Sherman was his name. One day I call him and we're talking and he says he works for the Phillies. And I said, 'Oh, I would like to work for the Phillies.' And he says, 'All you have to do is go to the Phillies and ask for an application form."

He didn't know much about baseball or the Phillies at the time, he readily admits. But he went to Citizens Bank Park in January or February in 2005—he can't remember exactly what month it was--and picked up an application. "They told me that they were not interviewing," he recalls, "but if something came up, they'd let me know. Within a few weeks, something came up."

The first time he saw the inside of a baseball park was when he reported to Citizens Bank Park for a training session prior to the season opener. "There was a meeting. We were told about the very, very strict code of conduct that we had to follow. They showed us around the ballpark. That was my first time of being at the ballpark. I said, this is a beautiful park."

The first baseball game he saw…professional, amateur, semi-professional…was the Phillies 2005 season opener. "It seemed like a slow game, at first," he recalled. Three years later, he knows a lot more about baseball. And he now considers himself a "big fan" of the game and, of course, the team. He puts it this way: "I love it. It is a very beautiful game."

He also understands his obligations to the paying customers. "Guests," he calls them. "We take the guests to their seats. We make sure their seats are clean. We make sure that every guest who comes in has a ticket for your section. Some people, the first time they come to the ballpark, they aren't sure where they should be. So we very kindly direct him to where he belongs. And then if the guests have questions...well we try to answer them for them.

"The guests...everybody is different. They come in different character, different behavior, different attitude. It is always interesting to deal with them. If somebody is acting bad, we try just to calm them down. If that doesn't work then we contact the supervisor. It always is not good to talk nasty to the guest.

"I like the fans. I like to meet people...meet different people. I like them especially when they cheer the players. I like it in Ashburn Alley. I like it when they do batting practice when they always try to catch a ball. I see the young people, very young people. People that have families...that have children. I feel good when I see them dressed up in a Philly T-shirt, a jersey and a cap. Especially the kids. The kids look really good."

The hardest part of the job? "When somebody misbehaves. You have to be nice to the person. But once in a while, people will think they are right and you are wrong. So you have to call a supervisor. It happens, but it certainly doesn't happen very often." With 40,000 to 45,000 "guests" visiting virtually every night...over 3 million a season...it's a wonder it doesn't happen more often than it does.

It just doesn't, not in Stephen Prince Apfum's section at least.

As Allen Davis sees it, a host at Citizens Bank Park has two primary allegiances to honor each home game. The first is to the fans. The second is to the Phillies organization itself. Both in his view are of equal imperative.

Of his allegiance to the fans, he has this to say:

"What I do, in whatever section I'm working, is to greet the people…say, hello, how you doing; can I help you with anything about the ballpark…where you can get cheese steak sandwiches… where the restrooms are…where you can go to smoke a cigarette… There's nothing you can't ask me and I won't try to help you. If I don't know the answer, I'm going to try to find it for you."

And his allegiance to his game day employer, the Phillies?

"I think that's being there on time, being there for all of the games, being there where they can depend on me…being there to know that if they ask me to do something, if they ask, Allen will try to find a way to do it. Whatever needs to be done, I'm going to do."

Pat McCoy is extroverted and high energy. Stephen Apfum is quiet and unassuming. Allen Davis is gregarious and enthusiastic.

He is a self-described "people person." It's a personality trait he traces back to his 30-year military career. He retired in 1990 as a Non-Commissioned Officer (1st sergeant) with a U. S. Army Dental Detachment. His military tours took him throughout the world including such diverse duty stations as Germany (3 times) and Korea (twice).

He is, however, first and foremost a Philadelphian. "I went all around the world," he says, "and then I came back to Philadelphia because there is no place like home." He lives with his wife, Michele, and daughter, Caroline at the outer edge of the city. "It's funny," he observes. "When I graduated (from West Catholic High School in 1958) our graduation was held in the St. Joseph's University field house. Now I live right across the street from the St. Joe's campus. Went all around the world and came back to my home base."

Among the memories he carries with him of his military service—dental assistant, dental radiology, dental prosthesis, dental record management and, ultimately, ranking dental Non-Commissioned Officer—are the opportunities he had to witness not one but two world Olympics.

The first didn't play out as scheduled and the world watched in sorrow and horror. It was the 1972 Munich Olympics. A group of Palestinian terrorists attacked the Olympic compound in an assault which ultimately took the lives of 11 Israeli Olympians and coaches. "That was the 5th of September," he informs. "I will never forget it because it was my birthday. When the massacre occurred, everything was pushed back one day; then they had one day for a memorial service. So I was not able to see my event. Considering what happened, that wasn't very important. I still have the tickets, however."

His second Olympic opportunity came on his second tour in South Korea, his last duty station before his separation from the service in 1990. "I was there for that one," he says. "It's coincidental, but my first assignment was in Korea and my last assignment was in Korea. I went to Korea as a private in 1960. I ended as a first sergeant in 1990. I was amazed (on his second tour), just amazed at the development of the (South) Korean continent. In 1960, I could hardly find a paved road. 30 years later, they had superhighways and superstructures—skyscrapers."

Allen Davis has a now-defunct hot dog company to thank for his eventual employment by the Phillies in 2000.

"This company had this offer. If you bought five pounds of hot dogs, you would get four tickets to a Phillies game. General admission. That was kinda neat. I would take my wife and my daughter to the Phillies game. We would go to the 700 level…as far up as you could go at Veterans Stadium."

It was on those trips to the Vet that Davis met a Phillies usher by the name of Joe Schnellenberg. "What a marvelous man he was," Davis explained. "We would always go to his section because he was so pleasant to us. We would go just as many times as we could. And we would always go to see Joe Schnellenberg."

On one of those visits, Schnellenberg asked Davis if he would like to usher at Vet Stadium. Davis immediately answered, yes. Schnellenberg got him an application to file, which he did. But there was no immediate response from the Phillies. "I would go to the park and see Joe," Davis continued, "and he would ask me if I had heard anything yet, and I would say, 'No.'"

So Schnellenberg gave Davis a second application to submit. This time, he was called in for an interview with Eric Tobin. "The rest," as Davis observes, "is history."

Schnellenberg retired in 2007 (his son and daughter were Philly employees when this conversation occurred after the 2008 season) but Davis never forgot the example his mentor set for him in serving the Phillies paying customers.

"This is really not a job," he concludes. "It's an opportunity to meet and talk with wonderful Phillies fans and wonderful people. I've had the chance to develop a relationship with some of the people who come back to our area. They know me and I know them. When they're not there, I might ask them how everything is going the next time I see them. It's almost like a family atmosphere over in that area (where he works)."

Davis is not by nature a man to idle his time away. Before he was hired at Citizens Bank Park, he worked in the premier services department for the Philadelphia Eagles across the street at Lincoln Financial Field.

As the years passed, the overlap between the end of the baseball season and the beginning of the football season got just a bit much for him to handle. He had to make a choice. "The Eagles have beautiful people over there," he stipulates. "Great working conditions. But when the Phillies would have a game and the Eagles would have a game, I would have to rush from one place to another. Finally, I said to myself, I'm not getting any younger so let me just concentrate on one. Nothing negative about the Eagles at all. But that's the only reason I'm here and not there."

In addition to his game day job with the Phillies, Allen Davis also volunteers once a week at Lankenau Hospital where his wife, Michele, is employed as a social caseworker. And he also volunteers as a guide at the Philadelphia Zoo. "We talk about the animals in an exhibition area and we take pelts or artifacts to share with the guests who visit." The latter has landed him more than one interview on Philadelphia radio and/or television through the years.

Fans can regularly find Davis stationed on the concourse level behind home plate where family or friends of the visiting team are seated. True to his nature, he goes out of his way to make the visitors feel welcome and comfortable. "They may feel like they're going to be resented when they come, so I open up my arms to them. Welcome to the Phillies, to Citizens Bank Park. We are happy to have you here. Sometimes they kinda look askance at me. You know, 'Is this guy serious? I'm a Met fan and he's telling me welcome!'

"But I really mean it. I want it to be a fun experience. Interfacing with the people on a daily basis is so enjoyable to me. Every time it is a new experience. Today is never the same as yesterday."

Most of the time, Davis reports, most of the people who are seated in his section are "100 percent good. And that makes my job that much easier."

Every once in a while, a few fans can kind of get out of hand. That's when the 1st Sergeant in Allen Davis comes out. "I just have to let 'em know that this or that kind of talk or conduct is unacceptable, that the ballpark and the ballgame are for everybody," he says. Whatever he does, it usually works.

The Phillies have been very much a part of the summer lives of Pat McCoy, Stephen Apfum and Allen Davis. And, if they have anything to say about it, that's not going to change anytime soon.

"I'll probably do it until I can't do it anymore," says McCoy. "Sometimes the legs are tired; you stand an awful long time. And I don't like to cold weather…April and Mays upstairs, sometimes. But I go home…put it this way: Your adrenalin is flowing, you don't even realize you were standing five, six hours. I take my wrap and my gel and into bed I go. I'm not getting any younger, but I suspect I'll be doing this as long as my legs let me run up and down. I live and die for this team."

Stephen Prince Apfum, by his own admission, went to work for the Phillies to earn extra money for his family. He agrees in that quiet way of his that he still needs the money. But now that he's learned about baseball and developed an interest in the game, there's more to his Phillies affiliation than just income. The electricity in the ballpark in the race to the 2008 World Series championship registered very strongly with him. "The mood was great," he remembers. "Love that mood. It's a beautiful mood. Everybody was so happy. They were giving us a high five, from left to right. And we responded. And two of them said, 'See you next year.' I said, 'You bet.'"

Pose the question, "How long are you going to be doing this?" to Allen Davis and you get this succinct reply: "As long as I'm able to walk!"

So if you should have the opportunity to encounter Pat McCoy, Stephen Apfum and/or Allen Davis on your next visit to Citizens Bank Park, take a moment to say hello. You're sure to get a "Welcome, glad you're here," in return.

CHAPTER 12

Premium Services

Terry Pier had only a half-hour notice when she was asked to sing "God Bless America" for the first time at a Philadelphia Phillies baseball game. She liked it that way. She still does.

Harold Palmer, on the other hand, was thankful for the brown shoes his staff wears at Citizens Bank Park. Otherwise, one of his premium seating attendants might still be among the missing.

Terry Pier and Harold Palmer are two of the Phillies 110-or-so-member premium services staff. Pier is a premium seating hostess. Palmer is, in fact, the director of premium services.

Both are Phillies game day employees and both are graduates of Temple University: Pier in 1977 with a degree in social sciences; Palmer in 1981 with a business administration degree in IT. Both also have professional careers separate and apart from their affiliations with the Phillies. Pier is a behavioral health counselor with a Fort Washington, Pa. hospital in suburban Philadelphia. Palmer is director of Application Systems Development for the Philadelphia Common Pleas Court system.

Both have long associations with the Phillies—since 1991 in the case of the former; since 1979 in the case of the latter. So where do the singing and the brown shoes fit into their respective stories? Well, it's like this...

Pier was a member of the Resurrection Lutheran Church choir in Horsham when, in 1992, in her second year working for the Phillies, she sent in an audition tape in hopes the group would be invited to sing the National Anthem before a Phillies home game. The choir was good enough, and so they were...several times, in fact, over the ensuing years.

In the process, Pier came to know Chris Long, the Phillies director of Entertainment. So it was that on a Sunday in 2002, Pier was asked on to sing "God Bless America" during the 7th inning break. It was a tradition the Phillies initiated shortly after the never-to-be-forgotten September 11, 2001 terrorist assault on New York City and Washington, DC.

"I had like a half-hour notice," she recalled in a conversation some seven years later. "Which is the way I would rather have it. I walked out to the field at the Vet. Just walking out there, looking at the crowd, it was like living a dream. I stood there and couldn't really believe it. I was a little nervous. Even just holding the microphone, I started to shake a little bit."

Now, in truth, Terry Pier is not just your average gal who just happens to like to sing in a church choir. She also took voice lessons at the Philadelphia Musical Academy on Broad Street while in high school and in college. And she sang on television on several occasions with the legendary Larry Ferrari, host of a popular local Sunday TV program.

An amateur, yes. A novice, no.

Pier is asked three, four times a season to serve as a substitute soloist for the Phillies. She never knows exactly when the call might come and she almost never knows "the real reason that somebody didn't show up. I think most of the time it is something like somebody got stuck in traffic. But they'd call my supervisor; they would locate me; I would go down to office area and someone would escort me out to the field."

Singing that first solo was, in her words, "a very thrilling moment for me." But ranking right up there had to be the opportunity to sing "God Bless America" on the closing day of the 2008 regular season—Fan Appreciation Day. The Phillies, it seems, recognize and appreciate the talent the organization has right on its own staff. In Terry Pier's case, with good reason.

The tale of the brown shoes is a story best told in Harold Palmer's own words. First, a word or two of background. While white or blue shirts with kakhi trousers are standard wear for Phillies game day employees, there are two distinguishing features to the premium seating staff attire: blue sweater vests and (as opposed to white sneakers) brown shoes. Now allow Palmer take over the narrative.

"When we came to Citizens Bank Park, Eric Tobin (director of Event Operations) wanted our premium services department staff to have distinctive footwear. So while everyone else in the ballpark has a white sneaker, premium services wear brown shoes.

"When we opened the ballpark, it was just chaos the first couple of days. And we couldn't find one of our staff members. I never met him…you know it was just somebody on my staff. I knew he was in the ballpark, but he wasn't where he was supposed to be. As I said, it was a little chaotic.

"So we put out his picture. And we kept walking around the ballpark looking for him. We walked through one gate and all of a sudden, one of my assistants looks at me and says, 'I found him.' I said, 'How did you find him?' He says, 'Look at his feet.' And there he was, one guy standing at the first base gate with brown shoes. He had gone there for two days and nobody knew who he was or where he was supposed to be. Like I said, there was a lot of new stuff that we have never seen before and we were trying to get things together, get them organized, and we just couldn't find this one guy. We found him thanks to the brown shoes."

The Phillies, as an organization, are not into class distinctions among its fan base. Be it the bleachers or the box seats…as a paying customer once you enter the stadium you're entitled to the same degree of service and courtesy as any other patron. That is, however, not to say that there is no difference between accommodations from which fans may choose.

That's where the premium services department comes into play. Premium services would accurately be described as the "high end" seating options of the ballpark…the luxury suites, club boxes and the best of the best, the Diamond Club. It's the bailiwick which Harold Palmer manages and in which Terry Pier and her associates work.

There are 70 luxury suites rimming Citizens Bank Park. The Hall of Fame Club is available to all premium seating customers, including access to the Hall of Fame restaurant and memorabilia which dot the area. And Diamond Club membership includes field level seating behind home plate and access to the upscale Diamond Club restaurant.

Only those patrons with a hole-punched ticket and wearing a Diamond Club ID bracelet have access to Diamond Club seating. "If the ticket has a hole in it, the hand that holds the ticket needs to have a bracelet on it," Director Palmer explains. "That prevents someone with a whole lot of punched tickets in their pocket from bringing down some friends because they're not going to have bracelets with their hole-punched tickets." While the bracelets are removable, they can't be removed without breaking them. If the bracelet is broken, that patron is not going to gain access to the Diamond Club seating area.

As Palmer explains it, a primary function of the Premium Services Department host and hostesses is to "grant or deny access" based on the appropriate credential or ticket to the appropriate area. Then, once a patron is admitted, it's a matter of helping them when necessary navigate the building. There are some areas of the building where you need direction to get exactly where you want to go. If directions won't work, the attendant will escort them to the proper location. "Higher end personalized customer service," Palmer calls it.

Terry Pier has her mother to thank for her interest in baseball in general and the Phillies in particular. "She was always a very big Phillies fan," Pier relates. "She could tell you the batting average of any Philly. When they were out on the West Coast, she wouldn't go to bed until she heard the final score, even if it was 2 in the morning. That's how I got involved with baseball."

So involved that she and her Mother were regular Sunday attendees at the Vet. Her mother passed away in 1989 from ALS, the Lou Gerhig disease. "After my Mom died, I came in for an interview," Pier said. "I came to so many games, I thought I would love to be surrounded by this every day." She started as a hostess (usherette) at Veterans Stadium in 1991. She moved to the Premium Services Department when the Phillies moved into Citizens Bank Park in 2004.

Harold Palmer took a neighborhood route to Phillies employ.

"I was a local (South Philadelphia) kid and I could see the Vet from my house," he explains. "As a young boy, my parents used to take me down to the games and they had friends there that worked in security and ushering. They would always say hello to them when they went to the stadium. My mom and my dad and my brother would go. My Dad would buy tickets…the four of us…up in the 700 level. I'd sit in the last row of the building behind home plate or first or third base.

"As I got a little older, I was walking down to games myself or with friends from the neighborhood…neighborhood kids, and being neighborhood kids we found ways to get into the ballpark without having a ticket."

It so happened that a close family friend, Joe Iancale ("Joe Yank," for short) was working for the Phillies at the time. "He called my house one night and said, 'You're down here every night. Why don't you come down here and work? The next night I showed up and started working."

Palmer spent a year in security when tragedy struck the Iancale family. "Joe Yank's" son, Sammie, was killed in a winter auto accident. Sammie worked the super box level at the time. Months later, Iancale approached Palmer. "I look to you as a son, also. So I'd like to move you up to his place." Which is what he did.

"I never forgot Joe for saying that and putting me up there in the super boxes," Palmer reflected. "He passed away a couple of years ago. He retired from the Phillies in the early to mid-'80s. But I never forgot him. Joe had a gold pass. He would come to the ballpark after he retired. He was one of the special people that I remember…one that kinda helped me along the way. There were a couple of them, but he was one of them."

The department was called Super Box Services at the time. Through the years, Palmer worked his way through the ranks. He became director of the Super Box staff in the early 1990's. The title changed with the move to Citizens Bank Park. But the essentials of the job didn't.

It's impossible for Pier and Palmer to have spent as much time with the Phillies as they have without collecting their own set of special memories.

2001 was one for Terry Pier. She went to Phillies Fantasy Camp, one of three women to do so that year. She remembers calling time in one game because she had to answer nature's call. Bobby Wine and Milt Thompson were two of her coaches. "I knew I was holding up the game. But I couldn't help it. As I was running down the steps, Bobby Wine looked at me and said: 'Where do you think you're going?' Bobby, I said, I really have to go to the bathroom. Real loud, he yells: 'There's no peeing in baseball!'" Sorry, Bobby, this was one time there was.

Terry Pier also remembers getting a base hit during that camp. She has the ball at home. It was signed by all her camp mates.

Pier also has other Phillies memorabilia in her home. Vet memorabilia, to be more accurate. When she turned 50 "a few years ago," right after the Vet closed, her friends surprised her with a party. Her gift: two seats from the Vet. They also occupy a special place in her home.

But her most poignant memories are of the Vet and the games she spent there with her Mother. "The Vet was just something very special to me because of my Mother," she reveals. "The day they tore it down, I was watching it on TV. I was at work. And I just stood there with tears in my eyes watching it come down. And I remembered my mother and the seats we had in Section 350. It was my Mother's permanent home."

Harold Palmer also remembers the Vet as a special place...so much so that he once thought there was no way he was going to get acclimated to Citizens Bank Park. "When I first got to Citizens Bank Park, I hated it," he confesses...quietly to be sure, but confesses nonetheless. "I absolutely hated it.

"The Vet...it was round. Easy to get around. I mean the Super Box level was just in a circle. I had been there 25 years. I knew it like the back of my hand. If I had to get to an area, I knew the quickest way to get there. When I got to Citizens Bank Park, I had to go up, go down, go over. Never thought I'd get used to it."

And now? Now, he says, he'd have to be hauled bodily out of Citizens Bank Park. What changed? Time and familiarity, he says. "The Vet, I was used to. Now, Citizens Bank Park…there is no better place. This ballpark just wraps its arms around you. Maybe it's the ivy, the color scheme…the steel, the grass, maybe it's just the sport. I don't know. But when you walk into the ballpark, you just feel welcome. I love being here."

As he rummaged through his memory bank, Harold Palmer came up with a number of special moments to share…like the '80, '83 and '93 World Series teams. The 2008 series championship, of course. Not to mention that the wife of then- Vice Presidential candidate Joe Biden was in attendance with her Secret Service contingent for the clinching Game 5 contest, and all the additional logistics that entailed.

And, he surely will never forget the brown shoes.

But here's one story you won't hear every day. It happened in the 2008 season.

"I was sitting at my desk and one of the staff hands me a little baggie," he reveals. "It didn't even have a twist tie on it; it was kind of opened at the top. Well, she just drops it on my desk and says, 'You're the boss. You handle this.'

"I said, what is it?

"She said some woman came to the game yesterday and said her Dad died last month and he loved the Phillies. She wanted to know if she could put his ashes here at the ballpark.

"I looked up at her and said, 'You mean this guy is in this bag? And there's not even a twist tie at the top of it.' So I just kind of stammered and stuttered and I said I would see what I could do.

"So I picked him up…real gingerly, you know. At the end of the night, I walked around to a certain part of the ballpark and kind of took care of what I wanted to do. I never knew his name. But I remember saying as I was pouring the ashes out, I hope this makes you happy or whatever.

"Now, when a ball's hit out to that certain area, I'd think to myself, 'There's a Dusty ball. I hope Dusty is happy. Not too many people know that story." Now they do. But, it should be stipulated, the telling of it must not be construed as an open invitation for others to do likewise.

As the 2009 season opened for business, Terry Pier and Harold Palmer were entering their 18th and 31st year respectively working for the Phillies. Not surprisingly, they both expected to be at it much, much longer.

"It's the excitement of being at the ballgame every night," Pier says. "Especially when we are winning. I find it a thrill to be surrounded by baseball people every night because I love the game so much. And there are a lot of friendly people here."

For Palmer, it's a matter of location as much as a diversion. "I will keep doing it as long as it's fun," he says. "As long as I don't consider it a job. Because it really is not. It's something I look forward to doing. I don't know how many games that I've missed over the years. It is not many (he uses vacation or personal time from the Court system when necessary, he explains). But I can see the lights from the ballpark at my house. If they're on and I'm not here, it's a weird feeling."

Guest Services

She's a public school superintendent by day and a customer service representative for the Philadelphia Phillies by night. A curious mix for most people, perhaps. But for not Debra Bruner. For her, it's been pretty much a way of life.

Five days a week, she's in her superintendent's office in the Somerdale, New Jersey elementary school district tending to academic and administrative matters. Six months in the Spring and Summer—nights and weekends during Phillies home stand--she's in the Guest Service stations at Citizens Bank Park fielding fan inquiries and/or requests.

For Deb Bruner, it's always been a matter of choice more than necessity. Double duty is just something she's done for most of her 30-plus-year professional career. "When I was teaching, I always working part time jobs," she explains. "I had started on my masters degree (as a night student at Temple University) when I started working for the Phillies. I started as an usherette in 1981. And I've been here ever since."

Why the Phillies?

Well, she responds, from her teenaged years at Ridley High School in Delaware County, she'd always been "active" in and around sports and athletics…a majorette and featured twirler in high school; Temple Diamond Dancer in college, even a part time cheer leader with the old Philadelphia Stars and a back-up cheerleader for the Philadelphia Eagles.

Bruner was working part time in a Delaware County retail store when she decided to apply for an usherette's job with the Phillies. "I was tired of retail," she explained. "I was ready for a change. I learned that the Phillies had usherettes, they had a softball team. And I thought, 'Hmm, maybe I can get a job with the Phillies. That would be a nice environment. It's sports; I like baseball; I enjoy being around people. That would be a nice thing to do.' So I applied and got the job. The rest is history…28 years later, I'm still here."

In the meantime, there were degrees and certificates for her to pursue on her professional career path…A Bachelor of Science in elementary education from Temple; a Master's Degree in reading (she's a certified reading specialist); and a doctoral degree in educational administration. Not to mention the principal and superintendent's certificates she obtained along the way as she advanced from teacher, to assistant principal, to principal to superintendent.

Deb Bruner may be one of the very few Phillies game day employees who applied without a reference from a relative or family friend who already was working there. "I remember when I first interviewed," she laughed, "the question was: 'Who referred you? Who did you know? Who are you related to?' And my answer was, 'Nobody, nobody, nobody.' I just thought it would be a fun part time job."

So she signed up to be a Phillies usherette. Except they weren't called usherettes, exactly. Rather, they were better known as the Phillies "Hot Pants Patrol." In their signature short-shorts, jackets and go-go boots, they were a regular fixture in the newspapers and on television. In the ballpark and around town doing their community outreach and/or charity work, these attractive young ladies were plenty visible and immediately identifiable. Ambassadors of baseball in shorts and boots, you might say.

There came a time six or seven years into her Phillies employ that Bruner thought very seriously of leaving to concentrate on her academic career. She had just turned 30, she recalled, and had obtained her first administrative position—assistant principal in Gloucester Township, New Jersey. "It was time to hang up the hot pants and put the white boots in the closet," she thought.

Then fate intervened in the person of Mike DiMuzio.

DiMuzio was the Phillies game-day operations supervisor at the time and, as Bruner remembers it, had returned from an off-season visit with the Kansas City Royals. The Royals had a Fans Accommodation service staffed by two full time and one game-day employees. The Phils saw a lot of merit in the concept. So in the Spring of 1987, DiMuzio asked Deb Bruner if she'd be interested in switching to customer service. "That's great," she thought. "That'll allow me to stay working for the Phillies. It'll fit nicely into my administrative position. I'll give it a try."

At its inception, it was called Fan Accommodations. Today, it goes under the label of Guest Services. By whatever name, the shutters on the Citizen Bank Park Guest Services windows go up an hour to an-hour-and-one-half before the first pitch is thrown. They'll remain that way for about an hour after the last out is recorded.

Throughout, Deb Bruner, Tony Vetri (her customer services partner for the past eight years) and two other game-day staffers are prepared to field all kinds of inquiries from the paying customers.

Complaints…lost-and-found…information…ticket relocations…ticket problems…lost children…even, as happened one evening, a lost boy friend. Anything and everything that comes their way, staff stands ready to be of service.

They work from two locations—one on the main concourse behind home plate; the other on the third level where the quarters, while tighter, the atmosphere is much more relaxed and the action much more reduced. Their space is functional—larger than a ticket window, but not as big as an executive conference room—centrally located and virtually unadorned.

There fans can secure Phillies schedules, ask for wheelchair assistance, report lost items, ask questions—"How do I get on the waiting list to become a season ticket holder?"—receive certificates of attendance for their kids, learn how to enroll in the fan of the month club…even register complaints ranging from an allegedly rude ticket taker—"Thank you for telling us, we'll pass it along"—to some managerial decision made by Charlie Manuel. On the latter, it should be stipulated, there's little Guest Services can do to accommodate a paying customer. Not even pass it along.

This August night, Tony Vetri (who's employed at a city law firm by day) gets a report from a parent that her 12-year-old son can't be found. He immediately communicates with supervisors strategically located throughout the ballpark. "We have a lost boy, 12 years old," he reports. "His name is Shawn and he's wearing a Harvard T-shirt. He was last seen around Section 104. When you find him, please bring him to guest services." Let the record show, the Phillies have yet to lose a young boy or girl before the park closes for the day or night.

Pre-game and in-game activities are fairly predictable for the staff. It's post-game that can get problematic. "There are always issues after the game as far as lost children, lost items, people separated from their parties, wheelchair issues…" Deb Bruner explains. "We're here a good half-hour or longer after the game ends resolving everything that crosses our desk."

Give-away games are always a challenge. Bobble head figurines, in particular.

The staff keeps a limited supply of bobble heads on hand to replace those which may have been broken prior to their distribution. The fans turns in the broken bobble head and he or she gets a replacement in return.

It's the requests for an extra bobble head…and there are many…that are most troublesome. Fans continually appear at the window with what they identify as an extra ticket and ask for a second bobble head for a son or daughter at home doing their homework…or a wife or a friend who couldn't attend the game for one reason or another. This particular night Tony Vetri even fielded a request for another bobble head from a fan who identified himself as a "clergy person."

Cleric or not, it was to no avail. The Phillies, in fact, have a written policy on the subject which is passed out to any fan in search of another bobble head. It saves the Guest Services staff a lot of explaining and discussion. It reads as follows:

"Our policy is to distribute one giveaway item per eligible fan entering Citizens Bank Park. An eligible fan is a fan that meets the advertised age limits or other requirements (i.e., All kids 14 & under on a kids promotion). Extra tickets for a game may not be redeemed for giveaway items."

It also carries this admonition:

"GIVEAWAYS NOT FOR SALE

"We do not make giveaway items available for sale. Giveaway items are not licensed through Major League Baseball Properties, therefore they cannot be sold at retail. Remaining giveaway items are liquidated for charitable purposes through the Phillies Community Relations Department."

The Phillies, however, regularly offer bobble heads in return for some good work. This night each fan who approached the Guest Services window received a flyer promoting the Phillies fourth annual blood drive to be conducted at the ballpark a few games hence. The flyer prominently displayed a picture of a Jimmy Rollins "limited edition" bobble head, with this enticement: "All donors who make a donation appointment and present to donate will receive an away uniform JIMMY ROLLINS bobble figurine." Such is the drawing power of the bobble head.

When the Phillies instituted a Fan Accommodation window at the Vet in 1987, it was staffed on the Kansas City model—two full time employees plus one game dayer (in this instance, Deb Bruner). Today it's staffed by four game-day employees who rotate every 10 games between the third-level upstairs window and the main concourse down-stairs window.

Ask Deb Bruner why, with all the academic and disciplinary challenges of her day job at the Somerdale School District…why she subjects herself to customer service job at night and this is the response you get:

"People say that to me all the time. Obviously, it's such a nice diversion from what I do during the day. In a lot of ways, it's nice to come to a ballpark and deal with different kinds of issues…talk to people about sports and the fans, the team, the pitching and why we're winning or why we're losing. In a lot of ways, it keeps balance in my life."

Balance…it's safe to say without some "balance" to her life, Deb Bruner would find it very difficult if not overwhelming to put in the long hours she does most days during baseball season.

Her typical day during a Phillies home stand goes something like this:

5:30 AM—up and at 'em;

7:10 AM—off to the school district;

8 AM—at her desk in the superintendent's office;

4:30, 4:45 PM—off to the ballpark;

5:30 PM—arrive at the ballpark;

10:30-11 PM—drive home

Midnight—rest for the night, ready to go again in the morning.

A normal Phillies home stand regularly runs 8, 9 or 10 games. The longest consecutive home stand she's worked was 14 games. It can be fairly exhausting as the season wears on. But her batteries seem to recharge when the Phillies are on the road. And when they return, she's at her customer service window once again.

It's a given that when there's a conflict with the Phillies schedule, her superintendent's responsibilities must always take first call. The Phillies have been very good about that, she says.

"Invariably, I have some board meetings, committee meetings, school functions that I simply must attend," Bruner explains. "The Phillies allow me the flexibility to take off if I need to take off." She calculates she only misses 7 or 8 games a season because of her obligations as a superintendent.

To compensate for any scheduling conflicts, she makes it a point to be at the ballpark virtually every weekend home stand. "In my 28 years here, I could count on one hand the number of weekends I've missed," she says. "I mean, I just don't miss weekends. That's the trade-off."

The trade-off doesn't go without sacrifices in her personal life, however. "I just said this to somebody the other day: Over the last 28 years, I've missed a lot of family events—things like weddings, anniversaries, special birthdays, parties…things like that. You just have to say, 'Okay, I guess I'm not going to be able to go to that.' Really important events…yes, you do take the time off and you do it. But, again, the Phillies have been good with me. I owe it to them to be good to them in return."

May and June are her most demanding time. "Those are the two busiest months of the school year," she says. "The last six weeks are extremely busy, when we have graduation, awards ceremonies, honor society banquets, induction ceremonies…I had a six-week span, every workday between May and June, where there was either a baseball game or a school event. I just didn't think about it. I said we're just going to take it one day at a time."

Come the end of June, she readily admits, she needs some time off. "Now that I'm in the mid-50's range, I am feeling it. For the most part, I take my vitamins and I've always been a real upbeat person. Luckily, I'm usually somebody who can go on without a lot of sleep. But I do find as I get older, a few extra hours of sleep would be a good thing."

Fortunately, the Phillies are usually on the road when her school year ends. "The last couple of years I've actually saved vacation time (from her academic position) so I have the opportunity to recharge my batteries. My husband and I have a house at the Jersey Shore (North Wildwood). That's my little piece of heaven. The last couple of years, the last week in June, I've been able to hit the shore and decompress."

It also helps that the folks she works with at the ballpark over the course of a season have become like an extended family to her. "There are a lot of family ties here," she says. "There are a lot of people who have met and married because of their affiliation with the Phillies." Count Deb Bruner among them.

She met her husband, Greg Grillone, while he was the City of Philadelphia's representative at the city-owned Veteran Stadium. He was the city's primary and direct link with the Eagles and the Phillies on operational, administrative and financial matters.

It was in that capacity that he ambled into the Phillies Guest Services office one night to discuss an issue. The woman he came to see wasn't at her desk at the time. He talked with Deb Bruner, instead. That's how they met. They dated. In 1991, they married.

The fact that she and her husband shared time at the Vet may be one of the reasons she's stayed at her post for as long as she has. "When we first were married, I knew when I was at the Vet in my Guest Services office, my husband was upstairs, near by. Working with both teams, he put in long days and night. He was always here. And I thought, if I stay with the Phillies, we'd both be at the ballpark together."

Greg Grillone retired from city service when the Phillies moved to Citizens Bank Park and the Eagles to Lincoln Field. He joined the adjunct faculty at Neumann College in suburban Aston teaching undergraduate and graduate courses in Sports Administration, a curriculum he helped develop while representing the city at the Vet.

It was about that same time Deb Bruner again seriously considered calling it a day with the Phils. "At that point," she recollects, "I was really torn. Should I leave or should I stay?" Her husband gave her the answer.

"Deb, I've watched you do it now for over 15 years and you really enjoy it," he told her. "Give it a shot. I know you want to see the new ballpark. Play it by ear, see how it goes. You'll know if you want to give it up." Apparently, the mood hasn't struck yet. The 2008 World Series year was her fifth at CBP--needless to say, not a bad time to be at the ballpark.

She knows there'll soon come a day when she has to make some serious decisions about how her life should continue. One she's already contemplating is when to bring her academic career to a close. "If I retire from my administrative position in two years (2010), it'll be 34 years in education for me. I've always said 34, 35 years—that's a career. But I'll still be young enough to pursue something else."

That "something else" will most likely include the Phillies, assuming the arrangement continues to work to their mutual satisfaction. It may also include the Philadelphia Eagles. In the annual Christmas letter Greg and she send to family, friends and colleagues, she wrote in December, 2008: "I...completed my 28th season this year with the World Series championship Phillies, and what an exciting season it was...This past fall, I also began working for the Philadelphia Eagles organization (I've been lining up my post-retirement career)...as a member of their concierge staff. The sports environment continues to be such an integral part of our household's lives and interests!"

Her history suggests it will remain so for some time to come.

Peanuts and Beer

The mist lay like a thin veil over Citizens Bank Park this Tuesday evening in May. Phillies vs. Florida Marlins. A 7:05 start. Mist or no mist, the Phillies faithful began their steady stream into the ballpark. But Cheryl Spielvogel and John Culin knew instinctively: This probably wasn't going to be a good night for them.

Spielvogel and Culin are but two of the army of food, beverage and memorabilia vendors who patrol the aisles of CBP for each Phillies home game. Between them, they have a combined 72 years of hawking beer and peanuts for the Phillies contract food service concessionaire.

If nothing else, you learn some rules about the vending business over 72 years. The first is: To be a successful vendor, you have to "hustle," really hustle! The second is: To sell your wares, you have to have people in their seats. This night, in the cool, damp, persistent drizzle of the evening, there understandably weren't many fans in their seats. They were in the ballpark, alright. But they were protecting themselves pre-game from the inclement weather by milling around the concourse.

"Not goin' to be good," Cheryl laments to Culin. "Can't sell to people while they're standing around." And this crowd, which eventually would approach capacity before the first pitch was thrown in a half-hour or so, seemed none too eager to make their way to their seats earlier than absolutely necessary.

John Culin and Cheryl Spielvogel spend half their summer nights peddling beer and peanuts at Philadelphia Phillies baseball games. For them, like so many of their Citizens Bank Park counterparts, it's a matter of choice; not of necessity.

Culin's been a "hawker'—that's the industry's trade name for a vendor, hence the term, "hawking"—since August of 1971. Cheryl's been selling her peanuts at Phillies games—and only

Phillies games ("I'm a one-sport woman," she proclaims)--since 1976.

Both have professional trades to ply during their daylight hours. Culin, a Ridley Township, Delaware County native and business management graduate of Widner University (College then), is a home owner claims adjuster for Nationwide Insurance working out of his North Wilmington, Delaware, residence.

Spielvogel is a psychology graduate of George Washington University in the nation's capital. When she couldn't find a position in her degree track after graduation in 1972, she found a job in IT data processing and development and has been in that line of work ever since.

So what drew them to vending in the first place? More to the point, what's kept them there so long?

"I'm a baseball fan, first off," Cheryl Spielvogel explains. "I was born and raised in Philly. When I was a kid, we used to go to my grandparents house every Sunday. My grandfather was a Phillies fan. The games were only on the radio at the time. So he would sit down on his bench with his radio and listen to the Phillies. And I would be sitting there listening with him.

"That's how it started. As I grew older, my parents would take me to baseball games. And when I graduated from college and I came home, I wanted to be here (at the ballpark) more often. As a baseball fan, when you walk out and you see that field—any baseball field—tell me that a thrill doesn't go through you. And I get to see that every day."

She called the Phillies to inquire about job possibilities. They were hiring for the "Hot Pants Patrol," but, she says, that wasn't for her. "They had to wear these leather boots—I mean, it was 90 degrees—and the heels and the dinky little outfits. I didn't want to be a hot pants girl. There were no other jobs. So I called up the Nilon brothers (the Phillies concessionaire at the time). They said come down (for an interview) and I came down. The rest is history, you know."

When it comes to employment at the ballpark, "the rest is history," it seems, is a common refrain among the employees.

John Culin's introduction to vending was a bit more direct. He was 16 years old at the time when he started to work as a busboy for the small restaurant Nilon Brothers ran in the 400 level of the Vet.

"I worked there one night and they had a problem with their liquor license," Culin recalled. "They said they couldn't open the restaurant for another couple of weeks. They asked if I wanted to do something else. Can you vend? And I said, sure. And I liked it." How's that go again? The rest, as they say, is history.

So why are they still at it so long after they entered the business?

Spielvogel has an answer at the ready: "This is real important to me, as far as my life goes. There's the baseball, the first thing. The exercise. It's also social…socializing with the fans. It's a bunch of different things. It's such a turnaround…180 degrees… from the professional job. It just balances me. (And haven't we heard that before?) As I get older and older, every year I say it stops when it stops feeling good. But it still feels good."

For Culin's part: "I just enjoy it. My wife asks me that all the time. She thinks sometimes that I am crazy. But I'm still here. Some people look at it as a job. I look at it as a hobby. I enjoy the fans. I've gotten to know different fans and I intermingle with some of them. I just like it!"

While John Culin and Cheryl Spielvogel are working the stands game in and game out, it falls to the likes of Brian Hastings and the Brigandi twins, Jim and Nick, to oversee and monitor the vending business from the administrative side.

Brian Hastings is the Regional Director of Operations for Aramark, the contract concessionaire for the Phillies, the Eagles at Lincoln Financial Field and the Philadelphia Flyers and 76ers at the Wachovia Center, as well as the Pennsylvania Convention Center in center city, Susquehanna Bank Center across the Delaware River in Camden and the Wachovia Arena in northeast Wilkes Barre, home of the Wilkes-Barre/Scranton Penguins of the American Hockey League.

By day, in their life's real work, you might say, Jim Brigandi, a graduate of Drexel University, is a general ledger manager at the Federal Reserve Bank in Philadelphia; Nick, also a Drexel grad, (both twins each have earned his MBA, incidentally) is an assistant vice president for business planning with Ace INA property and casualty insurance. By night, they double as vending managers monitoring vendor operations at Citizens Bank Park each game the Phillies are at home.

All three have a long history in the vending industry.

Hastings, a West Philly native, has been in the business since 1980, starting with the Nilon Brothers. When the Phillies food contract was won by Ogden Food Service in the mid-80's, Hastings moved to the company with the contract. When Aramark bought Ogden in the year 2000, Hastings went along again. He was promoted to regional director of the multiple Aramark operations in 2007 after 8 years as the company's general manager at the Vet and Citizens Bank Park. Along the line, he spent three years ('93-96) as an Aramark general manager at Wrigley Field in Chicago, the celebrated home of the Chicago Cubs.

The Brigandi twins, on the other hand, got into the vending business more as a matter of residency than design thanks to their South Philadelphia birthplace. "There's a South Philly custom with little kids," Nick explained to a non-Philadelphia visitor. "They sell pretzels on the streets of South Philly. It was kind of a South Philly institution. Kids 10, 15 years old, would go buy pretzels in the morning. You would have a shopping cart or something with wheels on it and you'd walk around the streets of South Philly and sell pretzels. We were probably 14, 15 years old. Couldn't get a real job. But you know, we made $20 bucks profit. Very minimal, even 1982, but we thought it was great."

So it was a natural extension for them to find jobs working the concession stands at Philadelphia Phillies and Eagles home game when they turned 16 in concert with Pennsylvania's child labor laws. "We worked behind the counter in a general concession stand," Jim said. "Nick would pour soda on one side of the stand. I poured soda on the other. Always soda. We weren't allowed to pour beer because we were only 16 years old."

As they reflected further, the Brigandi understood just how valuable this proved to their professional careers years later. "All of our friends worked at the Vet," they said. "Given all the time we spent at the Vet, it became our playground. As the years passed, our friends left. But we assumed additional responsibilities. We essentially developed our managerial skills at the Vet versus our fulltime careers. Vending operations, it turns out, were a natural progression in our managerial development."

Hastings, on the other hand, was introduced to the vending profession working for the Nilon Brothers in the summer. "My brother-in-law at the time was running the merchandising department and my father thought I had too much time on my hands. So he asked my brother-in-law to get me a job. I started out in the warehouse in 1980." He later was assigned to the vending room where he was in charge of all the in-seat vendors.

"It was a great way to learn the business," he remembers. "Hawkers are notoriously a different breed. They are all motivated by sales. The more they sold, the more they made. There's a great deal of intensity involved in delivering the product. If you didn't have any hotdogs…or you didn't have any soda or beer for them to sell, they'd be losing money. And they'd let you know about it. They're a very mercenary lot. You really got a full education when it comes to running food service with those guys."

There's a lot to "running food service" at a sport venue, if you stop to cogitate over it (not that many of us do.) A general manager like Brian Hastings used to be, at just one 21st century professional sport venue like Citizens Bank Park, would have under his supervision and authority a director of concessions; a director of premium services; an executive chef; a director of retail; a human resources manager; a warehouse manager; and a controller. Multiply it by the 8 or 9 venues in Hastings region and the magnitude of his responsibility becomes more transparent to the uninitiated eye.

Hastings summarizes his job this way: "It is all about making sure the right people are in the right jobs at the right place at the right times. I mean, I can't cook all the hot dogs for a baseball game; or stock all the beer like I used to. Or staff the stands. It's all about getting the right pieces in place and following a game plan. It's also about being able to react to changing situations. The whole dynamic of the game can change because of a rain shower…or the score. You have to be prepared. But you also have to be very flexible. Above all, you have to be able to make decisions."

One of the more significant decisions a concessionaire has to make involves ordering, particularly the perishables.

"We get deliveries every day," Hastings explains. "Like bread and produce and things like that. Beer, probably every two or three days ahead of time. You can only store so much. But we have deliveries every day. If we have a big home stand, and the Phillies have been selling out lately, the distribution will happen around the clock. A crew will come in and we have the game. And then a (new) crew will come in and re-stock and go all the way until game time until the next game."

And he notes, "We try to freeze as little as possible because the quality is much better when you don't freeze the food."

There's a sophisticated computer system in place to track food movement around the park, Hastings acknowledges. "We have a lot of records, a lot of history of previous games. If the Mets are in town, we know it will be close to a full house. If it's the Padres on a Wednesday night when the kids are in school, it's going to be much lower. Some of it is past knowledge. Some of it is also educated guess."

The Brigandi brothers also have experienced the vending business from a variety of perspectives..from the warehouse to the inventory, to the technology. Even to running a fork lift, though only briefly it should be stipulated. (As Jim recalls the incident, he was told to get on a fork lift at JFK Stadium and move a food trailer. He demurred for lack of experience. But to no avail. "I'm here with this fork lift trying to reposition the trailer," he recalls. "I don't know exactly what I did, but the thing almost fell over. I was told to get off the fork lift.") And he wasn't asked to touch a fork lift since.

When you inquire of the Brigandi boys what they do when they come into Citizens Bank Park each home game, they reply in unison: "What ever it takes to run the vending operation." They continue:

"We just don't come in here to sit and contemplate. There is an operation going on…five vending rooms going on…that are running up to 120 in-seat vendors. A vendor is a guy (or in Cheryl

Spielvogel's case, a gal) who is coming in and basically picking up a product and selling it to the people in the seats. This requires considerable operational and administrative support. Five rooms, five managers for those rooms; one cashier in each room. There is a very detailed reconciliation of cash and inventory that has to happen after each game at each location. What we do is provide the administration for the entire process, making sure it functions properly."

Food service, in many ways, is a game-by-game, stand-by-stand, employee-by-employee calculation. Citizens Bank Park has over 100 locations where food or beverage is sold. Each one has its own manager and its own inventory sheet. For a full house, there are approximately 600 concessionaires on hand for regular seating. Another 200 for premium seating; And 100 for retailing. It is, in short, a big business subject to many variables.

One, for sure, is how the team performs. "We live and die with team performance," Hastings notes. "We are very fortunate here (with the Phillies). A magnificent ballpark, which is an attraction in itself. The Phillies have created a destination where people can come just to see the ballpark. Then the team has been going well. When the team is going well, we get a good crowd. If they weren't, then it's not so good. Philadelphia had a very good year in 2008."

"The World Series of Vending," the Brigandi's would label it in a separate conversation.

That, by indirection if nothing else, raises the matter of pricing. Here, Hastings must necessarily tread lightly. "Our constant challenge is to balance price versus the value. We have certain, like any business, certain parameters that we have to operate within. Everybody believes food is high priced at sporting events. But one of the reasons we need to scale up and down with each event is that we are not open every day. Just 81 games in baseball; or 10 in football. We need a work force in place at all events. But it's not good selling the best hot dog we can sell if it costs, say $20. We need to make it affordable. We need to balance it against the economy. In some degree, we have a captive audience. But we found a long time ago that is not the way to be successful to exploit that. We have to be just as competitive with our offerings as you can get out on the street."

Finally, there is the staffing issue. "One of the biggest challenges in this business is staff," Hasting said. "Being able to source the people, getting them to show up when they're supposed to. Keeping a good, motivated work force. Keeping the employees happy so that they produce at a high level. Getting the building staffed. I mean you can have the food. You can have the staff. But if the staff is not motivated and trained in giving good customer service, the other two don't help you much."

Motivation and "good customer service" have never been a problem for vendors like Cheryl Spielvogel and John Culin. Hawkers are paid by commission. And they know from their many years of experience, they have only four or five good innings to make their money because once a game gets past the half way point, sales across the board begin to reach their point of diminishing returns.

Cheryl makes it a point to always arrive at the ballpark early. She usually spends an hour before she starts to sell sitting in Section 112…in the sun, reading, maybe watching batting practice…just relaxing. "There's nobody there but me…that's my hour of personal-in-the-ballpark time. Then John gets in and we talk. We talk about the game the night before. The game that is going to happen tonight, who's pitching, what the crowd is going to be like, how it was last night…"

Cheryl's always been in peanuts. She said she narrowed her choice when she started 34 years ago between peanuts and popcorn because "nobody was selling peanuts, nobody was selling pop corn." Ultimately she settled on peanuts even though she knew peanuts would be a "hard sell." She normally doesn't sell more than one bag at a time, and the pricier they get by the year (they were 40-cents a bag when she started out) the less their demand. Still, five loads, 40 bags to a load, are what she calls a good night.

John Culin, on the other hand, sold hot dogs before he sold beer. If, in fact, the Phillies were still playing in Veterans Stadium instead of Citizens Bank Park, he believes he'd probably still be selling hot dogs because of the easy access around the Vet. Not so with the more compartmentalized design of CBP. "This is a beautiful park," he says of his current domicile. "But you can't get from one side of the field to the other so easily."

In Culin's calculations, it took too much time in hot dogs to get from first base side to the third base side of CBP. So he switched to beer in 2005, the Phillies second year at the new ballpark. "Time is money," he says. "If you're losing time, you're losing money." It's a bit heavier lifting on his part, considering all the ice he must load to keep the beer cold, but the rewards are worth the effort.

There also are some rules to follow in beer sales. The age of the buyer, for one. IDs are requested when necessary. The amount purchased, for another (There's a two-beers-per-person limit at Citizens Bank Park.) Still, he expects to sell five or six loads on the average.

Five or six loads of beer; four or five loads of peanuts. That's what can make it a "good night" for John Culin and Cheryl Spielvogel, respectively. This night in late May did not figure to be a good night for either. But then, there's always the next game the next day to recoup…if the weather cooperates. Such is a vendor's lot at the ballpark. Culin and Spielvogel know that better than most.

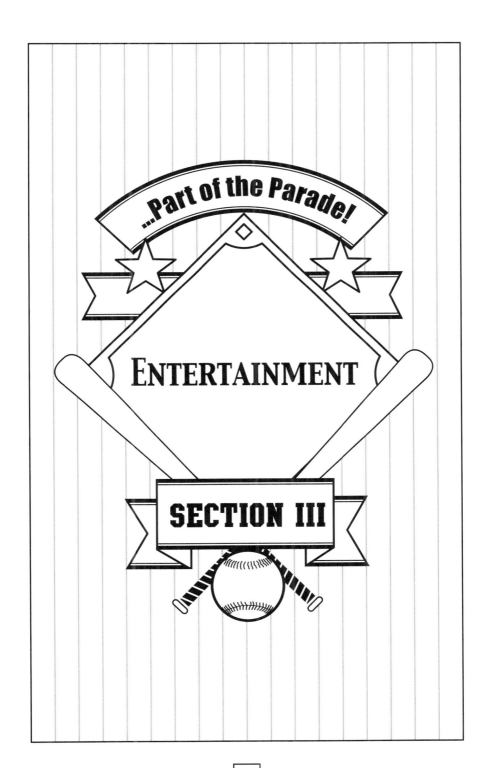

...Part of the Parade!

ENTERTAINMENT

SECTION III

Phanavision

Harvey Araton, writing in the New York Times about the retirement of John Madden, the death of Harry Kalas and the illness of the Yankees seemingly ageless public address announcer Bob Sheppard, coined a phrase to characterize fan expectations in this 21st century, technology-driven society of ours. A "video-obsessed, point-and-click culture," he called it. It takes someone like Mark DiNardo to appreciate better than most just how much on the mark Harvey Araton was when applied to professional sporting events.

Mark DiNardo is director of Video Services for the Philadelphia Phillies. With David Akers at the visual controls and Mark Wyatt at the audio, it's DiNardo and his 18-member Phanavision scoreboard staff which…night after night, game after game…attempt to create a sight and sound environment at Citizens Bank Park that not only entertains fans who are there to watch the Phillies play; but also encourages them to come back as often they wish and can afford. Giving the customer the "most bang for the buck," he calls it.

That, of course, presupposes an underlying question which is fundamental to this broader discussion. Just why is an extra "bang" necessary in the first place? Shouldn't the game in itself be "bang" enough? Not necessarily, DiNardo answers. Not when you consider the intense competition that's out there for the discretionary entertainment dollar across a broad spectrum of enterprises.

He puts it this way: When one considers all the entertainment options available to the consuming public, and the cost of admission in most cases, the consumer's expectations are very high. And the competition for that consumer dollar can get very intense. "The competition is out there. It's not even (just) within your own sport. Here (in the South Philadelphia sports complex) you (meaning the Phillies) don't get the corner. Here, you get the window. You have the Eagles on one corner; the Phantoms on the other corner; the Flyers and the Sixers on the other corner."

What's more, he added:

"We just don't compete with other sporting events. We're competing with concerts, with anything that people could spend their discretionary dollar on as individuals or as groups. I could take my kids and 10 of their friends to a birthday party at a roller skating rink or an ice skating rink. Or I could take them to a Phillies game or a Sixers game.

"The bottom line is that you want to create an experience for your fan that is memorable.. You want the fan to feel that their investment…the investment of their time, the investment of their money, was a good investment."

That's where skilled technicians like David Akers, Mark Wyatt and their associates on the Phanavision staff come into play.

Akers and Wyatt are seated each home game at the visual and audio consoles in the front row of the Phanavision control booth in the upper level of Citizens Bank Park adjacent to the Hall of Fame premium seating section. Akers is to the extreme left of the booth; Wyatt to the far right, separated by a glass panel. (The reverse if you happen to be looking up at them from the stands.) DiNardo is regularly standing quietly against a back wall as his troops execute their assigned duties.

Entertaining fans at the ballpark is an ages old tradition for professional sports. Remember the live organ music played by a live organist? Well, the organ and organist are gone now. Replaced by the 21st century technology which brings a variety of digital and computerized visuals and audio to the fans at the touch of a button.

Akers is the graphic artist/designer and statistics guru of the trio, combining animation, logos, and pictures with text and stats, all with the intent of serving the fans in a creative and informative way.

"My main job, basically, is to inform and entertain the fans," he explains. "Baseball is a statistics driven game. Most of what I do during a game is to get people information, as much as I can. You can never have enough in baseball.

"Everyone wants to know what's someone's batting average is…or what a certain pitcher's stats are. So I try to get as much out there as I can to the people who are in the stands so that they can ingest all this information.

"Then the second part is to do that in an entertaining way. If there's an ad out there (on the Phanavision scoreboard)… or a home run like a Ryan Howard home run, we try to create something that goes along with that. (Think a Burrell "bomb.") In the process, we may get the fans pumped up or making noise. But in the end, those are my goals—information and entertainment."

Mark Wyatt, on that other hand, might be called the mood control technician of the ballpark. Or the house disc jockey for lack of a better term.

His role is to create the right musical environment for the appropriate moment…nice background music as the fans are entering the ballpark, for example ("I try to get everyone in a good mood as soon as they arrive," he says); or soft, understated tones to accompany announcements from Public Address Announcer Dan Baker; more upbeat for the Phanatic and his live game performances and antics; and, of course, the foot-stompin', hand-clappin' kind of music that gets the crowd revved up when the Phillies are rallying…

"None of us can control the game," Wyatt is quick to acknowledge. "That's basically up to the team. But we can help. If we can get the fans behind them a little bit…or help out a little bit. The players say they often play off the energy of the crowd. If we're feeding the crowd, then everything's good."

There are certain rules of thumb he applies to his selections: Keep it current and popular, of course; make certain there's variety appealing to the different age levels in the ballpark on any given night; a mix of different songs from game to game; and, most important, music that captures the tone and tenor of the game at play.

"If the team is doing really well on a particular night," he continues, "then the music is going to reflect that. If we're not winning, then the music is going to reflect that. It's a lot easier when they are winning. The hardest part of my job is the nights when we're losing early in the game. It's more of a challenge because I can't come out and play a lot of happy music. We all have to work a little harder when we're not winning to keep the crowd into it."

DiNardo, Akers and Wyatt have spent considerable years gaining the experience which brought them to the place they are today.

DiNardo, born and raised in Wilmington, Delaware, is a 1983 graduate of the University of Delaware. A communications major, as might be expected given the track his career has taken him down. But, curiously given what he does for the Phils, from a curriculum which contained only two video production classes and a single winter term video project.

He earned an internship with PRISM at the Spectrum after graduation from Delaware—master control operator working the midnight to 8 AM shift. A year later—"I just got tired of the midnight to 8 shift"—he returned to Wilmington where he worked with a couple of small video production companies specializing in corporate video. He returned to PRISM in 1988 to run the scoreboard at the Spectrum—one of a 2-person staff doing 250 events a year at the facility. By the time he had moved with Spectacor to the Wachovia Center in 1997, the staff had grown to 12 and were doing in excess of 400 events a year. The Phillies approached him in 2005 after the move to Citizens Bank Park to assess the audio/visual capabilities of the new venue. He signed on with the organization the very next year.

Mark Wyatt started his professional career as a graphic designer. But his attraction to music took him very quickly to the disco world of entertainment. "I really liked the atmosphere," he revealed. "I enjoyed the music of the 70's and 80's very much. It was upbeat and full of energy. I always thought it would be fun to be involved with that kind of work." So he did, for 11 years (1978-89) while also continuing for a time with his graphic design profession.

The bug to get into professional sports bit him in 1997. "There are a lot of similarities in playing music for sports events, if you think about it, as there are working in a night club," he observes. Almost on a lark, he called Mark DiNardo at Spectacor to inquire about possible openings with the Flyers for an audio specialist. His timing was good. There was. After an interview, he was hired. Today, he not only plays music for the Phillies; but also the Flyers, the 76ers, the Eagles and the Wings. Even the Army-Navy game when it was played in Philly. About 225 events a year, by his calculation.

One of the lesser known but more informative aspects of his job is the music he plays when each of the Phillies come to bat, and how it is selected. Each player has the option of selecting the song or songs of his choice. Some like Jimmy Rollins and Ryan Howard do...several different times every season, in fact. Others like Chase Utley will pick one and stay with it for the entire season. Others, like Pedro Feliz, let Wyatt select for them.

For the record, here are some of the player selections from the 2008 World Series championship season;

Pat Burrell, "Dirty Laundry," Don Henley; Greg Dobbs, "Megalomaniac," Incubus; Matt Stairs, "Glass Shatters," Disturbed; Utley, "Kashmir," Led Zeppelin. Among the pitchers as they warm up: Cole Hamels, "Thunderstruck," AC/DC; Brett Myers, "Warrior," Kid Rock; Brad Lidge, "Soldiers," Drowning Pool.

"I like the idea of them choosing the songs," Wyatt says, "because it reflects their personalities a little bit and fans can get a better idea of who they are by the music they listen to. If I don't hear from them at the beginning of the year, I usually start out with the walk-up song(s) they had last year. If they want to change, they'll let me know. If a player is doing well with a certain song, they usually stick with it."

Wyatt's reputation in sports music is very highly regarded, as it turns out. "I was with NFL Films for 12 years," one of his associates on the Phanavision staff said, siding up to a visitor in the booth. "This guy is the best in the business!"

David Akers thought he'd like to get into movies or television before he found his creative niche in sports. A native of Manayunk, he was graduated from Archbishop Kennedy High

School and then, in 1995, a two-year program at the Art Institute of Philadelphia.

"As a young boy, I knew I liked to draw," he remembers. "Anything from regular pencil drawings to watercolors to paint to charcoal…anything I could get my hands on." He chose the Art Institute instead of other institutions, he said, because "it seemed like a place that was more up and coming in the field of animation. Most of the Disney movies had just come out that were pretty impressive, like 'The Lion King.' I wanted, I thought at the time, to get into animation and try to get a job with Disney."

Somewhere along the line, his aspirations were transformed, almost imperceptibly. "I have always been a baseball fan and, you know, football or hockey…anything that was Philadelphia based.

"When I would go down to the games, I would pay attention to what was on the boards. I really didn't see animation getting involved in baseball to any degree. So I was mainly drawn to movies and television. But when they (the Art Institute) said they had a position open at the Phillies, I said, 'Wow! I have to go down and see what this was about.'"

What it was about was getting hired in 1995 as a Phillies intern working the Theme Tower at the corner of the Veterans Stadium parking lot advertising upcoming events at the venue. It gave him an opportunity to use his training in hand drawn and computerized animation. Over the next several years, a decade, in fact, he made himself and his artistic talents as useful to the organization as he could wherever he could, (the year book, media guide, calendars, ads, video coaching aids…anything at all for which his background suited him). The enterprise and initiative paid off. He was hired for the fulltime Phillies staff in 2006.

There is one part of his job that is totally manual and requires no artistry at all. That's keeping the out-of-town teams scoreboard in right field in chronological sequence each day so fans can stay abreast of how the other major league teams are faring.

Hours before each home game, Akers walks through a narrow corridor behind the right field fence to arrange the games—visiting team and home teams—in their proper sequence according to starting times. He must physically slide the aluminum team signs from one spot on the board to another, according to starting times. That's important.

"You don't want a game that starts late in the middle of games that are underway," Akers explains. "It's much easier for the fans to follow. It's also more pleasing to the eye." It's the only component of the Citizen Bank scoreboard operation that is manually operated. Once Akers has the team lineups in place, the electronics take over.

—m—

The Phanavision booth where Akers and Wyatt work and DiNardo monitors is exactly what you might expect from your layman's eye. Think of those control studios you so often see on national telecasts of professional sporting events…a confined work space crammed with electronic monitors, gadgets and gizmo's economically stacked side by side, one on top of the other. A press row type table for those who work the front of the booth; headsets for all to go around.

DiNardo, for his part, is like the executive producer of the production. He's one "who has the big picture in mind and then puts together a team and allows them to execute a plan on a nightly basis."

But there's more…much more to what he does for the Phillies. He is their principal audio/visual specialist. As such, he advises and coordinates with the various administrative and baseball arms of the organization on their electronic needs. It's much like the role he played as vice president of technology overseeing the electronic media division at Spectacor before he joined the Phils. "Anything that had an electrical cord attached to it fell in my domain," he explains.

Much of his work day is spent in meetings with the various departments –sales, marketing, promotions—addressing, advising, assessing, evaluating their audio/electronic needs and capabilities…how, for example, it might be applied to explore and engage new avenues of revenue; or, for another, to help current sponsors.

Yet, the show that's on display on the Phanavision scoreboard every night remains his most visible work product. And he has a couple of rules to follow in planning and implementing the presentation.

1)—It's a given, he says, that the "sheer proliferation" of the entertainment supplement to professional sporting events "has shot through the roof." So it's a constant challenge to balance the entertainment components without assaulting the spectator. "We can never forget that, ultimately, the people are there to watch the game."

2)—Rev the crowd up when possible, but never as a cheerleader. "The fans know the game. They know what's going on."

3)—And perhaps, most important, be careful that the technological wizards in the booth, including himself, are programming for the fans and not themselves…always for the fans.

How do the staff and he know when they've had a good night? "By the crowd response," he replies. "If they're reacting or playing along with what we're doing, we know we got it right."

Right on, Akers and Wyatt agree.

Akers takes the challenge to stay fresh and creative at least 81 times a year very seriously. "We're always asking people…co-workers, visitors, fans…what did you like, what didn't you like about our presentation. We talk to people who travel around a lot, go to different ballparks, to national conventions to see what's out there…what are different teams doing to keep fans entertained… who would like to see more information. It's an on-going process. We never stop trying to learn what people want and what more we can do with the technology."

Ask David Akers if he gets any special, personal sense of satisfaction over some scoreboard display or animation he created, and he'll tell you:

"To hear the people in the stands reacting to something I did… some kind of animation or some kind of video that I did that had a blooper in it and people react to it by laughing. You can always judge how a piece does by people's reaction to it."

Another small moment of personal pride comes when some scoreboard background that he created is captured by national television cameras during a game-of-the-week telecast, or the play-offs, or, as in 2008, the World Series. "It's pretty nice to look in the background on a nationally televised game that a lot of people in baseball are watching and see one of my boards…one of my animations on the screen. I'm able to smile and say, 'Hey, I did that.'"

Mark Wyatt says he spends some time before the game begins surveying the crowd from his perch in the Phanavision booth. "I will sit up in my booth and look around to see who's there that night. Baseball always draws a pretty diverse crowd, but if, for example, we have a lot of college kids there, or little leaguers, or some group, I might try to play a little more music directed to them than I would on any other night. It's always good to know the type of crowd that you're playing to."

Another rule to follow: "You don't want to burn your music too early or too late. In a dance club, you wanted your best material to be happening at the prime time of your night. It's the same in baseball. You don't want to get the crowd fired up by the 3rd inning and sitting on their hands by the 6th. And I need to have appropriate music ready to go if there are many pitching changes, a rain delay, extra innings, what have you. I need to be ready for anything that might happen. And things can happen fast once the game is underway."

And how does he know when he got it right? "It's just a feeling when all the music goes well. I can tell when the crowd is really into it. Especially when the team won. Everybody is in a good mood. People are out having a good time, clapping, singing whatever else they want to do out there…dancing to the music, whatever. Then I feel like I'm doing a good job."

Taken collectively, that, good friends, is what they call in the trade getting "the most bang for the buck!" And it's an exercise that goes on each and every time the Phillies take the field at Citizens Bank Park. No resting on your laurels allowed.

That's Entertainment!

Chris Long of the Philadelphia Phillies has only 15, 20 minutes…30, tops…to get her acts in order. That's all the time she has as the club's director of Entertainment before the National Anthem is sung and the ballgame starts. And the time line for the Anthem and the first pitch always, but always must prevail.

Now exactly what is it that a director of Entertainment for a major league baseball team does? Which actually begs a second question which was posed in another form earlier: Why is one needed in the first place? Isn't the baseball game itself entertainment enough?

A two-part question merits a two-part answer:

To the first: A director of entertainment in layman's terms is a coordinator of pre-game and in-game events designed to supplement the entertainment environment of a day or night at the ballpark.

To the second: Apparently not.

More than just the game in today's MTV culture is required to attract the newer generation of fans to the ball park, in the first place. Even more importantly: To bring them back again…and again…and again, if possible. .

Providing pre-game and in-game entertainment has long been a staple of professional baseball at all levels. It certainly is not new or unique to the Phillies or their fandom, dating back to their days at Veterans Stadium, for sure. And Chris Long has been doing it for the Phils for sometime now.

But the intrinsic value of these events to the totality of a night or day at the ballpark was reinforced for the Phillies after their move to Citizens Bank Park in 2004. This is the way Chris Long described it in a conversation she had with author Tom Jones for his 2008 book, "Working the Ballpark:"

"One of the things we found is that by the third, maybe the fourth inning, people begin to get out of their seats and walk around the ballpark. Whereas before, people would sit in their seats and watch the game inning by inning.

"You find that people now, adults as well as people with kids, will sit only so long. Then, people will go back to their seats and sit, and then you will see them get up and walk around again in the 7th or 8th inning, or leave depending on how long the game as been.

"We found that you would see people walking the concourse, so we began to look at what we could do to entertain them, or make that experience more entertaining; perhaps to teach them a little bit about the game.

"Once we identified that, we knew we had to make sure that we did things to keep their attention and to make it fun to come out to a game because, although the baseball game itself is the primary focus, you need all those ancillary things to bring people back; to keep them coming back. There always has to be something going on."

So, for each Phillies home game, Long and her entertainment/marketing/fan development associates work from a very precisely timed script—a "timeline," Long calls it--leading up to the singing of the National Anthem. Some are relatively routine. Like the one for the August 20, 2008, Toyota/Chase Utley Bobble Figurine Night prior to a 7:05 contest against the Washington Nationals:

> 6:42PM—Reminder about the silent auction at first base (1 minute)
>
> 6:54 PM—Presentation of Southwest Airlines Phan of the Month (1 minute)
>
> 6:55 PM—First ball pitch, Jameer Nelson of the Orlando Magic (1 minute)
>
> 6:56 PM—Toyota first ball pitch (1 minute)
>
> 6:57 PM—National Anthem, Union League Glee Club (2 minutes)

6:59 PM—Introduction of the ball girls for the night
(1 minute)

7:00 PM—Introduction of the Nationals, Phillies lineup,
umpires (3 minutes)

7:08 PM—Play Ball!

Some timelines are more involved. Consider this one for a
September 23, 2008 Baseball Academy Reunion Night/Special
Welcome Penn Medicine Night prior to a 7:05 game against the
Atlanta Braves:

6:28 PM—Dan Baker, welcome and reminder about
Hurricane Ike assistance (1 minute)

6:29 PM—North Penn School District 9th Grade Marching
Band (2 minutes)

6:31 PM—Baseball Academy Reunion Parade (18 minutes)

6:49 PM—Southwest Airline Phan of the Month (1 minute)

6:50 PM—Coke Honorary Batgirl (1 minute)

6:51 PM—First Ball, Wilmington Friends School camper
(1 minute)

6:52 PM—First Ball, Children's Hospital of Philadelphia
(1 minute)

6:53 PM—Paul Owens Award presented to pitcher J. A.
Happ and catcher Lou Marson (4 minutes)

6:57 PM—National Anthem, Immaculata University
Chorale (2 minutes)

6:59 PM—Introduction of the ball girls (1 minute)

7:00 PM—Introduction of Braves, Phillies, umpires

7:08 PM—Play Ball

Involved or routine, Chris Long, battery-operated head set
and microphone in place, is on the field behind home plate with
staff moving folks about...whether for a check presentation, a
community or sponsors night, a civic award, a heritage night...
whatever's on the program. She and her associates are there to
make certain the events come off as scheduled. The participants

have been booked well in advance; having them in the right place at the right time is the most challenging part of the festivities.

"Getting it all to mesh together," was the way Long put it. "Some of the bigger nights (like September 23) are the bigger challenge. Smaller nights (like August 20), when it's just a presentation or two, it's just making sure everybody is where they're supposed to be; that we've got it organized, that the timing is set and ready to go."

The logistics associated with nights like September 23, Long concedes, can be a cause of concern. "We've had instances where we literally have had to juggle on the fly because somebody was delayed or they didn't get here. We had an instance earlier this year where the person throwing out one of the ceremonial balls was caught in traffic. He kept calling. We, fortunately, were able to juggle things around so that he didn't miss the opportunity."

In case you missed is it: 6:57 PM for a 7:05 game is the magical minute. That's when the National Anthem must be sung. Why? Well, television, primarily. "We need to get it sung before the hour," Long explains. "Number 1, we have to do the lineups at 7 PM in order to get them finished when the team comes out on the field. Also, with live TV, if they come up and we're in the middle of the Anthem..."

Well, in that case, no elaboration would be required.

Chris Long lives in New Jersey, but like so many of her Phillies counterparts, she's a born and bred Philadelphian. Southwest Philly, to be exact; a proud graduate of West Catholic High School. After liberal arts studies at Gloucester County Community College and Rutgers University, she worked as a secretary at the Philadelphia Naval Yard before joining the Phillies in 1971.

"I was first hired as a 'Hot Pants' girl,'" she recalls. "Then there was an opening in the (Promotions) office. I applied for the job but my girlfriend got it. I continued to work for the Navy. Then there was another opening in the office. I was meeting her for lunch. She introduced me to my eventual boss."

From there, her career gradually built upon itself. Initially, she would assist in booking the bands and coordinating events on the field until, in her words, "eventually, it just became my fulltime job." January of 2009 marked the beginning of her 39th year in the employ of the Phillies.

Her days usually start about 9 in the morning. On game nights, she doesn't leave until 10:30 or so. When the Phils are away, her schedule's "a little more manageable." Then she can leave for home at the more reasonable hour of 6 or 7 o'clock.

As noted earlier, she's usually on the field a half an hour ahead of the Anthem to be certain all the parts for that night's festivities are in place. Once the game starts, she's checking on a host of odds and ends…the Phanstormers in their retro jerseys and khaki pants/shorts who have "little skits" to perform or "little tattoos" to give away to youngsters, or "Happy Birthday" to sing to celebrants throughout the park. Then there are the events involving the Philly Phanatic—the hot dog shoot, or the Phanatic Dance, to name just two. And, often, a marriage proposal to conduct. More on that, later. By the middle of the 8th inning and she can call it a night or a day. Of course, it starts up all over again the next day when the Phils are at home. It just goes with the territory.

Planning for a new season of events actually gets underway in the late summer, early Fall of the preceding season.

"One of the things people always ask is: What do you do in the Winter?" she told author Jones. "People feel that once the team leaves town in September or October, you don't come back again until April. (But) We prepare.

"There is a large group of us that meets. We have to decide what the promotional items are that are going to be given away. We have to put the promotions on our calendars—the staples: fireworks nights; photo days; the Phanatic's birthday; opening day; Fan Appreciation Day. They all have to be plotted in.

"And then there's groundwork that you have to do for preparing for the season. We have a winter tour that goes out to malls and to dinners throughout the area where we take players out to meet people to remind them that baseball is coming…to get people thinking about baseball."

By January of each year, the skeleton of an events schedule is pretty much in place. It can be supplemented, Long says, if "something comes up and we hear about it and we think we can do a good show. But January, we have a pretty decent idea of what we're doing."

Much of what happens in this planning stage requires, of course, considerable coordination with other major arms of the organization —community relations, merchandising and marketing, corporate sponsorships, fan development. Put it all together and what have you got? That's entertainment!

With so much to coordinate over such an extended period of time, the real wonder is that something doesn't go off script more often that it does. The possibility, obviously, is always there.

Rainouts or rain delays, for example. What happens in those instances?

"Rain delays, you just sit and wait. There can come a point where I offer people the option of leaving if they want to. Most people, they'll wait if we believe there's a chance to get the game started. If it's a rainout, then we have to work on rescheduling. Sometimes, it does have to go until the following year. Then what I'll do is try my best to contract them first and give them a first option on a date for the following year." The formula seems to work, for the guest and for the Phillies.

Other potential problems? Like bookings for the National Anthem, for one. Long begins to line up the Anthem singers in January or February of each year. There's a different group or singer for the Anthem each night. Sometimes, a member of the Phillies staff like Terry Pier will fill the spot. But not often. Choirs or choral groups are preferred.

Why, she was asked.

"For two reasons, actually," came the answer. "One, because in most cases, if there is somebody who's not the best singer in the world, the rest of the singers can cover that. That's not possible with an individual. And we've had instances where people have forgotten the words, or started off key and gotten themselves in trouble. So by going to groups it does help with that."

One notable example she shared in "Working the Ballpark."

"We had a lovely woman once. When she began to sing, she got through 'Oh, say can you…' I don't think she got much further than that and she looked me right in the eye and said, 'Oh, Lordy, I forgot the words. Can I start again?'

"I said, 'Just begin to sing.' She started to get herself together and began to sing. I knew she was struggling again. I could see her fear. I started singing with her. So did the crowd. People just supported her. It was a beautiful moment, even though I was dying at that second." (Think Maurice Cheeks in Portland some years ago.) Still, it was enough to persuade Long and the entertainment planners to shift more in the direction of group rather than individual Anthem singers.

What about engagements? They would seem to be a recipe for surprise in more ways than one.

Not usually, Long responds. The parties purchase tickets and pay a fee. One of the principals, at least, knows the event is about to happen in a ballpark crammed with 40,000-to 45,000 people. The ceremony—is that the right word?—comes off at the end of the 4th inning. A cameraman unobtrusively approaches the couple. The music begins. The man—in some cases the woman, but most often the man—will turn to his sweetheart and say something to the effect of: "Look up at Phanavision." And there they'll be, picture for all to see and witness. The man (sometimes but not often, the woman) gets down on his (or her knee) and proposes in full view of the capacity crowd.

Has anyone ever said, "No!"

Long thought about it for only a moment or two before responding.

"We've had one or two that it was pretty evident that somebody jumped the gun. But, no, I haven't seen anybody say flat out, 'No!' You can tell they're not really saying, 'Yes!' There's a real hesitancy. Whether that was just because they were uncomfortable with the whole situation, or whether they didn't want to marry this person, I don't know."

So what do you do in situations like that?

"Well, there's nothing you can do. It's literally happening in front of you. As long as it's not a fight that's happening. I try to be there and if I would see it developing where I think it would be a problem, I would call up to the scoreboard room and say, 'You know what, let's not do this live. Continue videotaping, just don't do it live. These people pay for this so you can't take it upon yourself to say, 'Well, this isn't a good one. So we're not going to show it.'"

As previously noted, it doesn't happen very often. But as she can attest, it only takes one to make an impression.

So as this conversation came to a close, one final question was posed. "With so much on you plate, night after night, month after month, during the season, when do you breathe a sigh of relief?" She didn't hesitate a moment. "The day after the final day of the season," she replied.

But her respite is really brief, if at all. Marketing and entertainment are fulltime occupations. And there is a new season to begin planning for. If not immediately, then certainly, only shortly thereafter.

The Program Vendors

It used to be…not that long ago, actually…that you couldn't tell the players without a scorecard. Not so much anymore. The technological wonders of this contemporary era may have made the scorecard all but obsolete. But not the scorecard vendor. Carmen Maniaci, Tom "Pep" Payne, and David DiMuzio are but three living testimonials to the role the program vendor still plays in 21st century professional sport.

Carmen Maniaci is the program room supervisor for the Philadelphia Phillies at Citizens Bank Park. He and David DiMuzio essentially shared that role for six years before DiMuzio took a 10-year leave of absence in 1998 so that he could be about as his six-year-old daughter, Stephanie, grew into her teenaged years. Tom "Pep" Payne, meanwhile, is the epitome of what a classic vendor should be…high energy, personable and stylish in his own way.

All three are veterans in the program vending department.

It began for Carmen Maniaci 25 years ago, in 1985. He was a young boy of 14 when he walked to Veterans Stadium from his nearby South Philadelphia home looking for a job to earn some spend money. He remembers knocking on the door…"old Courtesy 8," he said…at Veterans Stadium and who should answer but David DiMuzio.

As Maniaci tells it, "He (DiMuzio) said, 'Can I help you?' I said, 'Yeah, I'm looking to sell programs.' He said, 'You're in the right spot. Come in here.'" Maniaci was hired that very night.

"I actually walked the stadium with one of the bags…those red vendor bags…with 25 programs, 25 year books," he continues. "The bag probably weighed more than me at the time. And I went from all the brown seats in the old Vet, first base to 3rd base, and I sold the bag out. I was shocked. I didn't know what to do. One of the other vendors said, 'You go back and get some more.' It was a beautiful thing. I made 30 bucks, maybe. It was opening night so everybody was buying. I was thrilled to death."

Maniaci moved into the "back room"—the program distribution center—in 1991,'92 as best as he can recall. He's been administering the vending program ever since.

Tom "Pep" Payne, on the other hand, got into the vending business primarily to remember his father, Raymond, who had passed away some months earlier. Payne was an Olney North Philadelphia boy at the time—he moved to Manayunk in the late 90's—and his father and he were regular attendees at the Vet for Phillies games. "Basically, every good memory I had with my father...mainly good memories...I can relate to the Vet. I was doing construction at the time. I didn't know if I wanted to continue doing construction. I was young. I had lost my father. So I was searching a bit. So when I was thinking about what I wanted to do, for some reason it jumped into my head that I wanted to be at the Vet. I wanted to be somewhere where the memories could live..." What better way than to search out job opportunities with the Phillies? He was interviewed. He was one of four additions to the vending staff that year. Payne is the only one of the four who's still on the job. "I think the three of them lasted, maybe three innings," he quipped.

In the case of David DiMuzio, by now the DiMuzio family connection is a well-established fact in Phillies employment lore. David is the youngest of the six DiMuzio boys....St. Edmond's Elementary School and St. John Neumann High School, just like his five brothers.

He started in the program room for the Phillies in 1976 as a teenager. Brother Michael, the director of Ballpark Operations whom you've already met, was working there. The organization was in need of some additional help. "I came in," David recalls, "actually to help him out by assisting in setting up the carts for the vendors."

Even though he took a fulltime job with the Philadelphia Stock Exchange after his graduation from high school in 1981, he continued to work for the Phillies in his spare time. (David rose through the ranks at the Stock Exchange from a stock certificate clerk to a manager to an assistant vice president to a vice president of operations until he was moved to IT as a manager of quality control when the paper stock certificates were rendered obsolete thanks to technology. Carmen Maniaci, incidentally, also landed a position with the Stock Exchange after his high school graduation in 1989—with help, he says, from David, six years his senior. He worked the trading floor doing a "little bit of everything"—customer service, phone clerk, key puncher, IT guy. "Did everything that had to be done," he said. (Editor's Note: In August, 2008, Maniaci and David DiMuzio were caught up in a 150-person downsizing lay-off at the Stock Exchange. In May of 2009, David DiMuzio signed on with a directorship at Drexel University. In the interim, he continued to work the Phillies program room as needed. Carmen Maniaci, in May of 2009, still was hunting the limited job market while he continued to supervise the program vendor room at Citizens Bank Park. Maniaci also runs the program operations for the Philadelphia Eagles and Temple University football and basketball)

If there's one person who personifies the high-energy program vendor, Tom Payne would be that person. And he's been very successful at it, at that. He has his very distinctive code of dress…a voice that bellows as he hawks his wares, and a permanent station in a one-man program stand that the fan encounters as soon as he or she enter the Ashburn Alley gate of Citizens Bank Park.

In many ways, Tom "Pep" Payne may have been born for the job.

"I am a vendor," he proudly proclaims. "I work directly for the Philadelphia Phillies (as a game day employee) and that means a lot to me. The signature on my paycheck is the same signature on Chase Utley's paycheck. I take pride in that."

Exactly what is it that makes him so enthusiastic, so committed to vending? "Just being here," he responds. "Just being here and selling and doing what it is that I do. I like the immediate gratification. I like knowing that I'm selling somebody something, something they can immediately take into their hands.

"I love being at sporting events. There's nothing like the rush of the crowd. There's no other job in the world where you immediately get to make 45,000 friends in one night. It's the best job. I get to come to work and be around 45,000 like-minded people…45,000 people who are cheering, who're excited about the same things I'm excited about. I can't think of any other sales job that's like that."

Vending is embedded so deeply in Tom Payne's blood stream that he resigned from a job in 2003 rather than miss a Phillies game. It was the last year of play at the Vet. A Hurricane weather system swept the Northeast, forcing cancellation of a Phillies contest the night before. The game was rescheduled for the next afternoon. Payne can take the story from there.

"I had a great job. I had been there for about a year or so. When the hurricane hit, they had to change the game to a 1 o'clock game. So I went to my boss the next morning and I said, 'Jim, got a problem. I have to go to the Phillies game. They changed it to a 1 o'clock game.' And he said, 'Tommy, I've given you off every time you've requested it. I just can't give you off any more.' So I said, 'I understand, Jim.' Went back to my desk and typed up my resignation and handed it in. 'Jim, I have to go to that game,' I said." And he did.

Payne is proud of the fact that he hasn't missed a Phillies game in four years. Not one. He's also not one to stay idle when the Phils are away. On those days or nights, you'll find him selling snow cones for the Camden River Sharks in the independent Atlantic Baseball League. During the baseball off-season, he's still selling…cotton candy and peanuts at Flyers and Sixers games across the street at the Wachovia Center. "I can sell anything to anybody," he says matter of factly. "I don't care what it is that you might put in front of me. If there's a need for it, I am going to be able to sell it."

Maniaci (and/or David DiMuzio if need be) begins working up a vendor distribution sheet and assigning vendor locations about two hours before the gates to Citizens Bank Park open. The vendors, themselves, report an hour-and-one-half before the fans are admitted.

The vendor sheet itself is very elementary: Name, date, location, series, and an item-by-item summary of the material distributed and to whom. For example, Phillies Magazine, $5; 2009 year book, $10; 2009 Media guide, $10; scorecard, $2; Photo card set, $5; Phanatic Activity Book, $5; team set, $8; Phillies cards, $5; Perfect season, DVD, $20; 2009 calendar, $5.

There is a signature line for each vendor to sign when the sales are reconciled at the end of the night; also total sales and taxable commissions. The vendors are paid a 10 per cent commission on what they sell each night. Sell $400 worth of items and a vendor makes $40 for that night. There was a time not long ago, when the vendors would walk out of Veterans Stadium with their commission cash in hand. Now they receive it in a pay check every two weeks.

A standard allotment for a vendor…like this one for a mid-May game against the Florida Marlins…would be 50 programs; 10 year books, 10 media guides, 10 scorecards and 10 photo sets.

And, of course, a supply of scorecards.

Once the vendors reach their assigned location, Maniaci and/or DiMuzio will motor through the ballpark to ensure that a plentiful supply always is on hand. As an alternative, there's always the cell phone, of course. The process was more labor intensive at the Vet. Like pushing handcarts to a designated location. Now they have little John Deer tractors to load up and drive around.

At the end of each night, the vendors must reconcile their sales with their distribution sheets. If one goes out with 50 programs and returns 10, that means they sold 40 at $5 per. Maniaci must get $200 to close the account for the night. The vendor, meanwhile, will have $20 credited to his payroll account.

"If you hustle, you will make money down here," Maniaci explains. "But you have to hustle. If you stay behind your stand, you'll sell next to nothing. If you go out every night and battle for the high goal, you work the stands, you hustle, you can make up to $80-$100 on a good Saturday or Sunday. But you've gotta hustle for it."

If "Pep" Payne is anything, he's a hustler.

He begins to set up his stand at the Ashburn Alley gate, the first gate to open, about a half-hour before the 4:30 PM opening time. He usually has four or five different items on hand at any one time: A program, a scorecard, the Phillies team cards, some Richie Ashburn and 2008 World Series DVD's. Buy a program or a scorecard, or any item from him, in fact, and he'll give you a complimentary pencil. It's a sales technique he's honed through the years. "If you're on the edge of buying and haven't quite made of your mind, what better to put you over the edge than some balsam wood with lead inside of it, right?"

You don't have to look hard to find him. You'll probably hear him first because he bellows as he hawks, and his bellow is very recognizable to Phillies regulars. And there is his distinctive dress—the red T-Shirt; the Khaki shorts; and, most distinctive, his knee-length red baseball socks, red sneakers and wrist band. (The wrist band, he says, never comes off, except when he sleeps and when he showers. "My wrist band is my heart, the Phillies are my heart and I wear my heart on my sleeve," is the way he put it.)

The red baseball socks are another story. When he first started working, his legs would get cold in those first spring weeks. So he decided he was going to wear the red socks for some warmth. They were also his connection of sorts with some of the Phillies players Players like Jim Thome, initially; Jamie Moyer, still; and Joe Blanton, most recently. Once or twice he tried to go without the socks and some fans complained. "Baseball is a game of superstition, after all," he reminds himself. So the socks stayed and became a trademark of sorts for him.

So, too, are his red sneakers. "Always red sneaks, a new pair every season. Before every new season, I retire the old ones. I keep the old ones and retire them every year. One day, I will set up my own museum," he jokes.

Payne will work his stand until the Star Spangled Banner is sung. Once the Banner is done, he packs up his material, pushes his booth to the side, grabs his little vendor bag and starts working the stands. The easiest part of the job, he says, is selling when the Phillies are winning or rallying. "Anytime the team does something good, anything that gets people into the game, helps spark sales. If the team is winning, fans are more inclined to go, 'Wow, a set of (photo) cards.' If Ryan Howard hits his second home run in a game, I'd better have 30 cards because I'll blow out 30 in the aisle before everybody sits downs from that home run."

And the hardest part? That's a two-part answer. First, the weather, rain or shine. "When it rains, people are not going to buy," he explains. "It also makes it tough to keep the product dry, that kinda thing." Then there's the stifling heat of a hot Philadelphia summer afternoon or evening. "In the intense heat, it gets a little tough going up and down the aisles with a 50-pound bag over my shoulder. The books aren't the lightest thing in the world."

Which begs the second issue: The legs and the knees. Payne works out during the off-season at a local gym. "I want to be at the gym so I can get my legs right for the next year. I want to be there doing the things I need to do for the couple of months leading up to the season so I can be in physical shape to endure the rigors of going up and down the steps. I work out strictly for that. This is definitely not the easiest job in the world. So yeah, I've got to make sure I'm in decent shape. Because I put a lot of wear and tear on the legs and the knees."

Payne's day or night at the ballpark doesn't end with the last pitch, either. By that time, he's back at his stand near the Ashburn Alley exit.

It's called "the blow-off" in the trade. "Every vendor knows the 'blow-off,'" Payne educates the unitiated. "That's when people are leaving and they're blowing off. If you're a vendor, you understand the 'blow-off.' You try to get your last bit of business during that time." The "blow-off" is better after a Phillies win, obviously. It was particularly lucrative during the 2008 play-offs and World Series championship.

When and if Carmen Maniaci finds other employment in the short term, it's pretty clear he's going to stay in the vending business. It's not for a lack of other endeavors. He is, for one, a member of the Avalon String Band—25 years in the annual Mummers' Parade, 20 years on the saxophone. ("I took lessons," he quips. "My buddies say (after hearing him play) I only took one lesson!") He and his wife, Jean, also are the parents of two children, Isabella (9) and Carmen Jr. (6). Their busiest days are probably still ahead of them, in that regard. But vending is as much a part of his life today, more so, than it was when he first knocked on that Veterans Stadium door in 1984.

"If I stopped doing this…I don't know what I'd do," he says. "It's been part of my life. I've been doing this a long time. And there are times I bring my kids down, and they just sit in the room. And they love it. So you know what I mean."

The same might be said in a different degree for David DiMuzio. Give the DiMuzio family's protracted connection with the Phillies. David probably couldn't completely break the traces if he wanted to. He took that 10-year break in 1998 to spend more time around the house as Stephanie was growing. His wife, Cathy, has worked one of the news stands at the Vet and Citizens Bank Park since 1985. Stephanie, now 16, joined her in the 2008 season. Their South Philadelphia home is less than five minutes from the ball park. He was on-call during his decade interregnum; he'll undoubtedly continue to be on as-needed basis for the foreseeable future.

"Pep" Payne, meanwhile, knows the day will come when he'll have to find something outside or in addition to vending. But for now, he's satisfied (he's somewhere between his mid-20's and 30) it's enough to sustain him financially. For him, it's a perfectly acceptable way of life at the moment. Though there are surely higher income opportunities out there if he wished to pursue them, he's fine with where he's at and what he has right now. He may even attempt to start up his own concession company at some point. Until that day comes, however, stop by his stand at Ashburn Alley. Buy a scorecard. You'll be sure to get a complimentary pencil in return.

Penny

Penny DiMuzio's not one who much cares to talk about herself. Though she's been in the work force for almost 40 years (32 of them in Philadelphia Phillies "novelties and souvenirs"), she still considers herself, first and foremost, a wife, a homemaker and a mother. And wives, homemakers and mothers, as often as not, prefer to talk less about themselves and more about their families.

"I've been blessed a million times," she says in that quiet way of hers. "My kids (six boys born between the years 1948 and 1963) are my life. They're all healthy. They're all working. They're compassionate. Good to their wives. I have five good daughter in-laws. They all get along together. We do Christmas together. Thanksgiving together, no matter how many people we are. Our kids, their kids, everybody's kids. They have such a good time. It's been a good life."

For the DiMuzio family, a good part of that life was spent in and around Phillies baseball. Son Tom, the University of Delaware quarterback, was on the summer sales crew as a young man. Son Ted was a bartender in the super boxes at Veterans Stadium. Son Mike is, of course, the director of Ballpark Operations at Citizens Bank Park. Son Mark worked the newsstand in the 500 level of Veterans Stadium.   Son David works in the program vendor shop. Danny has been working on the grounds crew for 30 years now. By Penny's count, no less than 18 DiMuzio's worked for the Phillies at one time or another over the last 30 years—her six boys, six of her grandchildren, 2 daughters-in-law; a nephew, Scott; herself, and for a time, her late husband, Ted. A sister-in-law, Rita Salerno, came along for good measure in 2009.

It's an association that's worked well for the Phillies and the family. As one Philly official put it: "Why wouldn't you hire people you knew and trusted?" For her part, Penny DiMuzio has this to say: "The Phillies are a good organization. They're good to their people. They're very active in support of Philly charities."

In the Phillies Table of Organization chart, you'll find Penny DiMuzio listed as "Coordinator of Retail Customer Service." She was bumped up from "Representative of Retail Customer Service" in 2009.

In practice, retail customer service involves processing and shipping the thousands of orders that flow into the Phillies organization by telephone, catalogue or by mail. It's a merchandising operation separate and apart from the Majestic Store outlets and kiosks operated by Aramark vendors in various locations throughout Citizens Bank Park.

So what exactly is it that the "Coordinator" of retail customer services does? Penny DiMuzio has a succinct response: "Make sure the customer is happy when they need something. You have to try to satisfy the fans who couldn't make the game and want a promotional item. Like the one today (in April, 2009), a 90-year-old grandmother wanted a Charlie Manuel Bobble Head Doll. That kind of stuff."

Retail Customer Service works out of a cramped, three-desk office space sequestered in the basement level of Citizens Bank Park. The administrative space is adjacent to a larger storage room stocked with everything from caps to tee-shirts to jackets and anything in between—a veritable if miniature warehouse of promotional Phillies items of all sizes, assortments and species.

The unit is a five-person operation—Penny and four young men. John Hollinger, 30, is the Coordinator of Retail Merchandising. Three 20-somethings—Eric Pesce, Rich Zeo and Gregg Beck—assist. Essentially, they do the heavy lifting. Penny is like the dispatcher. She keeps her fingers on all the buttons. Sometimes, she says, she even sits "in front of the computer like I know what I'm doing." Fundamentally, she keeps the orders straight, current and moving.

And lest it be ignored, she has another chore she's taken on by her own choosing—making certain "the boys have cookies to eat." Even in the basement of Citizens Bank Park, it's hard to break that motherly instinct.

For their part, the "boys" instinctively recognize the role Penny plays in the daily retail operation. And they're more than merely impressed with the commitment and stamina someone of her age goes about her business. When Penny was queried on the latter point, she admonished with a smile: "You don't want to go there." The query was dropped promptly. Nonetheless, her young wards are still impressed.

"She works a full 40-hour week and usually feels guilty about taking time off," John Hollinger says. "Even if she's taking vacation time, she still offers to come in if we get too busy. She handles the customer service side of the business very well and always looks to turn around projects and/or orders in as quick a time as possible.

"Outside of the holiday rush, we send orders out the same day they are taken. Penny's a big help with that. She's become quite comfortable over the years with the volume of customers we serve during the course of a season. And she's good at it. So much so, she'll receive random homemade gifts for doing nothing more than helping people over the phone. But that's Penny. Always making sure the customer is satisfied."

(Editor's Note: That her job comes first can be attested from personal experience. When a request for an interview originally was extended, she initially declined. She doesn't much like talking about herself, remember. After reconsideration (reluctantly and, one assumes, undoubtedly at the urging of her sons), she recanted. But only on the condition the interview be delayed until after the 2008/09 Christmas/New Year's holidays so that memorabilia orders could be filled without interruption. And that's exactly what happened.)

Penny DiMuzio is a transplanted Texan. San Antonio, to be exact. She remembers walking daily by the city's renowned "River Walk" on her way to work at Randolph Air Force Base. That's where she met Ted. He was stationed there with the military.

Her migration with Ted to Philadelphia was somewhat of a culture shock. "It was hard at first because the customs were so different, if you know what I mean," she says. It was also a climate shock. "In Texas, we didn't have any winter. I came up here with no coat at all. Got caught in the middle of a snowstorm…"

But she adjusted. And because Ted's job in Ft Monmouth, New Jersey, with the United States Government kept him away for the work week, much of the adjustment she did on her own as she tended to her growing family.

"I was home, believe it or not, until David (the youngest of the six boys) was in high school," she tells. "I never went to work." What she did go to were a lot of boy's athletic events.

"When the kids were small, they always played sandlot ball, little league ball, football," she recalls. "Then high school games, the college games. I used to see maybe…well, I couldn't tell you how many games a week I saw. I just wanted to be in a position if they came home heartbroken, or they came home on cloud nine… that I understood what it was about."

When Penny first entered the job market, it was with Strawbridge and Clothier department store-- first in sales, then in Human Resources. In 1977, she went to work at Veterans Stadium for the Nilon Brothers, a contract concessionaire, selling Phillies novelties and souvenirs. Thirty-two years later, she was in many respects still dealing in Phillies "novelties and souvenirs."

Why did she decide to go to work at the ballpark, she was asked? "Number one," she replied, "some of the kids were working down here. I thought, Hey, that was pretty neat. Number Two, like I said, he (Ted) lived out of town during the week. Number three…money-wise, it helped."

It was also convenient to the family's South Philadelphia home. The job was part time in the beginning. Then in the late '80's—"I really don't remember dates or years"--she went full time.

Why, the question was asked, was she still at it?

Once she got into the workplace, she replied, she simply could never settle to stay home all day. "I cringe at television," was the way she put it. "God forgive me for saying that…I can't sit and watch television. And what do you do in the house? You can only clean so many hours. So rather than sit and vegetate and watch TV, I would rather work. I really, thoroughly enjoy it. John and Eric and these kids that I work with…I feel like their mother."

There it was, once again…Penny DiMuzio's real self emerging. No prompting required. After all those years in the work place, she still thinks like a "mother." She knows exactly who she is and where she wanted her life to take her. For Penny, it was more than just a good place to be. It was the right place. For her…the only place!

Tours and Games

Their ages, their stations in life and their life experiences placed them at polar extremes. And their paths really never crossed. Yet for one rhapsodic summer, Ed Deal and the Ward brothers, Brian and Kevin, shared in the excitement, the electricity, the energy and the enthusiasm that was Citizens Bank Park as the Philadelphia Phillies marched steadfastly toward a 2008 World Series championship.

On the one hand, there was Ed Deal…a retired 30-year employee of the federal government and a former United States Army officer with a one-year tour in Vietnam to his background, no less. 2008 would mark his eighth year as a Phillies game day employee, doubling as a press box attendant and a CBP tour guide.

On the other, there were Brian and Kevin Ward…20 and 18-year old collegians respectively at the very beginning of their life's career paths. Brian had just completed his sophomore year as a business administration major at Muhlenberg College. Kevin was a few months away from the start of his freshman year at the University of Delaware enrolled as a political science major. 2008 was their first year as part time Phillies attendants manning the various entertainment venues available throughout the ballpark for youngsters ages 2-to-9 primarily.

If all three were destined to spend a baseball season in relative proximity of, if not relative familiarity with each other, they would agree: There was no better time in which to do it than 2008.

Ed Deal, like so many of his game day counterparts, was a born and raised Philadelphian—the Fairmount section of the city, he discloses. He was graduated from Roman Catholic High School in 1963 and earned a Bachelor of Arts Degree in English from LaSalle College in 1968. Thirteen years later, he would receive an MBA in Financial Management from St. Joseph's College…an academic version of the equal time principle.

Deal came by his love of baseball quite naturally and quite early. He was 8 or 9 years old, he recollects, when his father took him to his first major league game in old Connie Mack Stadium. How devoted a baseball fan was his Dad? So devoted he took young Ed a year or two later to Connie Mack's wake in February, 1956. That's how devoted he was.

A half-century later, Deal can still relate precisely two experiences at that event.

The first was just the "throngs" of people who stood in line to bid Connie Mack farewell. "I don't want to exaggerate," Deal recalls, "but there were thousands of people there. A Philadelphia policeman was directing the mourners up the steps. I remember him saying as my Father and I climbed the stairs: 'If this many people came to the games when he still was alive, he would still be around.'"

The second is best told in Deal's own words:

"When we got up to the viewing room, we were waiting in line and an old man went up to Connie Mack's open casket and patted his hand. My father didn't know who the man was. A photographer from the Philadelphia Bulletin (the also now-deceased afternoon newspaper) asked the old man to pat Mr. Mack's hand again. The next day the Bulletin ran the picture on the front page. The old man was "Home Run" Baker, one of Mr. Mack's more famous players. He was an old man himself. And he patted Mr. Mack's hand to say his good bye. I'll always remember that."

For a young collegian in the turbulent 60's era on college campuses across the country, Ed Deal was a rarity if not an anomaly. He was a member of a ROTC unit at LaSalle. After his graduation and commissioning as a second lieutenant, he volunteered to serve in Vietnam. "I thought I might end up making the service a career," he reflected in a conversation some 40 years after the fact. "I didn't have a girlfriend at the time so I wasn't committed to any one. I had no qualms about beginning my military career in Vietnam."

Emily Carver

Pat McCoy - "Drexel Hill Pat" - Hostess

R. Rahn

Stephen Afum - "The Prince" Host

Allen Davis - Host, Section 126

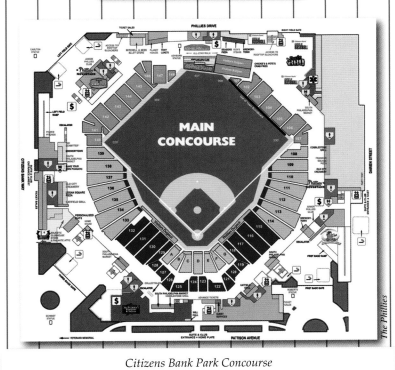

Citizens Bank Park Concourse

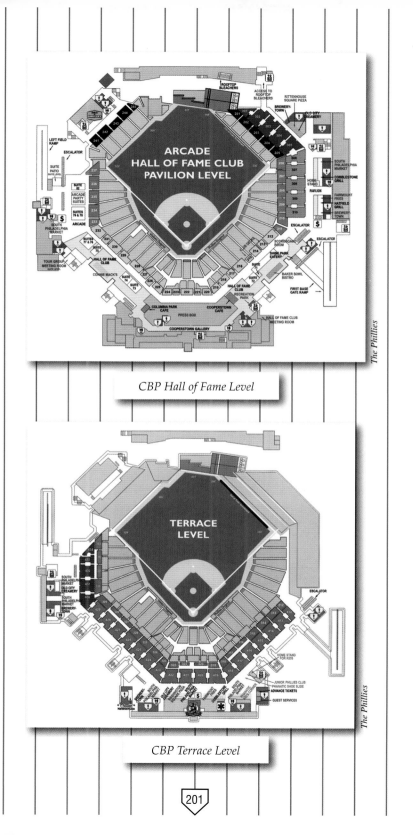

CBP Hall of Fame Level

CBP Terrace Level

The Phillies

Heddy Bergsman

Terry Pier
Premium Seating Hostess
Singer

James Villare

Harold Palmer - Director of Premium Services

N. Mawby

Brian Hastings
Aramark • Regional Director of Operations

R. Rahn

The Brigiandi Twins - Jim & Nick
Aramark • Vending Managers

N. Mawby

Cheryl Spielvogel - "The Peanut Lady"
Peanut Purveyor

N. Mawby

John Culin - "Beer Man"

N. Mawby

Deb Bruner - "The Super"
Guest Services

S. Mucha

Veterans Stadium, Citizens Bank Park

N. Mawby

Chris Long - Director, Entertainment

N. Mawby

Mark DiNardo - Director Broadcasting and Video Services

David Akers - Phanavision Representative

Mark Wyatt - Ballpark Music

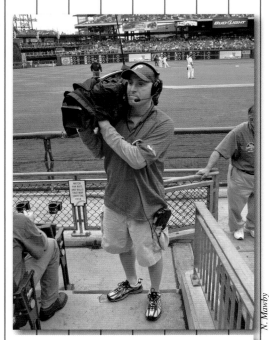

David Quinn - Cameraman Phanavision

Ryan McKenna - "The Rookie"
Cameraman Phanavision

R. Rahn

Bill Egbert - "Eggie" - Comcast Cameraman

N. Mawby

Third Base Dugout Camera View

Ward Brothers - Kevin & Brian - Kids Amusements 2008

Ed Deal - Press Room Attendant, Tour Guide

N. Mawby

Dan Stephenson - "Video Dan"
Manager, Video Production

S. Mucha

"Young Video Dan"

Penny DiMuzio - Coordinator Retail Customer Services

Penny & Mike - Mother and Son

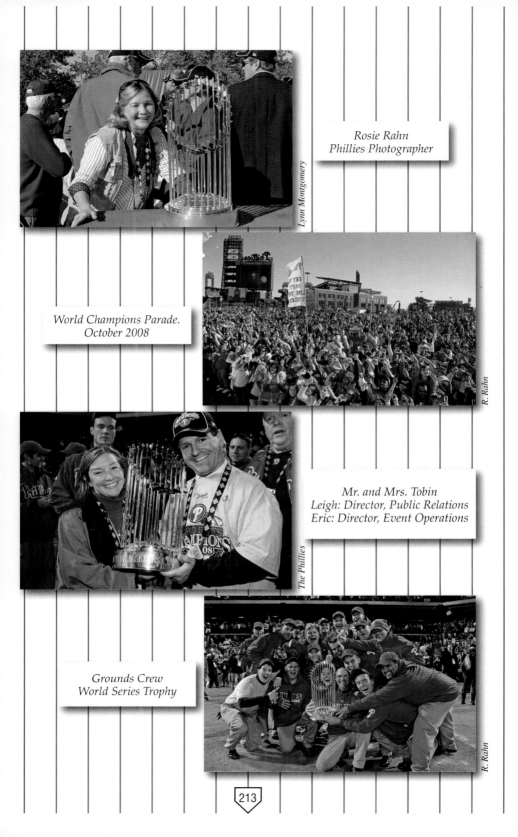

Rosie Rahn
Phillies Photographer

Lynn Montgomery

World Champions Parade.
October 2008

R. Rahn

Mr. and Mrs. Tobin
Leigh: Director, Public Relations
Eric: Director, Event Operations

The Phillies

Grounds Crew
World Series Trophy

R. Rahn

Infield Preparation
Grounds Crew

N. Mawby

Pregame
Ball Girls, Phanatic,
David Quinn

N. Mawby

First Base Gate
Greeters

N. Mawby

Tarp
Grounds Crew

S. Mucha

His relationship status soon would change. His military assignment didn't. After an eight-week officer training course at Fort Bliss, Texas, on November 10, 1968...his 23rd birthday, to be exact...he shipped out for Southeast Asia to serve first as a Hawk Missal Unit officer and then an advisor in the Military Assistance Command. Fate, as it so often does, intervened in the interim.

Six months before he went on active duty, Deal began dating Maureen Liberatore of Drexel Hill. Their relationship deepened. They were engaged while he was home on his 30-day leave prior to departing for Vietnam. They even had a church in Drexel Hill selected for their wedding.

It didn't quite play out that way. Again, it's best for Deal to explain in his own words.

""We wrote each other every day while I was in Vietnam. We talked about meeting in Hawaii on my R & R leave. Our letters began to get serious about getting married in Hawaii. I wrote to her father to ask him if he had any objections. He did not. We got his blessing and made our Hawaii plans." So it was on July 24, 1969, Ed Deal and Maureen Liberatore took each other as husband and wife in St. Augustine Catholic Church in Hawaii. And the qualms that Deal said he did not have about serving in Vietnam soon surfaced with his changed reality. "I had a little over three months to go in Vietnam. I was more nervous about returning. I was thinking, 'Now I'm going to get it.' Fortunately, I survived."

Deal returned to the United States in November, 1969. He was assigned as a Public Information Officer for an Army Defense Unit at Stewart Air Force Base in Newburgh, NY. A very tight job market—"It wasn't very good," he recalls—persuaded him to extend his active duty status for a third year where he served as executive officer of a Nike Hercules Missile unit in Clementon, NJ...close enough to the home he and Maureen had purchased in Delaware County for him to commute each day.

Deal separated from the military in June of 1970 and moved immediately into a position with the federal government. His first assignment was with the Veterans Administration. Shortly thereafter, he was transferred to the Small Business Administration where he stayed 15 years before moving on to the U.S. Treasury Department for another 15. He retired from Treasury in January, 2001.

Early on in his federal tenure, he worked part time (1970-1973) with WCAU-TV in Philadelphia. He also joined the U.S. Army Reserve. "I didn't have a single day off for 9 months," he remembered. "None of the three jobs paid a whole lot of money, but between the three of them, we were making out pretty well."

The workload became too much so in 1973, he dropped his spot with WCAU. In 2000, with his federal career about to close, he remembers asking himself, "What would I really like to do in life after retirement?" His answer: "Now I can get back to my true love…baseball and the Phillies."

In anticipation of just such a move, he submitted an application to the Phillies. He was hired as a host and, with the federal government's permission, worked both jobs for just short of a year. "My supervisor liked baseball and since he knew that I was going to be retiring soon, he gave me the okay to work for the Phils." The arrangement worked just fine, for him, the federal government and the Phils.

If Ed Deal's affiliation with the Phillies was very much by design, Brian and Kevin Ward's association was more on a lark.

"Kevin had this flier advertising about working for the Phillies," Brian explains "and he E-mailed the lady who was identified as the contact. Then I found out about it and (in true sibling rivalry) got kind of jealous because I wanted to work for the Phillies, too. So he gave me the E-mail address and I E-mailed her, as well. We both got interviews. We got the job. That was about it."

To those who knew them, it wouldn't have come as any surprise to learn the Ward boys were interested in working around a ballpark.

The sons of Robert and Diane Ward of Coatesville, Brian and Kevin were three-sport athletes at Bishop Shanahan High School in Downingtown. Brian played soccer, basketball and baseball all four of his years at Shanahan; Kevin competed in soccer and basketball all four years as well, and baseball as a freshman before dropping the latter to concentrate on tennis.

Both also had other jobs to work that summer of 2008—Brian as a camp counselor and Kevin as a tennis instructor. Still they pursued the Phillies position since it only required their presence 40-to-45 times during the season.

"We had been Phillies fans our whole lives," Brian said. "Working at the ballpark seemed like awesome stuff. So we just kind of applied. It was going to be a fun job and a chance to earn some extra money."

The drive to Citizens Bank Park and the sagging national economy had a different outcome in mind, however.

"It was a lot of fun," Kevin acknowledged. "The atmosphere was great every day. But money wise, because of our commute (45-to-50 minutes each way) and the high price of gas (soaring to $4 a gallon or more at the time), we really didn't make that much money. Still, it was nice to be at the ballpark."

"The kids were great, " Brian stipulated. "So was the atmosphere…the cheers and all that. It was also great people watching. That was always interesting, watching the fans come in."

Their primary responsibility was to be certain the kids were having fun and not getting hurt. So they didn't get to see much if any of the games they worked. But the noise would tell them when something good was happening for the Phillies. "You could tell what was going on from the cheers," Brian explained. "We came to know the sound of a home run cheer, for example. Double cheers were a little different. But you could kind of keep track."

Except, they admitted, when the Mets were in town. "The Mets games are a little different," was the way Brian put it (and haven't we heard that before). "There are so many Mets fans at those games. Something will happen and you'll hear a big cheer and you'd think it's for the Phillies. But it's actually for the Mets. It seems like the sounds of a Mets-Phillies game are almost half and half."

This conversation took place two-and-one-half months after the Phillies won the World Series. It was, the Ward boys said, a rare experience to be part of that environment. But they didn't think at the time that they would be returning for the summer of 2009. The commute and the cost were two factors they would have to contemplate a bit more precisely.

—ᗰ—

Before Ed Deal was a Phillies tour guide at Citizens Bank Park, he was (and remains) a press box attendant. Before he was a press box attendant, he was a host…an usher, to the more traditionalist fan.

When he first called the Phillies to inquire about job openings, he was told nothing was available at that moment. Still, he filed an application for future consideration. In February, 2000, the Phillies called him down for an interview. He was hired and for the 2000 baseball season, he worked two jobs—the feds during the day and the Phillies at night.

"I loved ushering," he remembered. "I met some great Phillies game day people who became close friends." He would have been content to stay as an usher if it weren't for a call he received in August of 2002 from Eric Tobin, director of Event Operations, asking if he would like to work the Vet Press Box.

Deal wasn't exactly a novice when it came to the media. He was sports editor of the LaSalle Collegian while in college. He also worked part time while in college as a teleprompter typist for WCAU-TV. It was the era of the legendary John Facenda, Herb Clarke and Tom Brookshire. "The Big News" era they called it at 'CAU. And Deal couldn't have been more pleased.

"Here I was, still in college, with thoughts of entering the news or sports writing field," he recalled. "And here I was, working for one of my idols, John Facenda. It was quite a thrill." Let the record show that while at CAU, Deal also "became friends" with a young broadcaster who was making his own way on his own time to the Phillies. Chris Wheeler was his name. And as Deal tells it, they became reacquainted years later in the Citizens Bank Park press box.

The siren call of the military preempted Deal's notion of becoming a journalist. But it never fully extinguished his interest in journalism. He stretched his collegiate career out for five years, he admits, to get an extra year with 'CAU under his belt, better to prepare him if he sought to return to the station after his active duty military service.

He did, in fact, return to the station for a short period of time until Maureen gave birth to their second child. "I left WCAU because my work load was getting to be too much," he said matter of factly.

Deal still doesn't know for certain whether Tobin knew of his background at 'CAU when he asked him to work in the press box. But he's certain it didn't hurt to have that on his resume.

In the meantime, Deal took it upon himself to become a Phillies the tour guide. "I used to see groups of tourists coming through the press box, and I asked how one became a tour guide." He was put in touch with Stephanie Nieland, the woman in charge of the Phillies tour. "She needed another tour guide and after interviewing with her, she hired me."

This time, his other-life experience had to have been an asset. As his federal government career was winding down, Deal was a financial program specialist making presentations about electronic payments to banks, financial institutions and other government agencies.

"It was a very boring job," he confesses. "I do these Phillies tours now and I see the interest that people have in what I have to say about Phillies baseball and Phillies history. When I was talking to these bankers about electronic payments, I sometimes put myself to sleep. But it was a good career."

So what's a tour of Citizens Bank Park like. Take a short one, courtesy of Ed Deal.

The tours are conducted year around Monday through Saturday, beginning at 10:30 AM when the Phillies are on the road. On game days, the tours are run Monday through Saturday at 10:30 AM and again at 12:30 PM. In the off-season, the tours are available Monday, Wednesday and Fridays at 10:30AM. No tours are conducted on Sundays, major holidays or days when the Phils play an afternoon game.

The tours cost $10 for an adult and $7 for youngsters. The tour groups have been as small as two or three people and as large 24. More than 24 in a group makes it difficult to guide easily around the ballpark, Deal explains, (though sometimes exceptions may be made.).

The tours always start in a second floor tour room above the Majestic paraphernalia Store. A 10-minute video educates the group about the construction of Citizens Bank Park and a bit about the demolition of Veterans Stadium. There are also a few clips of the season highlights. By December of 2008, highlights of the World Championship season were already part of the video. "The video is pretty exciting and gets the tourists really psyched up," Deal stipulates. "They leave the tour room in a good state of mind and are anxious to see behind-the-scenes aspects of the ball park."

And so they do. From the tour room, the group passes by the corporate suites, Harry the K's restaurant area to Ashburn Alley where they can walk down memory lane to view the Phillies "Wall of Fame." These are the plaques commemorating those Phillies voted to the wall by the fans. Here, the group also gets an up-close-and-personal look at the bullpen area.

Then it's down to the premium seating Diamond Club and Diamond Club restaurant and on to the playing field where they get a first-hand view of the Phillies dugout. "They can walk on the dirt area behind home plate," Deal reveals. "They can sit in the dugout and take pictures. But they're not allowed on the grass. That is a no-no."

If the Phillies are away, the tourists also get to visit the team's clubhouse. This particular day, most of the lockers—except for those of Chase Utley (who was rehabbing in Philly), Ryan Howard and Cole Hamels—had been cleared out. Reliever Ryan Madson also happened to walk by on his way to do some off-season work in the batting cage area.

Then it's on to the media interview room (where a lot of them again will take pictures behind the Phillies podium), then past the Umpires Dressing Room and Lounge and the Philly Phanatic's quarters. "The kids get a kick out of seeing the Phanatic's room," Deal adds. "I always tease the little kids when we are passing the Phanatic's door. I have them knock to see if they can wake him. Their eyes get so big when they knock on the door to have him come out."

From there it's to the elevator where the tour heads to the Press Box level and the Hall of Fame Club. The group will tour the Richie Ashburn radio booth and the newly designated Harry

Kalas television booth, the latter a stop that takes on considerable poignancy with the passing of the club's legendary broadcaster.

Next, it's on to the Hall of Fame Club where Phillies history and legend is recorded for posterity. The tours conclude with a brief look in one of the luxury suites.

"Overall, they get a real good tour of the ballpark," Deal observes. "They leave the ballpark very happy. I gave hundreds of presentations for the federal government during my career. By the time I was done, people would be yawning. I would have to wake them up and tell them they were done.

"The tours that I do at Citizens Bank Park represent the only time that I receive applause at the end of the tour. The applause is not for me. It's for the good time the people had in seeing behind the scenes at Citizens Bank Park."

The tours regularly last an hour and one-half. But Deal concedes, if the group connects with him or vice versa, one can last as long as two hours, two-and-one-half hours. "If I'm doing a public tour and I have very interested baseball fans who remember the Athletics and other Philadelphia baseball history, I'll tell baseball war stories," he says. "If people are interested, I let them tour as long they want to absorb all the history."

And how does he know when a tour goes well? A couple of ways, actually.

Eye contact, for one. "I can always tell by eye contact whether they're interested or not," Deal says. "Most of the groups do, but sometimes a few of the younger children will seem bored. They're looking the other way, or they're having side conversations. Last week I did a tour for a birthday party group. There were several mothers in attendance who could have cared less about what I was saying."

There's also, by his own admission, his "corny attempts" at humor.

"There's a music boom box in the Phillies batting cage area," he discloses. "People sometimes ask me what kind of music the Phillies listen to. I say their favorites are Beethoven and Bach."

Now if they laugh at that, then Ed Deal knows he's connected.

Take it from the Phillies marketing material...Citizens Bank Park "is not your typical ballpark" in so many ways. Brian and Kevin Ward can attest to some of that first hand. Specifically, those features which are designed solely for the enjoyment pleasure of young kids, ages in the main, 2 to 9.

Features like the "Phanatic Phun Zone," located inside the first base gate plaza for children 8 and under (with a junior Phanatic Phun Zone nearby for kids as young as 2 and under);

Or the "Phanatic Shoe Slide and Rock Climbing," located on the Terrace Level behind Section 317;

Or the "Citizens Bank Games of Baseball," featuring "Run the Bases," "Ballpark Pinball" and "Pitch 'Em and Tip 'Em" near the right field gate entrance for the bit older set.

There's also the "Phanatic Attic," with Phanatic retail merchandise for sale on the second level of the Majestic Clubhouse Store; and the "Phanatic Phood Cart" (near Kids Zone behind Section 117) or "Phanatic Kid's Corner" (behind Section 318), two concessions offering kids-sized portions; even a "Junior Phillies Club" for fans 14 and under featuring a "junior Phillies Club bag, players photos, posters and discounts on Phillies merchandise.

Much of this has an obvious marketing component to it. But for the kids, the features are intended for them to have fun. And it was Brian and Kevin Ward's responsibility to ensure they didn't get hurt doing it.

It wasn't always that easy. Kid being kids tend to run around a lot burning off that excess energy that goes with that age. Parents, the Ward brothers reported, were almost always present to help—"I only saw one instance where a parent actually just left his kid there," Brian said. Mothers seemed more focused on what their children were doing; Dads tended to sneak a peek or two or three at the TVs where available to keep track of what was happening with the game. A few Dads even asked the attendants to tell their youngsters the "Phun Zone" was closing so they could return to their seats to watch the game. But not that often, it was stipulated.

Weekend games, for obvious reasons, were usually their busiest of times. "The day games were always packed with kids," Brian observed. So much so that, for example, when the "Phun Zone" reached its 50-child capacity, the attendants would give the overflow wrists bands for them to return later.

And then there were the Phillies dollars to give the youngsters for playing a game, or running the bases or scoring a run in "Giant Pinball." Brian reported: "I was always blown away at how much these kids cared about getting the Phillies dollars. One Phillies dollar would get you a sticker, two would get you a pencil and 50 would get you a T-shirt.

"Kids would continuously get in line for the sole purpose of getting a lot of Phillies dollars. You could always get a kid to stop crying by giving him some Phillies dollars. A kid's face always would light up when you gave him some extra dollars…like he had just won the lottery or something."

The "Phun" sites open with the gates to Citizens Bank Park. They regularly close on or about the 7th inning, 9 or 930 PM for a normally paced game.

And for as much a fun experience as it was for the kids, it was similarly a learning experience for Brian and Kevin.

"A lot of times you were just working with one other person," was the way Brian put it. "So for five hours you had to make small talk with this person you really didn't know because this was our first year. It took a lot of communication skills not to be awkward with the person you were working with for the entire game. That's one thing—developing better communication skills—that I took with me from the experience."

Kevin added: "It was just interesting because I have always been employed locally and I always knew the employer who hired me. It was interesting to step out of the comfort zone just a little and go into the big city…meet new people in a job where you didn't know anyone. You had to make it work on your own… kind of."

Both brothers also remembered those bus rides from the employees parking lot to the ballpark where they witnessed the interplay and interchange between the veteran game day employees.

"Those bus rides always were interesting," they said. "All different types of people were on those buses…different people from different places with different functions to perform. We weren't in a real clique because this was our first year. But the two-or-three-year guys, the older guys all seemed to be pretty close to each other."

And then there were the program vendors. "The program people were really pumped and the more the Phillies were winning, the more really pumped they'd get. They were loud on the bus. And they were really fired up by the time we reached the park. But they had to be. Because that's what they'd do for an entire game. They got their game face on early."

When it came time for a decision, the Ward brothers opted not to return to Citizens Bank Park for the 2009 season. They chose, instead, to serve as camp counselors for Pope John Paul Elementary School in Coatesville, just minutes from home.

But they took one momento from the 2008 season they won't easily forget. Even though they didn't work during the post-season play-offs or the World Series, still they received a $25 dollar gift certificate from the Phillies organization after the year was over. "Our World Series cut," they called it. "It was kinda neat being a part of it, if only a little bit."

The Camera Men

Picture this…

Better yet, picture you….

Picture you smiling down on 45,000 of your dearest friends and baseball compatriots from the giant Phanavision scoreboard at Citizens Bank Park as the Phillies do battle with the Los Angeles Dodgers. It can happen. And you probably have David Quinn, Brian McKenna or one of their Phanavision crew to thank for the pub.

Or, imagine this…

Imagine, it's a calm, comfortable evening in South Philadelphia. You're taking in the Phillies versus the Florida Marlins from your field level seat along the home plate to first base foul line. Your cell rings. It's a family member or a friend watching the Phillies telecast on Comcast Sports Net from the comforts of their home or their favorite watering hole. You're on live TV! You're only one of the dozens of fans caught by the cameras in the background, to be sure. But you're clearly recognizable, nonetheless. You probably wave back (they usually do). And when you do, you're probably waving back to Bill "Eggie" Egbert's camera.

David Quinn, Brian McKenna, Bill Egbert…just three of the many television camera men who work the game and the Citizens Bank crowd in this telegenic era of professional sports. Quinn and McKenna are Phillies game day employees, members of the Phanavision unit which adds to the entertainment atmosphere of the ballpark for the fans in the seats. Egbert is a contract employee with the Comcast network which has brought televised Phillies baseball to fans throughout the city and beyond for most of the last decade.

Each of the three has been at it for a long time. And each is very good at what he does

David Quinn is a corporate tax accountant in real life. He holds a dual undergraduate degree in accounting and finance from Temple University; and a master in tax (2004) and an MBA (2007) from Philadelphia University. He also passed the State of Pennsylvania CPA examination in 2008. He started with the Phillies television crew in 1994 as a substitute cable puller at Veterans Stadium. This was the age before wireless where the hand held camera was "plugged in" and its movement was limited to a few hundred feet of cable.

A regular puller was injured and asked Quinn to fill in. It was heavy duty, particularly for afternoon games at the Vet. "It would be 95 degrees outside the stadium, but 115 degrees on the field," he recalled. "Or at least it felt that way. There were times I thought the cable would melt because of the heat."

Still, he enjoyed it so much that he came back as a puller the next season. He moved up to camera work a few seasons after that. "A camera man didn't show up," he said by way of explanation. "I just picked up the camera and have been doing it ever since."

"Eggie" Egbert, on the hand, undoubtedly was destined to get into sports television from a very early age. A graduate of a Philadelphia advertising and journalism school--the Charles Morris Price School of Television and Journalism at 13th and Locust Streets--he originally thought he'd follow his father, Harry, into the advertising business. But his dad learned through a friend that the soon-to-open WPHL Channel 17 station was hiring for engineering and production. Egbert followed the lead. And his career aspirations went down a different track. "I said, Why not?" he remembered. He was hired by PHL in June of '65. His first job was to actually help in the construction of the station... "building tables, knocking down walls, that sort of thing."

The station went on the air in September of that year. One of "Eggie's" earliest assignments was to man the camera for Richie Ashburn's five-minute sports show which aired in the 11 o'clock hour. The first ballgame he televised was for Chicago television, the Chicago Cubs versus the Phillies from Connie Mack Stadium. It was fed to Chicago under a contract between WPHL and the

Chicago Tribune Company in an era before radio and television broadcasters traveled regularly with their visiting teams.

Brian McKenna's career had a different twist to it. He was a free-lance sports camera man before he moved on to his life's other work—being a policeman. He was graduated from the New Jersey police academy. He's been a patrolman with the Egg Harbor, NJ, Police Department since 2005. Roaming Citizens Bank Park with a television camera serves as a welcome diversion from his daily responsibilities of chasing down bad guys.

Brian "Rook" McKenna walks into the Phanavision control booth about 5:30 PM this mid-May evening, his equipment at the ready: Earphones on his head; antenna back pack on his back; his wireless camera at his side. There are still minutes to go before the pre-game production meeting with video director Mark DiNardo.

As David Quinn explains, the first thing the Phanavision cameramen do when they report to the ballpark is to check out their equipment. "If it's a 7 o'clock game," he says, "they want us down here two hours ahead of time. I check in...go to my locker, get my camera, take it up to the control room, make sure that everything is working okay...nothing is broken, transmitting properly."

DiNardo arrives five minutes after the staff gathers. He and the staff walk through the script for the night. This one, the opening game of a three-game series with the Dodgers, is relatively light. Pre-game, there's an awards presentation (it's "Disability Awareness Night" at the ballpark). Of course, the traditional the first-ball pitch. And the Washington Twp., NJ, high school choir singing the National Anthem. In-game, here are only three scheduled events this night: A promotional give-away in the middle of the third inning sponsored by a hamburger company; an engagement at the end of the fourth inning; and the Citizens Bank "Lucky Row" at the end of the sixth inning.

"Any questions?" DiNardo asks the crew. There are none. "Oh yes," he reminds the group. "Everybody get their pay checks?" Apparently, they had. This particular meeting is over in about five minutes. The crew goes for a bite to eat in the Phillies employees' cafeteria, to return in 30 to 40 minutes, pick up their equipment and move to their assigned locations.

McKenna is working a hand-held camera that evening (there are four stationary cameras and two hand-helds at Phanavision's disposal). He takes the elevator down to ground level and makes his way to the field itself. Walking the corridors amongst the capacity crowd, his antenna rising from his pack, he frankly looks a bit like a visitor from another planet. He draws some inquiring glances from the passing fans, but nothing more than curious. And it certainly beats having to haul cable around.

Batting practice has been completed. The area around home plate, however, is still a beehive of activity: ESPN broadcaster (and former major league pitcher) Rick Sutcliffe is chatting it up in advance of the network's national telecast scheduled for the second game of the series; Dodger coach (and former Phillies player and manager) Larry Bowa is seated on a standard metal folding chair doing an on-field interview with some unseen studio host somewhere; ESPN.com (and former Philadelphia Inquirer) sports reporter Jason Salisbury is interviewing Dodger pitcher Chad Billingsly, the scheduled second game starter; Comcast Sports Net beat reporter and anchor Leslie Gudel is rehearsing her pre-game stand-up.

Public Address Announcer and pre-game field host Dan Baker takes his position at the microphone around the home plate area. The festivities get under way. McKenna makes his way behind second base where a teen band is performing. His shot makes it on Phanavision. Then the traditional first pitch ceremony followed by the National Anthem. As the Washington Twp. school choir sings, McKenna's footage again graces the Phanavision scoreboard. Once the field festivities are over, McKenna heads for the stands.

He starts in the seats behind home plate, shooting anything that captures his fancy. Little kids are always inviting subjects. Infants in their parents' arms, particularly infants in a Phillies cap, are seldom passed by. Attractive women making their way to their seats, for some reason, have a way of capturing the cameras' attention. They usually make the Phanavision scoreboard screen, as well.

Four young girls, teenaged in their appearance and wearing Phillies red jerseys, are swaying to the beat of the music coming from the stadium sound system. McKenna stops to get his shot. Then he makes his way through the main concourse to the left field area. He'll be looking for crowd reaction shots as the game plays out. Along the way, he'll shoot anything that might grab his attention.

All that's being caught by the Phanavision cameras will be on simultaneous display on the monitors in the control booth upstairs. The booth director determines what gets aired live on the scoreboard. What doesn't is video-taped. At some point, the taped material will be reviewed. Some of it may turn up later in some pre-game promotional piece. Or a season-ending highlight reel; or commercial footage produced specifically for Phillies television advertising. Some it simply will be rewound and readied for reuse as early as the next night.

The four stationary cameras shoot most of the game action. Each batter is shown live settling into the batter's box. Once the pitch is about to be thrown, however, Phanavision will switch to a file photo…a head shot of the player in question with all his pertinent statistics current to the exact moment. Such is the instant access computerized technology provides the fans in their seats. (Think David Akers in the Phanavision booth upstairs.)

The two hand-held cameramen, meanwhile, roam the ballpark. McKenna will have to make his way to the third level for the first in-game give-away. But then it'll be back to roaming.

"The hand-held's job while the game is going on," David Quinn explains again, "is to shoot footage as it strikes him. We're always looking for the artsy shots, zooming in and out of a play with the fans in the background. We're always looking for different things…shots that would be interesting during the game…a funny sign, something like that. We have our standard shots (presentations, engagements, etc.) but a lot of it is instinct, as well. You just have to keep in mind that you can go live in a second and you don't want to have the camera pointing at the ground or at someone flashing an obscene gesture when you do."

It's interesting to a bystander to observe the different reaction different fans have to the presence of the cameras in their midst. Some will primp, pose or posture for the camera as soon they spot it. Others will act nonplussed, as though the camera was never there. And still others will turn away not particularly caring to be captured on television, live or delayed. The cameraman can tell them by the way they react to his presence. He has to make an immediate judgment whether or not to take the shot. As Quinn noted, it's really instinctive on their part. But they usually guess right.

—ɯ—

While David Quinn and Brian McKenna roam Citizens Bank Park with their hand held Phanovision cameras, Comcast's Bill "Eggie" Egbert is in a fixed position on a platform next to the visiting team dugout along the 3rd base line. He's immediately identifiable with his beat-up, trademark Monsignor Bonner baseball cap. He shares the field-level platform with a stationary Phanavision camera and a camera for the visiting team telecast crew. It's not the safest place in the ballpark to be.

There's only a short fence (about two feet high) to protect him. He's been hit with a batted ball five times since the Phillies moved to Citizens Bank Park—none seriously, fortunately, His camera's been hit four times (twice by Bobby Abreu in one at bat). "I started gesturing to him, and he started to laugh."

It wasn't quite as precarious at the Vet, he reveals. "The dugouts were longer at the Vet. You could back up at the Vet. Now, I'm on a platform and I feel like a duck on the pond.

"Being on the third-base side, at least you can see the left handed hitters. But you get a right handed batter like Pat Burrell. If he got in front of a ball, you would pray to God you could see it come off the bat. The players would yell, 'Watch Out!' But there's not much you could do. You just duck behind the camera and pray to old Almighty God that if the ball was going to hit something, it would hit the camera and not you."

For the first game of a home stand, Egbert and his associates are at the ballpark by 1 pm for a 7 PM game. That's so the equipment can be set up and checked out to ensure it's functioning properly. Overnight the cameras are covered and remain in place. Still the crew reports four hours before the starting time to check the equipment again.

Once the telecast goes live, Egbert and crew are in constant communication with the game director situated in the control room of Comcast studios in the Wachovia Center across the street from CBP.

The director, of course, is the traffic cop. Through his ear phones, Egbert can hear the steady drumbeat of commands from the control center. "Ready (camera) 2; ready, 3; Take 3!" Or, "Ready 4, Ready 6, Take 4!" And that's essentially the way it goes all game long. Egbert's camera, located as it is on the 3rd base side, usually will be focus on left handed batters, runners leading off first base and right handed pitchers. The first base field level camera will do the opposite.

Egbert's camera is going the entire game. When the red light is on, he knows his shot is live. When the green light is on, he is taping for the four tape machines that are running for each game and available on call for instant replay.

The director is always on the look-out for what the industry terms the "Atta-boy" play…"atta-boy" being the player making a great play. Jimmy Rollins and Chase Utley had a couple of "atta-boys" in the Division clinching game against Washington and then, again, in the play-offs and World Series that followed. Former Phillies Center Field Gary Maddox, an Egbert favorite, was worth "10 atta-boys-a-game" during his playing career. "He was a sweeper out there," Egbert says emphatically.

While rovers like Quinn and McKenna go largely by instinct, game cameramen like Egbert have two prerequisites to their profession: "You have to know the sport, and you have to know your director and what he wants." After that, the game takes over as it develops.

Egbert's been part of the commercial telecast crew for better than 30 years. As the Phillies contract floated from one entity to another--WPHL, PRISM, Channel 29 and finally to Comcast— Egbert floated along with it. PRISM, Egbert remembers, went dark at midnight, September 30, 1998. Comcast came on the air at 12:01 AM, October 1.

Egbert says it was never a particular ambition of his to become a sports television cameraman. "It's where the opportunity presented itself and I took advantage of it." Once he got into the business, however, he didn't limit himself to just baseball. He still does Flyers hockey and 76ers basketball. He remembers back to the mid-60's when Channel 17 telecasted 65 pro basketball games a year. "Wilt Chamberlain would come into our studios. Talk about a big guy!"

—m—

After 38 years of sports telecasting, Bill Egbert is looking a year or two down the road when he can spend "more time in Wildwood than in South Philly (the sports complex, at least)." Age 66 is his target.

He'll have a lot of good memories from 40 years in the trenches when he does takes his ear phones off for the last time: The Richie Ashburn interview shows in the earliest years; Ashburn's love of the high center field camera ("He was a centerfielder, after all"); his distaste for pitchers ("Richie had no time for pitchers. I can't remember him ever interviewing a pitcher"); the post game shows Ashburn and Harry Kalas had to do from the parking lot after the 1980 World Series games. (Major League Baseball rather than the competing teams and their television partners had exclusive rights to the Series. "I could only shoot Harry and Richie in the parking lot with a hand held")…

…Also, Gary Maddox, of course, patrolling centerfield in that gracefully athletic way of his; Tommy Hutton and Rico Brogna playing first base with such skill ("I played first base growing up," he says; "American Legion, and I tell ya, those two were something else playing that bag."); Mike Schmidt at 3rd base ("Schmidt was so cool, people forgot how really good he was."); Jim Lonborg, who earned his big league reputation with the Boston Red Sox but pitched for the Phillies as his career was winding down ("One of the most professional and nicest guys that I've ever met").

And not to forget those days in the 70's when Phillies players filmed commercials from the playing field and if Egbert wasn't the cameraman, he would be the "floor manager" holding the cue cards.

"Dave Cash was a really good salesman. He did a great commercial and he was a great guy, too.

"But some of the others…I won't name names. Let's just say if I wrote 'Hello, my name is blank,' on the cue card, they would go, 'Hello, my name is blank.' It was amazing. Here they were playing in front of 50,000 people with great skill. But when the camera was on them to say a few words, they'd need help."

Egbert is a baseball fan. But when he comes to the ballpark, he comes to work the game and not root for a team. He remembers the advice a veteran cameraman by the name of Red McMahon gave him when he was starting out: "Kid, all you want is an 8-1/2 inning game. After 8-1/2 innings, you want somebody to win." It's a motto that's stayed with him throughout his long career behind a camera.

If Egbert understandably is at the point in his career when he ponders a more relaxed lifestyle, Brian McKenna and David Quinn are still raring to go. "This fun," say "Rook" McKenna (He's called "Rook," incidentally, because when he started his television freelancing 12 years ago, there were other Brians on the scene. As the newest member of the crew, he was, naturally, the "rookie.") "This is getaway time for me."

David Quinn had a similar take on this avocation of his: "This is a fun job. I don't really need it. But it's fun to have and I'm not holding someone else's career back. (Several Phanavision cameramen have, in fact, gone on to work in network television.) I enjoy the environment. It's a fun activity…a release…even a sense of accomplishment. As long as they want to have me, I'll be back."

If the past is prologue, that shouldn't be a problem for him. David Quinn was the first Phanavision employee to be selected a Phillies "Employee of the Month" a year or so ago. He won the designation again in May, 2009.

"Video Dan"

In the span of six short months, from October of 2008 to April of 2009, Video Dan Stephenson came experience both the exhilaration of victory and the despair of death.

As the manager of Video Production for the Philadelphia Phillies (a formal title for what's fundamentally the club's videographer), it was his good fortune in the first instance and his misfortune in the second to record the two events as they happened…if not for posterity, then certainly for generations of Phillies fans—past, present and to come.

The victory, of course, was the Phillies 2008 World Series Championship. In less than 90 days after the final out, Stephenson had captured the highlights of that magical run in a video year book entitled, "The Perfect Season." The disc became an instant best seller. More than 50,000 copies were sold within four months.

The death…well, that was as personal to the Phillies family as much as it was professional…tragic and unexpected. Harry Kalas, the beloved Hall-of-Fame broadcaster, was in the booth at Nationals Park in the nation's capitol preparing for a Phils game against Washington when he was fatally stricken. Kalas died on a Monday. By Friday, Stephenson had prepared a six-minute video tribute as the Phillies nation bid farewell to the iconic broadcaster in solemn services at Citizens Bank Park.

For Dan Stephenson and others in the Phillies organization, Harry Kalas passing brought back painful, heart-tugging memories of the loss of another Phillies icon 11 years earlier… Kalas long time broadcast partner and Phillies All-Star outfielder, Richie Ashburn. Stephenson recorded video on that, as well.

But this was different. This was the end of an era. And everyone knew it.

As Stephenson reflected a short time after the fact: "Anthony Gargano (a Philadelphia radio talk-show host) had it right. He said, 'When Whitey died, at least we had Harry. Now we don't have Harry anymore.'"

The sense of loss which pervaded throughout all of Philadelphia and much of the Delaware Valley as well as the baseball world in general that week was as deep as it was palpable. Stephenson's video tribute was just one personification of it. But one that would memorialize the moment for years to come. That, after all, is what videographers do.

—〜〜—

In the Spring of 2009, thanks to a chance encounter years earlier with Phillies broadcaster Chris Wheeler, Dan Stephenson was entering his 28th year with the Philadelphia Phillies. As he recounted the meeting, he had started his own video company at the time. But, by his own admission, it "wasn't working out too well." So he was biding his time and supplementing his income by working a side job as a bartender in Downey's restaurant in the city.

"Chris came into the bar one night and we had a long conversation," Stephenson related. "He said, 'Is this all you do, tend bar?' I said, 'No, I do video work.' And he said, 'Well, we're looking for somebody because the guy who is doing it now is leaving for Chicago with Dallas Green.

"In any event, I just basically ignored it. I was a huge Phillies fan. But it seemed so ridiculous that I could get a job just by talking to somebody like that.

"About three weeks later, I got a call from the restaurant manager. He said, 'We need a bartender.' I said, 'No way, it's my night off.' He said, 'It's for the new Phillies owners.' I said, 'I'll be right over.'"

That night, the story went on, Stephenson was setting up the bar when Phillies publicist Larry Shenk approached. "He wanted to be certain we had this kind of scotch, this kind of brandy, you know. After all, these were the new owners we'd be serving. At some point, I'm not sure exactly what brought it on, he said, 'Hey, you're the video guy Chris Wheeler was telling me about.' I said, 'You're kidding. He was telling you about me?' He said, 'Yeah.

You know we need somebody.' And I'm like, wait a minute, this could be something here."

Actually, it was more than a minute. More like a couple of hours. "The party's in full swing," Stephenson continued. "Bill Giles comes up to the bar. And Larry, goes: 'Bill, this is our new video guy.' That was a long, long time ago. The rest is history." (And doesn't that have a familiar ring to it?)

Stephenson's hiring undoubtedly was a little more involved than that summary version. But the telling of the tale does capture its essence: Dan Stephenson was be hired in the early '80's as a part time video technician for the Philadelphia Phillies because of a chance conversation with Chris Wheeler in a Philadelphia area bar.

What's even more amazing to him today is that he's still at it the way he is. "I remember being with the club in Clearwater for Spring training for the first time and saying to myself: 'This is such a great job. There is no way I can keep it. I know that I'll never be back in Clearwater again.' And here it is, (in December of 2008) 28 years later, I'm still going back to Clearwater. And I'm still enjoying it."

Stephenson was born in Philadelphia, but raised in Merchantville, New Jersey, about five miles across the Delaware River from the city's South Philadelphia Sports Complex. He was a history major at Franklin and Marshall College in Lancaster. He went on to earn a Masters Degree in Broadcasting Production from Boston University.

His first experience in videography came as a video technician at a Boston area mental hospital where his father was a psychotherapist. His function: Taping interviews conducted in the psychiatric wing to be used in the study of patient behavior. After a year-and-one-half of that, he "came home" to the Philadelphia area. He started his aforementioned video company, which, in turn, led to his encounter with Chris Wheeler, which in turn, led to his affiliation with the Phillies.

When he joined up with the Phillies, he said, the art and the techniques of his chosen profession were very rudimentary at best.

"Back then, it was very simple. All we could do was take the tapes from the games and, basically, get each player's at bat. Or, in the case of the pitchers, every pitch they threw. We'd chop up the tapes from the broadcasts and each player would receive his own VHS tape. By the end of the season, they could have as many as seven two-hour tapes of how they performed through the year. That, essentially, was all I did for five or six years."

Stephenson's career took a major turn in the late 1980's. An independent filmmaker by the name of Mike Tollin persuaded the Phillies to do a documentary of Mike Schmidt's pursuit of 500 home runs. "They hired Mike and his film crew to follow Schmitty around. In turn, Mike hired me to use a camera whenever he was at bat and shoot it from a different angle than TV would have it. The documentary was called, 'That Ball is Outta Here!' The Phillies really liked it. So the next year they hired Mike's company to do the highlight film and he would hire me to do behind the scenes stuff. That gave me access to a lot of shots that the regular coverage couldn't get. A fresh look at some things the average fan would not have access to. The tapes were kind of successful."

Not long thereafter, Stephenson proposed that he do the editing of the tapes as well as the shooting. The Phillies agreed. So it was, almost a decade after he was first hired, Dan Stephenson had graduated from a video technician and camera man to a writer, a producer, a director and an editor wrapped into one technically skilled package. "I went full time in 1991 and I've basically been doing it ever since."

Stephenson still operates a camera when the occasion calls for it. This December day, he interrupts a conversation to video a press conference Chase Utley was having to give a status report on the progress of his rehab from hip surgery. Charlie Manuel was in the audience. New General Manager Ruben Amaro was at Utley's side.

"I'll hold on to this," he explained. "Chances are we won't have any reason to use it. But Chase might have said something. We might get a call from a station that for some reason might not have been able to make it. We'll provide it as a professional courtesy. It works vice versa. A lot of times a station will shoot something that I don't have and if I call and ask, 'Any chance of getting a copy of that,' they'll send it to us. Professional courtesy works two ways in this business."

While filming a press conference goes with his territory, it's the creative challenges of his job that get his professional juices flowing most intensely. A documentary or a highlight film, for example. Or, say, in the case of Harry Kalas, a video tribute to a Phillies legend. A couple of examples in point.

In 2003, Stephenson produced a documentary on Veterans Stadium. It was entitled: "The Vet…The complete history of Phillies Baseball at Veterans Stadium." It came in a two-disc package: Disc One—"Field of Memories;" Disc Two—"The Final Innings."

The case holding the discs reads, in part: "From its debut on a chilly Saturday afternoon in April, 1971 to its emotional farewell on a sun-splashed day in September, 2003, Veterans Stadium served Philadelphia proudly as the home of Phillies baseball for 33 memorable years…Packed with over three hours of content including a special bonus feature on 'The Vet's Implosion,' this Collector's Edition, two-disc set, available for the first time, serves as a final tribute to the old stadium at Broad and Pattison."

Phillies chairman Bill Giles narrated "Field of Memories." Harry Kalas, who else, was the narrator for "The Final Innings."

Actually, it was Stephenson's idea for the Phillies to do the Vet video in the first place. "The Eagles chose not to do any kind of tribute to Veterans Stadium. I was upset. I thought there should be a tribute of some sort. The Vet belonged to the fans. I just felt I had to make a documentary about what it meant to the players, to the people, to those of us who worked there." So he did. Three years after it hit the streets, he was remained convinced as ever that the end product more than justified the effort.

The first video he wrote, shot and produced was in 1994. It was a video a biography of Hall of Fame Pitcher Steve Carlton, entitled, appropriately enough, "The Life and Times of Steve Carlton." "That was a lot of fun," Stephenson said, "because he was one of my favorite guys…one of the best guys ever. He refused to show that side to the media, but I tried to show a little bit of it for the fans. We produced it in time for him to go to Cooperstown to be inducted into the Hall of Fame."

Two others of his favorites were "Glory Days," the story of the 1980 World Champion Phillies, and "High Hopes," the triumphs and the tribulations of the 1993 World Series finalist Phillies. "The fun part of that is that they were two teams where I knew most of the guys," Stephenson says. "We sat down and did interviews… kind of told the story inside and out."

But for a pure and treasured labor of loves, one stands out. It was a 10-year-project involving 600 to 700 hours of work (compared to the average 500-to-600 hours for a traditional highlight video) before it finally was released in 2008. "Richie Asburn: A Baseball Life" it was called. It had its genesis in the short video Stephenson produced in honor and memory of the special place Ashburn occupied in Phillies legend and lore.

"We didn't do a highlight video that year (of Ashburn's death in 1997)," Stephenson explained. "But we did a short thing and we included that in what we called, "Flashback—A Hundred Year History of the Phillies (1900-2000)." That was followed by "Great Moments in Phillies History," a sequel which included snippets of Schmidt and Ashburn being inducted into the Hall of Fame. Footage of Ashburn's funeral, with Harry Kalas' tear-provoking eulogy, was included, as well. And that's when the thought occurred to Stephenson: "Oh, my God, it would be great to do a whole biography on Richie some day."

He continued: "It was such a big project. Encompassed the entire 70 years of a man's life. The good thing was that it was a story that everybody loved. Everybody loved Richie Ashburn. The guy had no enemies. The fun part was going through hours and hours of old game audio. Listening to he and Harry talk… You couldn't beat that."

He started collecting interviews. Don Zimmer, a friend of Ashburn's, was interviewed when he came in town. Bill Campbell, another of the Philadelphia sports broadcasting elites, also. Robin Roberts. Over 55 interviews in all.

Then an even more creative idea came to mind. The Phillies had a road trip scheduled to Kansas City in 2007. Stephenson checked how close that was to Tilden, Nebraska, Ashburn's birthplace. He called Ashburn's son, also Richie, and asked if he would care to drive to Tilden with him when the Phils were in Kansas City. Son Ashburn said he'd love it. So the two went to Tilden together and walked the Ashburn homestead as the camera rolled.

The result was a 2 DVD, three-hour set, the synopsis of which reads: "Richie Ashburn is arguably the most beloved figure in the long and storied history of Philadelphia sports. His Midwestern wit and dry sense of humor seemed to be in sharp contrast with the gritty atmosphere of East Coast baseball, but 'Whitey" won over this tough town with his straightforward approach and playful charm. It's all lovingly narrated by his best friend and broadcast partner, fellow Hall of Famer Harry Kalas."

Little could Stephenson have known when the Ashburn video debuted that in just little over a year's time, the other half of that revered broadcasting team would pass from the Philadelphia scene, as well.

Selecting the narrator for a Stephenson video is not an idle matter to be left to chance. Quite the contrary. The narrators are every bit as integral to the product as the script and editing of the disc itself.

Harry Kalas, Ashburn's broadcast partner and a best friend, was the obvious choice for Ashburn's " …Baseball Life." Ditto the Vet's "…Final Innings" where Kalas established his reputation as an outstanding broadcaster.

So, too, was Phillies executive Bill Giles for the Vet's "Field of Memories." When Owner Ruly Carpenter recruited Giles from Houston, he was reputed to have told him: "We've got to fill this place. I don't know how to do it." If Yankee Stadium was "The House that Ruth Built," the Vet, in Stephenson's view, was the "House that Giles filled."

Similarly, it was no coincidence that Relief Pitcher Brad Lidge was chosen to narrate "The Perfect Season," the Phillies 2008 video yearbook. After all, without Lidge's perfect season in relief, there might have been no World Series championship to celebrate. The jubilant Lidge, kneeling in joy after the last strikeout, graces the disc cover. "The World Series was the goal of this team from the first day of Spring training," Stephenson reported. "And who better to demonstrate that than the relief pitcher without whom it might not have been possible."

So, too, went the selections of the narrators for the 1980 World Series winner and the 1993 World Series runners-up. Manager Dallas Green narrated much of the former; John Kruk and Larry Andersen, much of the latter. "I did 1980 through the eyes of Dallas Green," Stephenson explains. "I had done a long interview with him and then wrote the script and used his voice over. In '93, it was Larry Andersen and John Kruk—two of my favorite guys. I sorta told the story through their eyes. And I was proud of both. Two great seasons, two totally different seasons. It was a lot of fun to get into the nuts and bolts of both campaigns. One ended well, obviously. '93—it would've been nice to win two more games, but it just didn't happen."

Larry Andersen was the choice again for the Harry Kalas tribute. "They knew each other for 25 years," Stephenson explained. "Harry had great empathy for the players and what they do. From the biggest stars to that guy down on the roster. He never criticized a player directly. 'Whitey' sometimes would. But Harry didn't. Larry Andersen was one of those guys down on the roster. He became a broadcast colleague. In the case of Harry Kalas, Larry Andersen spoke from both sides of the fence, the players' side and the broadcasters' side."

Whether the Kalas tribute would be enlarged into a memorial disc ala the Ashburn memorial had not been decided in the immediate aftermath of Kalas' passing. "I just don't know, yet," Stephenson said. "We wanted to say goodbye to our friend in the proper way. When it was all over, I think we did."

What, if anything, is to come beyond that will come in its own due course.

There is an obvious commercial aspect to what Dan Stephenson does as a videographer. "We (the Phillies) produce it and sell it ourselves," he concedes. "It's worth the investment."

But there's more to his work than just commercial enterprise. Much more. With his special set of technological and editorial skills, he is as much a visual historian as he is a video producer. And that's his primary goal. To record and preserve a piece of major league baseball history for the fans of the Philadelphia Phillies. "We're here for the fans," he said. "We can't help with the team on the field. But we can help to bring to the fans insight and access to the players that they would not otherwise have. We try to give them a window to the players and their personalities beyond what they see on the playing field."

Because of his special access as club videographer, he's in a position to do it in a special way.

In the 2008 yearbook, for example, he captured Charlie Manuel's address to the team in a closed clubhouse as Spring Training began. "In all the year's I've been in baseball," Manuel, the baseball lifer, tells his 2008 squad, the 2007 team "played the best of any I've been around. (But) we've got a couple of more stairs to go. Winning is where it's at. I know what kind of guys we have. Believe me, winning is where it's at. Let's go get it. That's all I've got to say." And Dan Stephenson captured the moment for everyone to look back on now that the Phillies did, indeed, "go get it!".

He also caught Chase Utley when the second baseman made a surprise visit to the Phillies game day employees who passed out the All-Star ballots for the 2008 star fest. Utley was the leading vote getter on the National League Squad.

"I just want to take some time to thank the game-day staff who handed out the ballots at the ballpark," Utley, in game togs, told the appreciative and applauding Phillies crew as they chanted "MVP, MVP" in unison. "I heard this park had one of the highest ballpark balloting in the whole league. And I wanted to thank you all. We got two All-Stars out of it. And we're extremely excited. Thank you." Utley, incidentally, also, almost as an afterthought, cautioned the staff in a percipient way not to get ahead of themselves with that MVP thing. Another moment most of us would not have seen without Dan Stephenson's videography.

And there was the poignant interview with Brett Myers in the aftermath of the deaths of Charlie Manuel's mother and Shane Victorino's grandmother during the Phillies play-off march to the World Series. "We're family here," Myers spoke into the cameras.

"When somebody in the family passes away, we all feel like we lost somebody, too."

So much so that the 2008 video yearbook ended on this note:

"Dedicated to the memories of June Manuel and Irene Victorino."

That was Stephenson's touch. He is, first and foremost, a video historian for the Philadelphia Phillies baseball organization. But he's also a member of the Phillies family. "It's a reward to me that the ball club let's me do what I do," he says.

Index

Y

Z